The Cornwallis Papers

The Campaigns of 1780 and 1781

in

The Southern Theatre of the American Revolutionary War

Volume IV

Arranged and edited by

Ian Saberton

The Naval & Military Press Ltd

Published by
The Naval & Military Press Ltd

Unit 10 Ridgewood Industrial Park,
Uckfield, East Sussex,
TN22 5QE England

Tel: +44 (0) 1825 749494
Fax: +44 (0) 1825 765701

www.naval-military-press.com
www.military-genealogy.com
www.militarymaproom.com

Documents hitherto unpublished © Crown copyright 2010

Documents previously published in which Crown copyright subsists © Crown copyright

Introductory chapters, footnotes and other editorial matter © Ian Saberton 2010

The right of Ian Saberton to be identified as author of the introductory chapters, footnotes and other editorial matter in this work has been asserted in accordance with sections 77 and 78 of the UK Copyright, Designs and Patents Act 1988

ISBN Volume I   9781845747923
ISBN Volume II   9781845747916
ISBN Volume III 9781845747909
ISBN Volume IV   9781845747893
ISBN Volume V   9781845747886
ISBN Volume VI   9781845747879

Printed and bound in Great Britain by
CPI Antony Rowe, Chippenham and Eastbourne

CONTENTS

Editorial Method ... vii

PART SEVEN
THE REST OF THE WINTER CAMPAIGN
1st February to 7th April 1781

39.	Introduction to the rest of Part Seven	3
40.	Letters to Germain and Arnold	
	1 – To Germain	11
	2 – To Arnold	21
41.	Miscellaneous correspondence etc	
	1 – Between Cornwallis and O'Hara or Tarleton	22
	2 – Between Cornwallis and Craig	25
	3 – Between Balfour and Craig	30
	4 – From Cornwallis to Balfour	41
	5 – Between Cornwallis and Rawdon	44
	6 – From Colonel Phillips of the South Carolina royal militia	53
	7 – Proclamations, warrants, and summons to arms	55
42.	Return of troops etc and Care of wounded	
	1 – Returns of British etc troops, casualties, and captured weaponry	61
	2 – Care of certain British etc troops seriously wounded at Guilford and left at New Garden Meeting House	70
43.	Other papers	
	1 – Cartel for the exchange and relief of prisoners etc	74
	2 – Extracts from the Davidson Papers	89
	3 – Intercepted letters	96

PART EIGHT
REFITMENT AT WILMINGTON
8th to 24th April 1781

44.	Introduction to the rest of Part Eight	101
45.	Letters to or from England, New York or Virginia	
	1 – To Germain	104
	2 – To Clinton	109
	3 – To Major General Phillips	114
	4 – To Amherst	117
	5 – From and to the Speaker of the House of Commons	118
46.	Miscellaneous letters etc	
	1 – To Rawdon or Balfour	121
	2 – To or from the Royal Navy	123
	3 – From Craig	133
	4 – From officers of the 71st Regiment and the Brigade of Guards	136
	5 – A proposed basis for offensive operations in North Carolina	138
	6 – Petition to become British subjects	140
	7 – Troop return	142

PART NINE
THE MARCH TO VIRGINIA
25th April to 19th May 1781

47.	Introduction to the rest of Part Nine	149
48.	Miscellaneous letters etc	
	1 – To or from Phillips or Arnold	151
	2 – To or from Tarleton	155
	3 – To or from Craig	165

4 – To or from Balfour	170
5 – From Rawdon	179
6 – Troop return	184
7 – Intercepted letters	184
Index	187

Editorial method

Subject to the following modifications, the editorial method remains the same as described in volume I.

Omitted papers

Though belonging to the period covered by this volume, the following papers in the series PRO 30/11/- are omitted on the ground that they do not relate to the southern campaigns or are too inconsequential: 2(408); 5(17), (40), (42), (73), (75), (92), (94), (96), (98), (101), (111), (115), (119), (121), (122), (125), (127), (129), (272), and (288); 6(15), (19), and (333); 67(81); 69(1) and (3); 71(11) and (13); 91(15); 104(11); 105((4), (5), (6), (12), (14), (16), (18) and (20); and 277(8).

Footnotes

As a general rule biographical footnotes on persons who are not the subject of such notes in this volume will be found in volume I, II or III.

Titles of works cited in abbreviated form in footnotes

Appletons'
  Appletons' Cyclopædia of American Biography (New York, 1888-)

Army Lists
  A list of the general and field officers... (London, 1754-77), together with *A list of all the officers of the army...* (London, 1778-)

Bass, *The Green Dragoon*
  Robert D Bass, *The Green Dragoon: The Lives of Banastre Tarleton and Mary Robinson* (Sandlapper Press Inc, 1973)

Clark, *Loyalists in the Southern Campaign*
  Murtie June Clark, *Loyalists in the Southern Campaign of the Revolutionary War,* volume I (Genealogical Publishing Co, 2003)

Coldham, *Loyalist Claims*
  Peter Wilson Coldham, *American Loyalist Claims* (National Genealogical Society, 1980)

DAB
  Dictionary of American Biography (New York, 1928-1958)

Davies ed, *Docs of the Am Rev*
  K G Davies ed, *Documents of the American Revolution 1770-1783,* volume XX (Irish Academic Press, 1979)

DeMond, *Loyalists in NC*
: Robert O DeMond, *The Loyalists in North Carolina during the Revolution* (Duke University Press, 1940)

Gibbes, *Documentary History*
: Robert W Gibbes, *Documentary History of the American Revolution* (The Reprint Company, 1972)

'Joseph Graham's Narrative', *The Murphey Papers*
: Joseph Graham, 'Narrative', in William Henry Hoyt ed, *The Papers of Archibald D Murphey* (Publications of the NC Historical Commission, 1914)

The Greene Papers
: *The Papers of General Nathanael Greene,* volumes VI to VIII, edited by Richard K Showman, Dennis M Conrad, Roger N Parks, et al (University of North Carolina Press, 1991-5)

Gwathmey, *Historical Register*
: John H Gwathmey, *Historical Register of Virginians in the Revolution 1775-1783* (The Dietz Press, 1938)

Hay ed, *Soldiers from NC*
: Gertrude Sloan Hay ed, *Roster of Soldiers from North Carolina in the American Revolution* (Reprint, Genealogical Publishing Co Inc, 1988)

Heitman, *Historical Register*
: Francis B Heitman, *Historical Register of the Officers of the Continental Army during the War of the Revolution* (Reprint, Clearfield Publishing Co Inc, 2000)

Lambert, *SC Loyalists*
: Robert Stansbury Lambert, *South Carolina Loyalists in the American Revolution* (University of South Carolina Press, 1987)

Lossing, *Pictorial Field-Book*
: Benson J Lossing, *The Pictorial Field-Book of the Revolution* (New York, 1855)

McCrady, *SC in the Rev 1780-1783*
: Edward McCrady, *The History of South Carolina in the Revolution 1780-1783* (The Macmillan Co, New York, 1902)

Moss, *SC Patriots*
: Bobby Gilmer Moss, *Roster of South Carolina Patriots in the American Revolution* (Genealogical Publishing Co Inc, 1983)

ODNB
: *Oxford Dictionary of National Biography* (Oxford University Press, 2004)

Raymond, 'British American Corps'
: W O Raymond, 'Roll of Officers of the British American or Loyalist Corps', *Collections of the New Brunswick Historical Society*, ii, 1899

Robinson, *NC Guide*
: Blackwell P Robinson ed, *The North Carolina Guide* (University of North Carolina Press, 1955)

Ross ed, *Cornwallis Correspondence*
: Charles Ross ed, *Correspondence of Charles, First Marquis Cornwallis*, volume I (London, 1859)

Royal Regiment of Artillery
: *List of Officers of the Royal Regiment of Artillery from the Year 1716 to the Year 1899* (London, 1900)

Sabine, *Biographical Sketches*
: Lorenzo Sabine, *Biographical Sketches of Loyalists of the American Revolution* (Boston, 1864)

Salley Jr, *Orangeburg County*
: A S Salley Jr, *The History of Orangeburg County, South Carolina, from its first Settlement to the close of the Revolutionary War* (Orangeburg, 1898)

Stevens, *Clinton-Cornwallis Controversy*
: Benjamin Franklin Stevens, *The Campaign in Virginia 1781: the Clinton Cornwallis Controversy* (London, 1887-8)

Syrett and DiNardo ed, *The Commissioned Sea Officers*
: David Syrett and R L DiNardo ed, *The Commissioned Sea Officers of the Royal Navy 1660-1815* (Navy Records Society, 1994)

Tarleton, *Campaigns*
: Banastre Tarleton, *A History of the Campaigns of 1780 and 1781 in the Southern Provinces of North America* (London, 1787)

Valentine, *The British Establishment*
: Alan Valentine, *The British Establishment, 1760-1784: An Eighteenth-Century Biographical Dictionary* (University of Oklahoma Press, 1970)

Wheeler, *Historical Sketches*
: John Hill Wheeler, *Historical Sketches of North Carolina from 1584 to 1851* (Reprint, Clearfield Company Inc, 2000)

Wheeler, *Reminiscences*
: John Hill Wheeler, *Reminiscences and Memoirs of North Carolina and Eminent North Carolinians* (Reprint, Genealogical Publishing Co, 1966)

The Cornwallis Papers

PART SEVEN

The Rest of the Winter Campaign

1st February to 7th April 1781

CHAPTER 39

Introduction to the rest of Part Seven

Crippled though he was by Cowpens and the loss of his light troops there, Cornwallis had resolved to press ahead with the winter campaign. Unfortunately for the Crown, it was a gamble that would not pay off.

In reaching his decision Cornwallis had been influenced by a combination of three factors. Militarily, he hoped to overtake Morgan and release the Cowpens prisoners, but if he could not prevent Morgan from forming a junction with Greene, he hoped to intercept the combined force between the barriers of the Yadkin and the Dan, compelling a general action which, given the disparity in seasoned troops, he was confident he would win.

Politically, he was conscious of the continuing imperative to make progress swiftly. In Britain there was a growing war weariness pervading all sections of society, compounded by the ruin of foreign and colonial trade, the knock-on effect on the rest of the economy, the weight of much increased taxation and public indebtedness, the collapse of private prosperity, and a rapid decline in the public finances. All in all, for a country of only eight million people, the costs of the war, both financial and otherwise, were becoming unsustainable.

Personally, he was aware how badly it would reflect on him if he made no attempt to release the Cowpens prisoners and abandoned the invasion of North Carolina a second time. Not only would his reputation be damaged but the effect on public opinion would undermine further the tenuous British hold on South Carolina and Georgia. As Rawdon had asserted on a similar occasion, 'as much is to be done by opinion as by arms'.

Cornwallis's pursuit of Morgan did not get off to a propitious start. He remained for two days after Cowpens at Turkey Creek, where he received news of the disaster. In the meantime Morgan rapidly retreated, sending his prisoners across the Catawba at Island Ford under an escort of militia and Washington's dragoons, while with the rest of his force he passed Ramsour's Mill to a lower ford, Sherrald's, where he crossed on 23rd January. There he was almost immediately joined by the prisoners, whom he soon sent on over the Yadkin to Virginia.

If Cornwallis had marched promptly to the northward, he might have intercepted Morgan at Ramsour's, but it was not to be. Apart from his delay in moving off, he mistakenly marched to the north-westward, eventually reaching Ramsour's by the 25th. There he remained for three days, during which he came to a momentous decision which, no matter the immediate improvement in his mobility, might well inhibit his remaining in the back parts of North Carolina unless his supplies were in due course replenished from Wilmington. Charles Stedman, a British commissary who was there, recounted the event: 'Lord Cornwallis, considering that the loss of his light troops could only be remedied by the activity of the whole army, resolved to destroy all the superfluous baggage. By first reducing the size and quantity of his own, he set an example which was cheerfully followed by all the officers under his command, although by so doing they sustained a considerable loss. No waggons were reserved except those loaded with hospital stores, salt, and ammunition, and four empty ones for the accommodation of the sick or wounded. The remainder of the waggons, baggage, and all the store of flour and rum were destroyed... And such was the ardour both of officers and soldiers, and their willingness to submit to any hardship for the promotion of the service, that this arrangement, which deprived them of all future prospect of spirituous liquors and even hazarded a regular supply of provisions, was acquiesced in without a murmur.' In the evening of the 29th Cornwallis arrived at the banks of the Catawba, but a heavy rain fell in the night and swelled the river so much that it was impassable for the next two days.

Meanwhile Greene, on learning of Cowpens, had set his troops in motion from Hick's Creek towards Salisbury, while he himself galloped across country to take personal command of Morgan's force. He reached Morgan at Sherrald's Ford on the 30th. When the Catawba began to drop the following day, he decided to hurry on with Morgan and his men to the Trading Ford on the Yadkin, leaving Davidson with some militia to dispute Cornwallis's passage of the Catawba. At dawn on 1st February Cornwallis crossed the river under a galling fire at Cowan's Ford and joined up with Webster, who had passed higher up at Beattie's. Davidson was killed. O'Hara with the van pressed ahead to the Trading Ford, which he reached on the 3rd just as the last of the enemy crossed on boats which Greene with admirable foresight had collected. With no boats available on the western bank, and with the swollen river unfordable, Cornwallis halted for two days at Salisbury to collect provisions, after which he turned north to the Shallow Ford ten miles up river, where, having been delayed by the height of creeks on a necessarily circuitous route, he crossed in the evening of the 7th. On the same day Greene's men from Hick's Creek arrived at Guilford. Joining up with them, Greene convened a council of war there on the 9th, which, taking into account that his combined force amounted to only 1,426 Continental infantry and 600 poorly armed and constantly fluctuating militia, decided not to risk a general action but to retreat immediately over the Dan. Detaching a light corps under Williams to mislead Cornwallis that he was headed for the upper fords of the river, he pressed ahead with his main body to Irwin's Ferry on the lower reach. There he crossed on the 14th, followed by Williams' corps during the night, having again assembled, with admirable foresight, all the available boats. In hot pursuit the British van arrived a few hours later.

We have already related the destruction of Cornwallis's baggage, stores and waggons at Ramsour's Mill. Another more serious consequence of Cowpens now ensued. If Cornwallis had not lost his light troops there, his total force would now have come to some 3,400 men[1] (excluding artillery) when a notional figure of 400 is allowed for losses incurred during his advance. Now that Greene had been driven into Virginia, it would have made sound strategic sense to keep him where he was while Cornwallis was left to assemble in relative security the numerous loyalists in North Carolina and re-establish British authority there. To this end a compelling course would have been for him to divide his force so that half remained on the Dan while the rest withdrew into the interior and set about reinstating government under the Crown. With so large a British force remaining on the Dan, Greene would have run the grave risk of being caught in the process of repassage if he had attempted it. Diversions might have been made and he may have succeeded, but even so, he would have faced entrapment between Cornwallis's two divisions and either a general action in which Cornwallis had a marked superiority in seasoned troops or, if at all possible, another ignominious flight across the Dan. Given that each of Cornwallis's divisions would have fallen not far short of the troops brought to the battlefield at Guilford, neither would have been easily defeated in detail.

Yet dividing Cornwallis's force was no longer an option. Reduced as he was to 2,600 men (excluding artillery), he saw no alternative, after halting for a while, but to proceed by easy marches to Hillsborough, where he arrived on the 20th. Erecting the King's standard, he invited by proclamation all loyal subjects to come forward and take an active part in restoring order and constitutional government.

With no force opposing a repassage of the Dan, Greene rightly concluded that it was essential to disrupt Cornwallis's operations, prevent the loyalists from assembling, and impress the revolutionaries with his presence. On the 19th Lee and his Legion were dispatched across the river with orders to intimidate the loyalists, to rouse the drooping spirits of the revolutionaries, 'to alarm the enemy by night, and to harass them by day'. Four days later he joined up with Pickens and his militia, who had remained behind in North Carolina. On the 20th Lee was followed across by Williams with a light corps, who was ordered to observe the motions of the British and embrace the first opportunity of giving them an advantageous blow. Reinforced by Stevens and several hundred Virginia militia, Greene passed with the main body on the 22nd, intent — when reinforced further — on 'ruining' Cornwallis.

Meanwhile Cornwallis was greatly disappointed in his expectations of being joined by the loyalists, almost all of whom, as Tarleton explained, were prepared to assembly only in perfect security: 'Soon after the King's standard was erected at Hillsborough, many hundred inhabitants of the surrounding districts rode into the British camp to talk over the proclamation, inquire the news of the day, and take a view of the King's troops. The generality of these visitors seemed desirous of peace but averse to every exertion that might tend to procure it. They acknowledged the Continentals were chased out of the province, but they declared they soon expected them to return and the dread of violence and persecution[2] prevented their taking a decided part in a cause which yet appeared dangerous.' An exception was Dr John Pyle, who assembled some 2 or 300 loyalists between the Haw and Deep Rivers

---

[1] This and later figures are extrapolated from the return of rank and file fit for duty, pp 61-2, by using a factor of 17.5% to cater additionally for officers, staff, serjeants and drummers.

[2] See vol I, p 153.

and began marching for Hillsborough. Mistaking Lee and Pickens' men for Tarleton's, they were inhumanly butchered on the 25th. 'This affair,' concluded Pickens, 'has been of infinite service. It has knocked up Toryism altogether in this part.' A final nail was soon after placed in the coffin of Cornwallis's expectations when another body of assembled loyalists was mistakenly attacked on 4th March by Tarleton's men, who killed four and badly cut up twenty or thirty. 'In the case of Pyle's men,' commented Joseph Graham, 'they were cut up by the Americans and thought it was the British; in this case they were cut up by the British and thought it was the Americans. These miscarriages so completely broke the spirit of the loyalists in those parts that no party was known afterwards to attempt to join the British in these or the adjoining counties.'

The attitude of the loyalists encountered by Cornwallis at Hillsborough is perhaps best described in the following anecdote related by his commissary, Stedman: 'The commissary, who considered it as his duty not only to furnish provisions to the army but also to learn the disposition of the inhabitants, fell in about this time with a very sensible man, a Quaker, who, being interrogated as to the state of the country, replied that it was the general wish of the people to be reunited to Britain; but that they had been so often deceived in promises of support, and the British had so frequently relinquished posts, that the people were now afraid to join the British army lest they should leave the province, in which case the resentment of the revolutioners would be exercised with more cruelty; that although the men might escape or go with the army, yet such was the diabolical conduct of those people that they would inflict the severest punishment upon their families. "Perhaps," said the Quaker, "thou art not acquainted with the conduct of thy enemies towards those who wish well to the cause thou art engaged in. There are some who have lived two and even three years in the woods without daring to go to their houses but have been secretly supported by their families. Others, having walked out of their houses under a promise of being safe, have proceeded but a few yards before they have been shot. Others have been tied to a tree and severely whipped. I will tell thee of one instance of cruelty: a party surrounded the house of a loyalist; a few entered; the man and his wife were in bed; the husband was shot dead by the side of his wife." The writer of this replied that those circumstances were horrid but under what government could they be so happy as when enjoying the privileges of Englishmen? "True," said the Quaker, "but the people have experienced such distress that I believe they would submit to any government in the world to obtain peace." The commissary, finding the gentleman to be a very sensible, intelligent man, took great pains to find out his character. Upon enquiry he proved to be a man of the most irreproachable manners and well known to some gentlemen of North Carolina then in our army, and whose veracity was undoubted.'

It was on 25th February that Cornwallis received certain intelligence that Greene, having been reinforced, had recrossed the Dan. Judging it no longer expedient to separate his force, he recalled a detachment commanded by Tarleton. Destitute of forage and provisions, and too distant – after Greene's return – to protect the great body of loyalists residing between the Haw and Deep Rivers, he next day quit Hillsborough, passed the Haw, and encamped near Alamance Creek. With Lee and Williams hovering around him, and with Greene constantly moving nearby between High Rock Ford, Boyd's Mill and Speedwell's Iron Works, he had no option but to remain compact, controlling no ground beyond his pickets. 'From that time..,' wrote O'Hara to the Duke of Grafton, 'the two armys were never above twenty miles asunder, they constantly avoiding a general action and we as industriously seeking it. These operations obliged the two armys to make numberless moves, which it is impossible to detail.'

On his tactics during this period Greene commented as follows: 'I have been obliged to practice that by finesse which I dare not attempt by force. I know the people have been in anxious suspence waiting the event of an action, but let the consequence of censure be what it may, nothing shall hurry me into a measure that is not suggested by prudence or connects with it the interest of the department in which I have the honor to command.'

Eventually, on 11th March, Greene formed a junction with a Virginia regiment of 18 months' men and a considerable body of North Carolina and Virginia militia. Thus reinforced, and despite sending Pickens back to South Carolina with a very small number of South Carolinians and Georgians, he now offered battle. It took place on the 15th at Guilford. From a British perspective Cornwallis provides a brief account of the affair in his letter of the 17th to Germain[3]. It is unnecessary to elaborate here, save to state the motives of the commanders, the disposition of the enemy, a few supplementary facts, and the sequel.

According to Cornwallis, 'I was determined to fight the rebel army if it approached me, being convinced that it would be impossible to succeed in that great object of our arduous campaign, the calling forth the numerous loyalists of North Carolina, whilst a doubt remained on their minds of the superiority of our arms.' In effect he was looking for as decisive a victory as at Camden, one that would demolish the revolutionary forces and compel the remnants to retreat over the Dan or, in the case of the militia, to flee to their homes. Such an outcome might well convince the timid loyalists at last to assemble, without whose assistance the reinstatement of constitutional government was a forlorn hope.

Greene explained his motives in a letter of the 18th to George Washington: 'Our force, as you will see by the returns, were respectable, and the probability of not being able to keep it long in the field, and the difficulty of subsisting men in this exhausted country, together with the great advantages which would result from the action if we were victorious and the little injury if we were otherwise, determin'd me to bring on an action as soon as possible.' At worst he hoped to leave Cornwallis with no decisive victory and a large number of wounded. In that event, if Cornwallis had to retire, the most serious cases would need to be left behind and fall into the revolutionaries' hands, whilst the rest, who remained with Cornwallis, would encumber his further operations. Such was indeed the outcome.

The battleground chosen by Greene was approachable from the west along a road through a narrow defile shouldered by rising ground on both sides and lined with dense copses that continued unbroken to within half a mile of Guilford Courthouse. At this point the ground had been cleared on both sides of the road, leaving an open space, broken only by fences, about 500 yards square. Ahead of this first clearing the woods again closed upon the road for another half mile, at the end of which there came another open space of cultivated ground, seamed by hollows, around the courthouse itself. Greene's first line, composed principally of North Carolina militia, was formed behind a rail fence along the edge of the first clearing. Ordered by Greene to fire only two rounds before retiring, they did so, appreciably thinning the British ranks.

---

[3] See p 17.

About 300 yards behind the first line was Greene's second, composed of Virginia militia. 'Posted in the woods and covering themselves with trees, they kept up for a considerable time a galling fire, which did great execution.' At last the right gave way, paving the way for the much depleted British left wing to attack the Continentals, who formed Greene's third and principal line. It was drawn up in a curve along the brow of the courthouse hill a few hundred yards behind the second line and somewhat out of alignment with it. A most bloody contest ensued, which might have gone either way, but true to his resolution not to risk the destruction of his entire army, Greene eventually decided to withdraw, although the remnants of his first line were still active on his left. He did so 'with order and regularity'. There was little pursuit, for Cornwallis's troops were spent with hard fighting and their long march to the battlefield.

There has been much uncertainty about the number of troops brought by Cornwallis to the battle, and sadly these Papers do not provide a definite answer. If, as stated in note 1 on page 5, we extrapolate from the return of rank and file fit for duty, we obtain an overall figure of 2,600 for all ranks (excluding artillery) as at 1st March. Between then and the battle there were several petty skirmishes, which would have reduced this figure to, say, 2,500. Before the battle the Royal North Carolina Regiment (232 rank and file), 100 infantry and 20 cavalry were detached with the remaining waggons and baggage towards Bell's Mill on Deep River. If we increase the total by 17.5% to cover all ranks, we arrive at an overall figure of approximately 400, leaving Cornwallis with an overall figure of some 2,100 men (excluding artillery) brought by him to the battle. Yet according to the return of troops who fought there (page 63), the number for all ranks was 1,924 (including 50 artillery), leaving, when we subtract the artillery, 226 men unaccounted for. Quite simply, the two returns do not correlate.

Greene's numbers are also imprecise, but they are generally reckoned to have amounted to some 4,500 (including artillery), of whom about 1,750 were Continentals and the rest militia.

As stated later in this Part[4], Cornwallis's casualties in the battle came to 93 killed, 413 wounded, and 26 missing – a total of 532. Of his Continentals, Greene admitted to losing 57 killed, 113 wounded, and 161 missing – a total of 331. No reliable figures for his militia have ever been published.

'Never perhaps has the prowess of the British soldier been seen to greater advantage than in this obstinate and bloody combat,' concluded Fortescue. 'Starting half-starved on a march of twelve miles, the troops attacked an enemy, fresh and strong, which not only outnumbered them by more than two to one, but which was so posted, by Greene's excellent judgment, as to afford every possible advantage to its natural superiority in bushcraft, armament, and marksmanship. Yet, though heavily punished, they forced the Americans from the shelter of the forest and drove them from the field.' Nevertheless, 'the victory, though a brilliant feat of arms, was no victory. Greene did indeed retreat, and the most part of his militia deserted to their homes so that his losses were never actually ascertained, but Cornwallis had gained no solid advantage to compensate for the sacrifice of life and he was now too weak farther

---

[4] See p 64.

to prosecute' his campaign. All in all, the victory was, as Phillips truly stated, the sort that ruins an army. If only Cornwallis had not lost his light troops at Cowpens, the story might well have been different.

Cornwallis's troops had cheerfully undergone hardships, fatigue and starvation, but they were now terribly reduced in numbers and almost destitute of provisions and other supplies. He had no choice but to accept the inevitable and on the third day after the battle he began to make his way towards Cross Creek, where, in expectation of being supplied by water carriage from Wilmington, he intended to halt as a proper place not only to refresh and refit the troops but also to dispose of his numerous wounded, sixty-four of whom he was obliged to leave behind at New Garden Meeting House.

Having lost a quarter of his men at Guilford, and encumbered with wounded, Cornwallis was in no position to face another engagement, for, if his losses were equally severe, they might involve the demolition of his entire army. Recognising this fact, Greene began to pursue him as far as Ramsey's Mill on Deep River, intent on giving battle. There, on the 28th, he found that the British had partly destroyed a temporary bridge which they had built across the river and had retired southward a few hours earlier. The country below was so barren, his provisions were so short, and the term of much of his Virginia militia was so soon to expire, that Greene could not pursue farther.

Cornwallis entered Cross Creek at the beginning of April. To his dismay he could not open a water communication with Wilmington. The distance, the narrowness of the Cape Fear River, the commanding elevation of the banks, and the hostile sentiments of great part of the adjoining inhabitants made the navigation impracticable. The Highlanders in and around Cross Creek remained loyal, but they declined to embody for the same reasons as the rest of the loyalists. Under these circumstances Cornwallis decided to march his whole force to Wilmington. Whether at a pinch he could have detached part to go there with the wounded and attempted with the rest to join Rawdon at Camden is debatable.

Cornwallis arrived in the vicinity of Wilmington on the 7th. Writing shortly after to the Duke of Grafton, O'Hara remarked, 'We feel at this moment the sad and fatal effects of our loss [*at the Battle of Guilford*]. Nearly one half of our best officers and soldiers were either killed or wounded and what remains are so completely worn out... [*that*], *entre nous*, the spirit of our little army has evaporated a good deal.'

In the meantime Greene had come to a decision of key strategic importance. Writing to George Washington on 29th March, he remarked, 'If the enemy falls down towards Wilmington, they will be in a position where it would be impossible for us to injure them if we had a force. In this critical and distressing situation I am determined to carry the war immediately into South Carolina. The enemy will be obliged to follow us or give up their posts in that State. If the former takes place, it will draw the war out of this State and give it an opportunity to raise its proportion of men. If they leave their posts to fall, they must lose more there than they can gain here. If we continue in this State, the enemy will hold their possessions in both.' Though brilliant in its concept, the decision was risky, for, as stated in *The Greene Papers*, he was violating established military principles by leaving an enemy army virtually unchallenged in his rear. Yet he was well aware of the unorthodoxy of his design, as he explained to James Emmet, a North Carolina officer: 'Don't be surpris'd if my movements don't correspond with your ideas of military propriety. War is an intricate business, and people are often sav'd by ways and means they least look for or expect.'

Sending Lee ahead to surprise British posts on the Santee and Congaree, Greene began his march from Ramsey's Mill on the 6th. The die was cast.

§ - §

Principal papers and works consulted in the writing of this chapter

The Cornwallis Papers (UK National Archives, Kew)

Sir John Fortescue, *A History of the British Army*, volume III (Macmillan and Co Ltd, 1902)

Don Higginbotham, *Daniel Morgan: Revolutionary Rifleman* (The University of North Carolina Press, 1961)

Joseph Graham, 'Narrative', in William Henry Hoyt ed, *The Papers of Archibald D Murphey* (Publications of the North Carolina Historical Commission, Raleigh, 1914)

The Papers of General Nathanael Greene, volumes VII and VIII, edited by Dennis M Conrad, Roger N Parks, Richard K Showman, et al (The University of North Carolina Press, 1994-5)

David Schenck, *North Carolina 1780-81* (Raleigh, 1889)

The South Carolina Historical Magazine, LXV (1964)

Charles Stedman, *History of the Origin, Progress, and Termination of the American War* (London, 1792)

Banastre Tarleton, *A History of the Campaigns of 1780 and 1781 in the Southern Provinces of North America* (London, 1787)

Theodore Thayer, *Nathanael Greene: Strategist of the American Revolution* (Twayne Publishers, NY, 1960)

Sir George Otto Trevelyan Bt, *The History of the American Revolution*, volume VI (Longmans, Green, and Co, 1915)

Christopher Ward, *The War of the Revolution* (The Macmillan Co, NY, 1952)

Franklin and Mary Wickwire, *Cornwallis: The American Adventure* (Houghton Mifflin Co, 1970)

§ - §

CHAPTER 40

Letters to Germain and Arnold

1 - To Germain

Cornwallis to Germain, 17th March 1781[1]　　　　　　　　5(258): C

N° 6　　　　　　　　　　　　　　　　　　　　　　　　　　　　Guildford
　　　　　　　　　　　　　　　　　　　　　　　　　　　　17th March 1781

Rt Hon Lord George Germain etc etc etc

My Lord

Your Lordship's dispatch N° 1 dated the 9th of November ultimo[2] was delivered to me by my aid de camp, Major Ross. The officers and soldiers who fought so gallantly on the 16th of August received with the warmest sense of gratitude the royal approbation of their behaviour, and it is particularly pleasing to me that my conduct has given satisfaction to His Majesty and to His Ministers.

By the long interruption of our communication with South Carolina I have not been informed whether Lt Governor Bull and the other civil officers have arrived in that province.

I shall pay proper attention to your Lordship's directions upon that subject as well as relating to the prisoners of war confined at Charlestown. There are at present some hopes that

---

[1] Published in Stevens, *Clinton-Cornwallis Controversy*, i, 353. There are no differences.

[2] *dispatch N° 1..*: see vol III, p 44.

a negociation now on foot between me and General Greene will terminate in a cartel for their exchange. If it fails, I shall endeavour to dispose of them in the manner recommended by your Lordship, the expence and inconvenience of keeping them being intolerable.

I have the honour to be with great respect, my Lord,
Your Lordship's most obedient and most humble servant

CORNWALLIS

Cornwallis to Germain, 17th March 1781[3]

5(281): C

N° 7

Guildford
17th March 1781

Rt Hon Lord George Germain etc etc etc

My Lord

Having occasion to dispatch my aide de camp, Captain Brodrick, with the particulars of the action of the 15th in compliance with general directions from Sir Henry Clinton, I shall embrace the opportunity to give your Lordship an account of the operations of the troops under my command previous to that event and of those subsequent untill the departure of Captain Brodrick.

My plan for the winter's campaign was to penetrate into North Carolina, leaving South Carolina in security against any probable attack in my absence.

Lord Rawdon with a considerable body of troops had charge of the defensive, and I proceeded about the middle of January upon the offensive operations. I decided to march by the upper in preference to the lower roads leading into North Carolina, because, fords being frequent above the forks of the rivers, my passage there could not easily be obstructed and, General Greene having taken post on the Pedee and there being few fords in any of the great rivers of this country below their forks, especially in winter, I apprehended being much delayed, if not entirely prevented, from penetrating by the latter route. I was the more induced to prefer this route as I hoped in my way to be able to destroy or drive out of South Carolina the corps of the enemy commanded by General Morgan, which threatned our valuable district of Ninety Six, and I likewise hoped by rapid marches to get between General Greene and Virginia and by that means force him to fight without receiving any reinforcement from that province or, failing of that, to oblige him to quit North Carolina with precipitation and thereby encourage our friends to make good their promises of a general rising to assist me in re-establishing His Majesty's Government.

The unfortunate affair of the 17th of January was a very unexpected and severe blow, for, besides reputation, our loss did not fall short of 600 men. However, being thoroughly

---

[3] Published in Stevens, op cit, i, 355. There are no material differences.

sensible that defensive measures would be certain ruin to the affairs of Britain in the southern colonies, this event did not deter me from prosecuting the original plan. That General Greene might be uncertain of my intended route as long as possible, I had left General Leslie at Camden untill I was ready to move from Wynnesborough, and he was now within a day's march of me. I employed the 18th in forming a junction with him and in collecting the remains of Lt Colonel Tarleton's corps, after which great exertions were made by part of the army, without baggage, to retake our prisoners and to intercept General Morgan's corps on its retreat to the Catawba, but the celerity of their movements and the swelling of numberless creeks in our way rendered all our efforts fruitless.

I therefore assembled the army on the 25th at Ramsoure's Mill on the South Fork of the Catawba, and as the loss of my light troops could only be remedied by the activity of the whole corps, I employed a halt of two days in collecting some flour and in destroying superfluous baggage and all my waggons except those loaded with hospital stores, salt and ammunition and four reserved empty in readiness for sick or wounded. In this measure, tho' at the expence of a great deal of officers' baggage and of all prospect in future of rum and even a regular supply of provisions to the soldiers, I must in justice to this army say that there was the most general and chearfull acquiescence.

In the mean time the rains had rendered the North Catawba impassable, and General Morgan's corps, the militia of the rebellious counties of Rowan and Mecklenburgh under General Davidson, or the gang of plunderers usually under the command of General Sumpter, not then recovered from his wounds, had occupied all the fords in a space of more than forty miles upwards from the fork. During its height I approached the river by short marches so as to give the enemy equal apprehensions for several fords, and after having procured the best information in my power, I resolved to attempt the passage at a private ford (then slightly guarded) near McCowan's Ford on the morning of the 1st of February.

Lt Colonel Webster was detached with part of the army and all the baggage to Beattie's Ford, six miles above McCowan's, where General Davidson was supposed to be posted with 500 militia, and was directed to make every possible demonstration, by cannonading and otherwise, of an intention to force a passage there, and I marched at one in the morning with the Brigade of Guards, Regiment of Bose, 23rd, 200 cavalry and two three pounders to the ford fixed upon for the real attempt.

The morning being very dark and rainy and part of our way through a wood where there was no road, one of the three pounders in front of the 23rd Regiment and the cavalry overset in a swamp and occasioned those corps to lose the line of march, and some of the artillery men belonging to the other gun (one of whom had the match), having stopped to assist, were likewise left behind. The head of the column in the mean while arrived at the bank of the river and day began to break. I could make no use of the gun that was up, and it was evident from the number of fires on the other side that the opposition would be greater than I had expected. However, as I knew that the rain then falling would soon render the river again impassable and I had received information the evening before that General Greene had arrived in General Morgan's camp and that his army was marching after him with the greatest expedition, I determined not to desist from the attempt; and therefore, full of confidence in the zeal and gallantry of Brigadier General O'Hara and of the Brigade of Guards under his command, I ordered them to march on but, to prevent confusion, not to fire untill they gained the opposite bank. Their behaviour justified my high opinion of them, for a constant fire from the enemy in a ford upwards of 500 yards wide, in many places up to their middle with a rocky bottom and strong current, made no impression on their cool and determined valour nor checked their passage. The light infantry, landing first, immediately formed and in a few minutes killed or dispersed every thing that appeared before them, the rest of the troops forming and advancing in succession. We now learned that we had been opposed by about 300 militia that had taken post there only the evening before under the command of General Davidson. Their general and two or three other officers were among the killed. The number of wounded was uncertain and a few were taken prisoners. On our side Lt Colonel Hall[4] and 3 men were killed and 36 men wounded, all of the light infantry and grenadiers of the Guards. By this time the rear of the column had joined and, the whole having passed with the greatest dispatch, I detached Lt Colonel Tarleton with the cavalry and 23rd Regiment to pursue the routed militia. A few were soon killed or taken and, Lt Colonel Tarleton having learned that 3 or 400 of the neighbouring militia were to assemble that day at Tarrants's House about 10 miles from the ford, leaving his infantry, he went on with the cavalry, and finding the militia as expected, he with excellent conduct and great spirit attacked them instantly and totally routed them with little loss on his side, and on theirs between 40 and 50 killed, wounded or prisoners. This stroke with our passage of the ford so effectually dispirited the militia that we met with no further opposition on our march to the Yadkin through one of the most rebellious tracts in America.

During this time, the rebels having quitted Beattie's Ford, Lt Colonel Webster was passing his detachment and the baggage of the army. This had become tedious and difficult by the continuance of the rain and the swelling of the river, but all joined us soon after dark about six miles from Beattie's Ford. The other fords were likewise abandoned by the enemy. The greatest part of the militia dispersed and General Morgan with his corps marched all that afternoon and the following night towards Salisbury. We pursued next morning in hopes to intercept him between the rivers, and after struggling with many difficulties arising from swelled creeks and bad roads, the Guards came up with his rear in the evening of the 3rd, routed it, and took a few waggons at the Trading Ford of the Yadkin. He had passed the body of his infantry in flats, and his cavalry and waggons by the ford, during that day and the preceding night, but at the time of our arrival the boats were secured on the other side and the ford had become impassable. The river continuing to rise and the weather appearing unsettled, I determined to march to the upper fords after procuring a small supply of provisions at Salisbury. This and the height of the creeks in our way detained me two days, and in that time, Morgan having quitted the banks of the river, I had information from our friends who crossed in canoes that General Greene's army was marching with the utmost dispatch to form a junction with him at Guildford. Not having had time to collect the North Carolina militia and having received no reinforcement from Virginia, I concluded that he would do every thing in his power to avoid an action on the south side of the Dan; and, it being my interest to force him to fight, I made great expedition and got between him and the upper fords, and being assured that the lower fords are seldom practicable in winter and that

---

[4] Francis Hall had spent his entire service in the 3rd Regiment of Foot Guards (the Scots Guards). Commissioned an ensign on 19th February 1757, he had been promoted to lieutenant on 20th September 1762 and to captain on 3rd May 1775, a rank which carried with it a lt colonelcy. No other officer was hurt in the passage of the Catawba. (*The Army Lists*; *The Cornwallis Papers*)

he could not collect many flats at any of the ferrys, I was in great hopes that he would not escape me without receiving a blow. Nothing could exceed the patience and alacrity of the officers and soldiers under every species of hardship and fatigue in endeavouring to overtake him, but our intelligence upon this occasion was exceedingly defective, which, with heavy rains, bad roads and the passage of many deep creeks and bridges destroyed by the enemy's light troops, rendered all our exertions vain, for, upon our arrival at Boyd's Ferry on the 15th, we learned that his rear guard had got over the night before, his baggage and main body having passed the preceding day at that and a neighbouring ferry, where more flats had been collected than had been represented to me as possible. My force being ill suited to enter by that quarter so powerfull a province as Virginia, and North Carolina being in the utmost confusion, after giving the troops a halt of one day, I proceeded by easy marches to Hillsborough, where I erected the King's standard and invited by proclamation[5] all loyal subjects to repair to it and to stand forth and take an active part in assisting me to restore order and constitutional government. As a considerable body of friends were said to reside between the Haw and Deep Rivers, I detached Lt Colonel Tarleton on the 23rd with the cavalry and a small body of infantry to prevent their being interrupted in assembling. Unluckily, a detachment of the rebel light troops had crossed the same day and by accident fell in with about 200 of our friends under Colonel Pyle[6] on their way to Hillsborough, who, mistaking the rebels for Lt Colonel Tarleton's corps, allowed themselves to be surrounded, and a number of them were most inhumanly butchered, when begging for quarter, without making the least resistance. The same day I had certain intelligence that General Greene, having been reinforced, had recrossed the Dan, which, rendering it imprudent to separate my corps, occasioned the recall of Lt Colonel Tarleton's detachment; and forage and provisions being scarce in the neighbourhood of Hillsborough, as well as the position too distant (upon the approach of the rebel army) for the protection of the body of our friends, I judged it expedient to cross the Haw and encamped near Allemance Creek, detaching Lt Colonel Tarleton with the cavalry, light company of the Guards and 150 men of Lt Colonel Webster's brigade a few miles from me on the road to Deep River more effectually to cover the country. General Greene's light troops soon made their appearance, and on the 2nd, a patrole having reported that they had seen both cavalry and infantry near his post, I directed Lt Colonel Tarleton to move forward with proper precautions and endeavour to discover the designs of the enemy. He had not advanced far when he fell in with a considerable corps, which he immediately attacked and routed, but, being ignorant of their force and whether they were supported, with great prudence desisted from pursuit. He soon learned from prisoners that

---

[5] *proclamation*: see p 55.

[6] Born in Concord, Pennsylvania, John Pyle (1723-1804) was sent as a young man to study medicine in Oxfordshire, England. Becoming an MD, he returned home about 1744. In 1767 he migrated to Chatham County, North Carolina, where he continued in medical practice and became a leading Regulator. In February 1776 he accepted from Governor Martin a commission as captain on the Provincial establishment but later swore an oath of allegiance to the revolutionary state. He nevertheless remained a covert loyalist and responded to Cornwallis's proclamation of 20th February by assembling a band of loyalist irregular militia from between the Haw and Deep Rivers. While marching to join Cornwallis at Hillsborough, he and his unresisting men were inhumanly butchered by Lee's Legion and Pickens' militia, an event which came to be known as 'Pyle's massacre'. According to tradition, he himself lost three fingers and the use of an eye in the affair and only escaped by concealing himself in a nearby pond. Of the surviving wounded, thirty-two were treated at HM Hospital, Wilmington. After the war he continued to reside in Chatham County, where he died. ('Ratcliff-Smith Genealogy' (Internet, 24th December 2005); Clark, *Loyalists in the Southern Campaign*, i, 347, 537; 'Joseph Graham's Narrative', *The Murphey Papers*, ii, 273-6)

those he had beat were Lee's Legion, 3 or 400 Back Mountain men under Colonel Preston[7], with a number of militia, and that General Greene with part of his army was not far distant. Our situation for the former few days had been amongst timid friends and adjoining to inveterate rebels. Between them I had been totally destitute of information, which lost me a very favourable opportunity of attacking the rebel army. General Greene fell back to Thompson's House near Boyd's Ford on the Reedy Fork, but his light troops and militia still remained near us, and as I was informed that they were posted carelessly at separate plantations for the convenience of subsisting, I marched on the 6th to drive them in and to attack General Greene if an opportunity offered. I succeeded compleatly in the first, and at Weitzell's Mill on the Reedy Fork, where they made a stand, the Back Mountain men and some militia[8] suffered considerably with little loss on our side, but a timely and precipitate retreat over the Haw prevented the latter. I knew that the Virginia reinforcements were upon their march, and it was apparent that the enemy would if possible avoid risquing an action before their arrival. The neighbourhood of the fords of the Dan in their rear and the extreme difficulty of subsisting my troops in that exhausted country putting it out of my power to force them, my resolution was to give our friends time to join us by covering their country as effectually as possible consistent with the subsistance of the troops, still approaching the communication with our shipping in Cape Fear River, which I saw it would soon become indispensibly necessary to open on account of the sufferings of the army from the want of supplies of every kind. At the same time I was determined to fight the rebel army if it approached me, being convinced that it would be impossible to succeed in that great object of our arduous campaign, the calling forth the numerous loyalists of North Carolina, whilst a doubt remained on their minds of the superiority of our arms. With these views I had moved to the Quaker Meeting in the forks of Deep River on the 13th, and on the 14th I received the information which occasioned the movement that brought on the action at Guildford, of which I shall give your Lordship an account in a separate letter.

I have the honour to be with great respect, my Lord,
Your Lordship's most obedient and most humble servant

CORNWALLIS

---

[7] Born in Donegal, Ireland, William Preston (1729-1783) was brought to Virginia in 1735. After receiving a rudimentary education, he went on to study history, mathematics and penmanship, qualifying in 1752 as a deputy surveyor in Augusta County. Having served under the Crown as a sheriff, coroner, colonel of militia and member of the House of Burgesses, he sided with the revolutionaries and by 1781 had been acting for four years as County Lieutenant of the newly formed Montgomery County. In mid February he had assembled some 350 riflemen and had with them only just placed himself under the command of Andrew Pickens. After being involved on 2nd March in the affair at Clapp's Mill (to which Cornwallis now refers), he would go on to take part in the action at Wetzell's Mill and the Battle of Guilford. He lived to rejoice in the victory at Yorktown but died eighteen months later, possibly of an apoplectic fit, while attending a regimental muster. He is described by his daughter as 5 feet 11 inches tall, inclined to corpulency, with a ruddy complexion, fair hair and hazel eyes. According to her, he was a person of well cultivated intellect, with a fine taste for poetry. (John Frederick Dorman, *The Prestons of Smithfield and Greenfield in Virginia...* (Filson Club, 1982); Patricia Givens Johnson, *William Preston and the Allegheny Patriots* (B D Smith & Bros VA, 1976); 'Joseph Graham's Narrative', *The Murphey Papers*, ii, 280-3)

[8] *some militia*: according to the draft of this letter (76(28)), 'some Virginia militia'.

Cornwallis to Germain, 17th March 1781[9]

76(38): C

Nº 8

Guildford
17th March 1781

Rt Hon Lord George Germain etc etc etc

My Lord

I have the satisfaction to inform your Lordship that His Majesty's troops under my command obtained a signal victory on the 15th instant over the rebel army commanded by General Greene.

In pursuance of my intended plan communicated to your Lordship in my dispatch Nº 7 I had encamped on the 13th instant at the Quaker Meeting between the forks of Deep River. On the 14th I received information that General Butler with a body of North Carolina militia and the expected reinforcements from Virginia — said to consist of a Virginia State regiment, a corps of Virginia eighteen months' men, 3,000 Virginia militia and recruits for the Maryland line — had joined General Greene, and that the whole army, which was reported to amount to 9 or 10,000 men, was marching to attack the British troops. During the afternoon intelligence was brought, which was confirmed in the night, that he had advanced that day to Guildford about 12 miles from our camp. Being now persuaded that he had resolved to hazard an engagement, after detaching Lt Colonel Hamilton with our waggons and baggage escorted by his own regiment, a detachment of 100 infantry and 20 cavalry towards Bell's Mill on Deep River, I marched with the rest of the corps at day break on the morning of the 15th to meet the enemy or to attack them in their encampment. About four miles from Guildford our advanced guard commanded by Lt Colonel Tarleton fell in with a corps of the enemy consisting of Lee's Legion, some Back Mountain men and Virginia militia, which he attacked with his usual good conduct and spirit and defeated; and continuing our march, we found the rebel army posted on rising grounds about a mile and a half from the court house. The prisoners taken by Lt Colonel Tarleton, having been several days with the advanced corps, could give me no account of the enemy's order or position, and the country people were extremely inaccurate in their description of the ground. Immediately between the head of the column and the enemy's line was a considerable plantation, one large field of which was on our left of the road, and two others, with a wood about 200 yards broad between them, on our right of it. Beyond these fields the wood continued for several miles to our right. The wood beyond the plantation in our front, in the skirt of which the enemy's first line was formed, was about a mile in depth, the road then leading into an extensive space of cleared ground about Guildford Court House. The woods on our right and left were reported to be impracticable for cannon, but as that on our right appeared to be most open, I resolved to attack the left wing of the enemy, and whilst my disposition was making for that purpose, I ordered Lieutenant Macleod to bring forward the guns and cannonade their center. The attack was directed to be made in the following order: on the right, the Regiment of Bose and the 71st Regiment led by Major General Leslie and supported by the 1st Battalion of Guards; on their left, the 23rd and 33rd Regiments led by Lt Colonel Webster and supported

---

[9] Published in Stevens, op cit, i, 363. There are no material differences.

by the Grenadiers and 2nd Battalion of Guards commanded by Brigadier General O'Hara. The Yaghers and light infantry of the Guards remained in the wood on the left of the guns, and the cavalry in the road, ready to act as circumstances might require. Our preparations being made, the action began about half an hour past one in the afternoon. Major General Leslie, after being obliged by the great extent of the enemy's line to bring up the 1st Battalion of Guards to the right of the Regiment of Bose, soon defeated every thing before him. Lt Colonel Webster, having joined the left of Major General Leslie's division, was no less successfull in his front, when, on finding that the left of the 33rd was exposed to a heavy fire from the right wing of the enemy, he changed his front to the left and, being supported by the Yaghers and light infantry of the Guards, attacked and routed it, the Grenadiers and 2nd Battalion of Guards moving forward to occupy the ground left vacant by the movement of Lt Colonel Webster.

All the infantry being now in the line, Lt Colonel Tarleton had directions to keep his cavalry compact and not to charge without positive orders, except to protect any of the corps from the most evident danger of being defeated. The excessive thickness of the woods rendered our bayonets of little use and enabled the broken enemy to make frequent stands with an irregular fire which occasioned some loss, and to several of the corps great delay, particularly on our right, where the 1st Battalion of Guards and the Regiment of Bose were warmly engaged in front, flank and rear with some of the enemy that had been routed on the 1st attack and with part of the extremity of their left wing, which by the closeness of the wood had been passed unbroken. The 71st Regiment and Grenadiers and 2nd Battalion of Guards, not knowing what was passing on their right and hearing the fire advance on their left, continued to move forward, the artillery keeping pace with them on the road, followed by the cavalry. The 2nd Battalion of Guards first gained the clear ground near Guildford Courthouse and found a corps of Continental infantry much superior in number formed in the open field on the left of the road. Glowing with impatience to signalize themselves, they instantly attacked and defeated them, taking two six pounders, but, pursuing into the wood with too much ardour, were thrown into confusion by a heavy fire and immediately charged and driven back into the field by Colonel Washington's dragoons with the loss of the six pounders they had taken. The enemy's cavalry was soon repulsed by a well directed fire from two three pounders just brought up by Lieutenant Macleod, and by the appearance of the Grenadiers of the Guards and of the 71st Regiment, which, having been impeded by some deep ravines, were now coming out of the wood on the right of the Guards opposite to the court house. By the spirited exertions of Brigadier General O'Hara, tho' wounded, the 2nd Battalion of Guards was soon rallied and, supported by the Grenadiers, returned to the charge with the greatest alacrity. The 23rd Regiment arriving at that instant from our left, and Lt Colonel Tarleton having advanced with part of the cavalry, the enemy were soon put to flight and the two six pounders once more fell into our hands. Two ammunition waggons and two other six pounders, being all the artillery they had in the field, were likewise taken. About this time the 33rd Regiment and the light infantry of the Guards, after overcoming many difficulties, compleatly routed the corps which was opposed to them and put an end to the action in this quarter. The 23rd and 71st Regiments with part of the cavalry were ordered to pursue. The remainder of the cavalry was detached with Lt Colonel Tarleton to our right, where a heavy fire still continued and where his appearance and spirited attack contributed much to a speedy termination of the action. The militia with which our right had been engaged dispersed in the woods. The Continentals went off by the Reedy Fork, beyond which it was not in my power to follow them, as their cavalry had suffered but little, our troops were excessively fatigued by an action which lasted an hour and a half, and our wounded[10], dispersed over an extensive space of country, required immediate attention. The care of our wounded and the total want of provisions in an exhausted country made it equally impossible for me to follow the blow next day. The enemy did not stop untill they got to the ironworks on Troublesome Creek, 18 miles from the field of battle.

From our own observation and the best accounts we could procure, we did not doubt but the strength of the enemy exceeded 7,000 men. Their militia composed their line with parties advanced to the rails of the fields in their front. The Continentals were posted obliquely in the rear of their right wing. Their cannon fired on us, whilst we were forming, from the center of the line of militia but were withdrawn to the Continentals before the attack.

I have the honour to inclose to your Lordship the list of our killed and wounded[11]. Captain Schutz's wound is supposed to be mortal, but the surgeons assure me that none of the other officers are in danger and that a great number of the men will soon recover. I cannot ascertain the loss of the enemy but it must have been considerable. Between 2 and 300 dead were left upon the field. Many of their wounded who were able to move, while we were employed in the care of our own, escaped and followed the routed enemy, and our cattle drivers and foraging parties have reported to me that the houses in a circle of 6 to 8 miles round us are full of others. Those that remained we have taken the best care of in our power. We took few prisoners owing to the excessive thickness of the wood facilitating their escape and every man of our army being repeatedly wanted for action.

The conduct and actions of the officers and soldiers that compose this little army will do more justice to their merit than I can by words. Their persevering intrepidity in action, their invincible patience in the hardships and fatigues of a march of above 600 miles in which they have forded several large rivers and numberless creeks, many of which would be reckoned large rivers in any other country in the world, without tents or covering against the climate and often without provisions, will sufficiently manifest their ardent zeal for the honour and interests of their Sovereign and their country.

I have been particularly indebted to Major General Leslie for his gallantry and exertion in the action as well as his assistance in every other part of the service. The zeal and spirit of Brigadier General O'Hara merit my highest commendations, for after receiving two dangerous wounds he continued in the field whilst the action lasted. By his earnest attention on all other occasions, seconded by the officers and soldiers of the brigade, His Majesty's Guards are no less distinguished by their order and discipline than by their spirit and valour. The Hessian Regiment of Bose deserves my warmest praises for its discipline, alacrity and courage and does honour to Major Du Buy[12], who commands it and who is an officer of superior merit.

---

[10] *our wounded*: according to the draft of this letter (76(34)), 'our numerous wounded'.

[11] *the list..*: no copy. For a later return of killed, wounded and missing, see p 64.

[12] See vol III, p 37, note 41.

I am much obliged to Brigadier General Howard, who served as volunteer, for his spirited example on all occasions.

Lt Colonel Webster conducted his brigade like an officer of experience and gallantry. Lt Colonel Tarleton's good conduct and spirit in the management of his cavalry was conspicuous during the whole action, and Lieutenant Macleod, who commanded the artillery, proved himself upon this as well as upon all former occasions a most capable and deserving officer. The attention and exertions of my aide de camps and of all the other publick officers of the army contributed very much to the success of the day.

I have constantly received the most zealous assistance from Governor Martin during my command in the Southern District. Hoping that his presence would tend to incite the loyal subjects of this province to take an active part with us, he has chearfully submitted to the fatigues and dangers of our campaign; but his delicate constitution has suffered by his publick spirit, for by the advice of the physicians he is now obliged to return to England for the recovery of his health.

This part of the country is so totally destitute of subsistance that forage is not nearer than nine miles and the soldiers have been two days without bread. I shall therefore leave about 70 of the worst of the wounded cases at the New Garden Quaker Meeting House with proper assistance and move the remainder with the army tomorrow morning to Bell's Mill. I hope our friends will heartily take an active part with us, to which I shall continue to encourage them, still approaching our shipping by easy marches that we may procure the necessary supplies for further operations and lodge our sick and wounded where proper attention can be paid to them.

This dispatch will be delivered to your Lordship by my aide de camp, Captain Brodrick, who is a very promising officer and whom I beg leave to recommend to your Lordship's countenance and favour.

I have the honour to be with great respect, my Lord,
Your Lordship's most obedient and most humble servant

[CORNWALLIS]

§ - §

2 - To Arnold

Cornwallis to Arnold, 21st February 1781[13]   *85(5): ADfS*

Hillsborough
February 21st 1781

Brigadier General Arnold commanding His Majesty's forces in Chesapeak Bay

Sir

Having pursued General Greene to Boyd's Ferry and driven the whole Continental force entirely out of North Carolina, I repaired to this place, where my first object will be to arm our friends and employ them to the best advantage for His Majesty's Service, the second to establish a communication with our fleet in Cape Fear River and get up such necessaries for the troops as are absolutely requisite after the length and rapidity of our march.[14] I flatter myself that the unfortunate action of the 17th of January has had no other ill effect than the loss of the men and the disgrace to our arms, as the enemy has been obliged ever since to retire with the utmost precipitation.

By accounts in the country I hear that Major Craig has taken possession of Wilmington and that our ships of war and store ships are in Cape Fear River.

I have heard nothing of you but from vague reports. So many persons, however, have asserted that you have burnt the enemy's stores at Richmond that I am inclined to believe it. From the best intelligence I can procure, Greene has about one thousand infantry (Continental and Virginia eighteen month men), Morgan three hundred Continental light infantry and one hundred rifle men, Washington seventy or eighty, and Lee with the remains of White's etc about one hundred and twenty dragoons. Seventy very active infantry are attached to Lee's corps. I shall be glad to hear from you as frequently as possible.

I am, sir,
Your most obedient and most humble servant

CORNWALLIS

§ - §

---

[13] According to an endorsement, the original was dispatched on 24th February by a man named Brewer but was taken by the enemy.

[14] After 'march' the following is deleted: 'and the excessive fatigue'.

CHAPTER 41

Miscellaneous correspondence etc

1 - Between Cornwallis and O'Hara or Tarleton

O'Hara to Cornwallis, 5th February 1781   *67(77): ALS*

Camp at the Trading Ford
February the 5th 1781

Earl Cornwallis etc etc etc

My dear Lord

The water has rose so considerably as to cover the waggon totally you saw yesterday overagainst the upper ford.

About nine last night we observed the number of their fires to decrease considerably, and at eleven two only could be seen. At the reveillée this morning we heared their bugle horn and saw their centrys posted upon the bank of the river retire from the water side. Till within this half hour we have not seen any people on the other side. About four or five with their arms (apparently a small guard) are all we see at present. They are posted in the house by the ford.

As my people do their duty of every sort perfectly well, I have just heard by accident that about *four yesterday evening* a number of batt horses were seen marching up the river.

Yesterday about forty men I was told had passed about one mile below me. I sent a party immediately after them but was not fortunate enough to fall in either with them or the flat.

This morning I was informed that a number of canoes were assembled at a ferry three miles from this camp. I have sent a detachment there to destroy them.

Without you mean that we should move this day or night towards Salisbury, I would wish to have my people join me I left at Salisbury. We are here without camp kettles or blankets.

Such as it is, that's all I have heard or seen since I have been here.

Yours most sincerely

COH

Tarleton to Cornwallis, 13th February 1781[1] 67(79): ALS

Iron Works
February 13th, 5 am

My Lord

I sent out spies to find the enemy's position. They only ventured five miles. My patroles took a militia man who says Green pass'd High Rock yesterday. The two corps will meet at the fork of the roads twenty miles from hence and ten from Dicks's Ferry. Every exertion shall be made to obtain intelligence to day.

I have the honor to be
Your Lordship's most devoted servant

BAN TARLETON

Tarleton to Cornwallis, 23rd February 1781 67(87): ALS

Haw River
February 23rd, 9 am

My Lord

I shall pass to day.

The enemy are gone to Butler *at Tar River*.

I have the honor to be
Your Lordship's most devoted servant

BAN TARLETON

---

[1] An inaccurate version of this letter appears in Bass, *The Green Dragoon*, 167.

Tarleton to Cornwallis, 23rd February 1781[2]   67(88): ALS

February 23rd 1781

My Lord

Want of your Lordship's *billets* stops me.

George Johnson and John Justin bear this. They wish to come out of town to night. Their property is near me. They may be entrusted. *I hear nothing of the enemy*.

I have the honor to be
Your most devoted servant

BAN TARLETON

Cornwallis to Tarleton, 24th February 1781[3]   85(11): ADfS

Hillsborough
February 24th 1781

Lt Colonel Tarleton

Dear Tarleton

I have received intelligence from two persons that Greene passed the Dan on the 22nd and was advancing to Dobbyns's. They mention so many particulars that I cannot help giving some credit. I therefore wish you join me as soon as possible.

Yours etc

CORNWALLIS

[*Subscribed*:]

I take up my ground this evening on the south side the Eno.

§ - §

---

[2] Published with a minor inaccuracy in Bass, *The Green Dragoon*, 168.

[3] According to an endorsement, the original (published in Tarleton, *Campaigns*, 257) was dispatched by a man named Holloway at 3 pm with three copies being sent between 4 and 8 pm, the last from the south side of the Eno.

2 - Between Cornwallis and Craig

Cornwallis to Craig, 21st February 1781[4]   *85(7): ADfS*

Hillsborough
February 21st 1781

Major Craig

Sir

After driving the whole Continental force into Virginia with such precipitation as to prevent their embodying any considerable number of militia in this province, I repaired to this place, where I shall be for some time busily employed in arming and modelling our friends. I must, however, soon open a communication with Cross Creek and receive some supplies from you. I do not at present know what measures it will be necessary to take to secure the navigation of the Cape Fear River. You will please to do every thing in your power to procure the most exact information on that subject. The articles which we are in the greatest want of are shoes for the infantry and saddles and boots for the cavalry. Of the former we require a very large supply.

If you apprehend a deficiency in any of those articles, you will lose no time in sending to Charlestown. You will please to inform Lt Colonel Balfour that I shall want cavalry appointments of all sorts, and desire him, if he finds difficulties in procuring them at Charlestown, to send immediately to New York. A quantity of shirts will likewise be much wanted for this army. Take every means of letting me hear from you.

I am, sir,
Your most obedient and most humble servant

CORNWALLIS

[*Subscribed*:]

Send a copy of this letter with the inclosed note to Lt Colonel Balfour[5].

Should any troops arrive in Cape Fear River from Europe, you will please to desire the commanding officer to come up with all possible expedition to Cross Creek, taking every means of giving me information of it. You will likewise acquaint him that we have no wheel carriages but three horses are allowed to a captain and two to a subaltern.

---

[4]   The subscriptions of 5th and 8th March were added to the triplicate, which was dispatched on the 19th of that month. The original miscarried, but the duplicate arrived safely.

[5]   *the inclosed note..*: Cornwallis to Balfour, 21st February, p 41.

Camp near Alamance Creek
March 5th 1781

General Greene having repassed the Dan and sent his light troops to prevent the assembling of our friends between the Haw and Deep River, I found it necessary to pass the Haw in order to protect them. I have since heard that General Greene has passed the Haw at High Rock Ford. I shall do every thing in my power to bring him to an action, as no material rising of our friends can be expected whilst his army is in the neighbourhood. Lt Colonel Tarleton had a successfull skirmish with the enemy's light troops on the 2nd.

Camp on Reedy Fork
March 8th 1781

On finding that Greene was in Guilford County south of Reedy Fork and that he had dispersed his light troops through the Irish settlement to awe our friends on Deep River, I moved to Whitesel's Mill on Reedy Fork east of Buffaloe, where we fell in with five or six hundred of his militia and light troops, who were obliged to retire with precipitation. General Greene marched immediately towards the iron works on Troublesome Creek. As I cannot engage in another pursuit to the Dan River, I intend now to march through Guilford County to Bell's Mill on Deep River, permitting our friends to punish their cruel persecutors in the Irish settlement as we pass.

Cornwallis to Craig, 19th March 1781[6]

85(16): ADf

Camp, Bell's Mill, Deep River
19th March 1781

Major Craig

Sir

I am now in my way towards Cross Creek. It is reported that the reinforcement from Ireland is arrived at Wilmington. I wish, if it is true, that the troops may be sent up to Cross Creek as soon as possible and the navigation secured, and that shoes, necessaries, rum, wine, and hospital stores for the wounded, which are very numerous, may be forwarded with expedition. Take every means of letting me hear from you.

[CORNWALLIS]

---

[6] According to an endorsement, the original was enclosed with the triplicate to Craig of 21st February.

Craig to Cornwallis, 22nd March 1781   *69(19): C*

22nd March

    Yesterday only I received the first dispatch with which I have been honoured from your Lordship, being the duplicate of the one of the 21st February. Since my arrival I have sent three messengers. The last was left in so fair a way that I hope he will have [reached] you safe. If so, your Lordship will be informed of our situation here. The rebel militia, now between five and six hundred under Brigadier Lillinton[7] with six pieces of cannon, continue at Heron's Bridge and prevent all communication with that part of the country. We have dispersed a party of about a hundred that were on the Brunswick side of the river and defeated another of a hundred and fifty a few days ago, killing twenty and taking a few prisoners, but it has had no effect on their main body. Both their numbers and position put it out of my power to attack them, nor can I hope to disperse them with my present force. Though our different actions have been attended with very little loss, yet we are much diminished by sickness and desertion. By the best information I can procure of the river between this and Cross Creek, it is in general about one hundred yards in breadth, the banks steep with frequent bluffs from sixty to a hundred feet high. These occurr at least every ten miles. The roads do not pass near the banks but at some distance back with communications to the plantations which are on the borders of the river. The water shallow, particularly about six miles below Elizabeth Town, not admitting boats that draw above three feet, for which reason large boats are constructed on purpose. Forty miles up you feel the tide, but above that the current is gentle except during the freshes, which are most frequent in the fall. The boats are generally from twenty to twenty five days going and returning. By this state of the river your Lordship will judge how impracticable it will be to send any thing up 'till the country is more settled. Lylington must at all events be dispersed, which I believe the appearance of a detachment between him and Duplin Court House will effect. When this body is dispersed, the east side of the river would be for the present pretty secure, the more so as the inhabitants of Black River, tho' few in number, are very well inclined. I should still, however, think the navigation in future precarious and requiring convoys, unless the whole country between your Lordship and Newbern was mastered, which would be very easily effected. The people here are so little used to turning out and so heartily tired of what they have had lately that, when once returned to their plantations, the most violent will not be compelled to assemble again easily. On the west side of the river Marion is to be guarded against. He is between us and the Pedee and, by the last information I could get of him, which, however, was not much to be depended on, was three or four hundred strong. One of his haunts is the White Marsh within twenty miles of the river. Plunder being his object, he must be well watched. Your Lordship will judge I am making difficulties only for your

---

[7]   Brought to Cape Fear in North Carolina in 1734, John Alexander Lillington (*c.* 1725-1786) was the son of a colonel in the British Army who, after settling in Barbados, had become a member of HM Council there. When the Provincial Congress met at Halifax in August 1775, he was commissioned colonel of the revolutionary militia in Wilmington District and six months later led a body of his men in the defeat of the Scots Highlanders at Moore's Creek Bridge. It was to be his only material involvement in the war. Now promoted to brigadier general, he was commanding a force of militia observing Craig at Wilmington. At the close of the war he would retire to Lillington Hall, beside the site of which his grave may still be seen. A mansion lying nine miles north-east of the present hamlet of Rocky Point near Wilmington, it stood for some two centuries before being burned. (Wheeler, *Reminiscences*, 47-8; Wheeler, *Historical Sketches*, i, 72; *Appletons'*; Lossing, *Pictorial Field-Book*, ii, 379-381; Robinson, *NC Guide*, 348)

information, which you have ordered me to give you. I was once in hopes to have removed the principal one Lyllington myself, but on serious reflection I thought too much at stake to justify the attempt. I wrote to Colonel Balfour for a reinforcement but he had it not in his power to send it me. The town of Wilmington itself would require at least six hundred men to garrison it properly. As it was impossible for us to attempt it, we chose a post below the town but commanding it. Our post is not very good and infinitely too extensive. However, I thought it tenable against the people we had to deal with. The stock of supplies of which your Lordship stands in need at present here is very small – totally inadequate to your wants. We have neither saddles, boots, or any appointments for cavalry, so that I shall take the most expeditious means of writing to Lt Colonel Balfour, to whom I shall observe your Lordship's directions. I subjoin some sketches of returns[8] for your information, and am with the greatest respect

Your Lordship's etc

[J H CRAIG]

Cornwallis to Craig, 3rd April 1781　　　　　　　　　　　　　　　85(20): C

Camp one mile below Elizabeth Town
3rd April 1781

Major Craig

Sir

I shall be at Livingston's Creek on the fifth of April and should be glad that boats could meet me there with some flour and rum, particularly flour.

CORNWALLIS

Craig to Cornwallis, 6th April 1781　　　　　　　　　　　　　　　5(181): ALS

Willmington
6th April, 11 o'clock

My Lord

About an hour ago an officer of the 82nd arrived with the letters I have the honor to send you, which I have lost no time in doing as I hope they will prove satisfactory to your Lordship. The change Captain Inglis has made with respect to the vessel to go to Charles Town will, I hope, meet with your Lordship's approbation as it was a good deal by my advice. The *Loyalist* by being below will probably sail a day or two before the *Delight* could get down, and I thought your Lordship might want the *Delight*.

---

[8] *some sketches..*: not extant.

I have receiv'd application from all the ships of war to return the marines who have been doing duty with me here. When they leave me, I shall be so extremely reduc'd in numbers as not to be able to furnish a guard for your Lordship when you do us the honour of a visit. May I beg your Lordship's directions. I have issued orders here that no sutler is to go near your Lordship's army without my leave, and at the same time have told them that on application I will give permission, but it shall be under such restrictions with respect to spirits as I hope will in some degree obviate the inconveniencies your Lordship apprehended from the intercourse of those gentry. Directions have been given about fitting up the transports, but they are so low down the river, and so many other unfortunate accidents concerning them happen, that I much fear your Lordship will find a difficulty in getting your wounded on board so soon as you expected. McLean's Bluff is, I am told, a dry, good situation. However, my time has as yet this morning been so much engrossed by the attention to your Lordship's other directions I have not made so many enquiries as I could have wish'd. Should I find any reason against your Lordship's going there, I will inform you before you march tomorrow.

I have the honor to be with the greatest respect
Your Lordship's most obedient and most humble servant

J H CRAIG

[*Subscribed*:]

War is declar'd against Holland. General Phillips with 3,000 men arriv'd in the Chesapeak.

Craig to Cornwallis, 6th April 1781   5(183): ALS

Willmington
6th April 1781, 11 o'clock

My Lord

As the shortest way of acquainting your Lordship with the purport of Colonel Balfour's letters to me, permit me to enclose them to you, requesting, when your Lordship has read them, Major Ross will be good enough to take charge of them to return them to me when convenient.

I have the honor to be
Your Lordship's most obedient servant

J H CRAIG

§ - §

3 - Between Balfour and Craig[9]

Balfour to Craig, 15th January 1781   109(2): C

Charles Town
January 15th 1781

Major Craig
82nd Regiment

Sir

You will be pleased to embark with the troops order'd to put themselves under your command and proceed from hence to Cape Fear River in North Carolina, to gain the navigation of which being the principal object of this expedition. You will take care to secure such a post on it as you shall find most calculated to attain this end and also afford protection to the victualers and other store ships which accompany you for Lord Cornwallis's army.

For this purpose I wou'd recommend to your consideration Wilmington as a most eligible post shou'd it be found tenable without too considerable a risque, which is on no account to be adventured; but on the contrary this town must be relinquished, even after possession, shou'd the approach of an enemy in force render the measure necessary.

In case, on your arrival at Cape Fear, you shou'd consider Wilmington for the above or other reasons (of which, being on the spot, you will be better enabled to judge) as an unfit post, I would point out Brunswick and Fort Johnston as places suited to these views, and which I conceive may be held without any essential hazard and have, besides, the advantage of effectually covering the shipping.

As one of the principal motives for this expedition is the supplying Lord Cornwallis's army at Cross Creek with provisions etc, the better to accomplish this you will secure what boats and small craft can be procured, and to this part of the service from its great necessity I must request your utmost attention.

On the first appearance of Lord Cornwallis's approach you will be pleased to attempt an immediate communication with him and also as soon as possible the sending a supply to his army; and to enable you to correspond securely with his Lordship as well as myself, several cyphers will be herewith delivered for your use when any possible risque renders such precaution necessary.

Your own judgment will direct the best mode of sending and guarding up provisions and stores and also point out the fittest posts for covering them, but in these and all other respects

---

[9] The letters are not necessarily in date order but in the order in which they were written and received by Craig. He forwarded them to Cornwallis with his letter of 6th April, p 29.

you will be guided by what information you are able to obtain from the country and the knowledge which, when there, you must acquire of it.

Captain Barclay, who commands the sea force, will on all necessary occasions cooperate with you and afford every assistance in his power to accomplish this service.

I have further to request you will communicate to me your arrival at Cape Fear, your situation there, and whatever else you may deem essential.

Wishing you every success, I have the honor to be, sir,
Your most obedient and humble servant

N BALFOUR

Craig to Balfour, 4th February 1781   5(67): ACS

Willmington
4th February 1781

Sir

As I had the honour of receiving my instructions from you and have at present no way of communicating with Lord Cornwallis, I think it my duty to make my report to his Lordship through you, requesting you to take the earliest opportunity of laying it before him.

Having at length after four days conquer'd the difficulties occasion'd by the intricacy of the navigation and the ignorance of the pilots, we landed on the 28th last month at a settlement about 12 miles from Willmington (Captain Barkley at my request landing with us the marines of the ships of war under his command) and the next day march'd and took possession of Willmington in conjunction with the gallies, who, with Captain Barkley on board, mov'd up the river at the same time, the inhabitants surrendering themselves prisoners at discretion.

I found that a body of militia under a Colonel Young[10] had been collecting for some time and had retir'd, but the night before we came into the town, to Heron's Bridge about ten miles off, where they intended waiting to collect strength and cover the vessels which had carried all their stores and ammunition up the river. The accounts of their numbers varied so much that I was at a loss to form any judgement of them. However, as the dispersing them as well as seizing their vessels might be of consequence to us, I determin'd to march to them the next day, thinking that, tho the great strength of their post, with which I was well acquainted, might make the first difficult, still an opportunity might be found, especially if

---

[10] On meeting at Halifax in April 1776, the North Carolina Provincial Congress had commissioned Henry Young as a major in the New Hanover County regiment of the revolutionary militia. Its catchment area lay in and around Wilmington. By now he had succeeded to the colonelcy of the regiment. (Wheeler, *Historical Sketches*, i, 81; Jack E Fryar Jr, 'When the British Came', *The Coastal Chronicles*, i (Dram Tree Books, Wilmington NC, 2002))

they attempted to support their vessels. The open attack of the post we knew to be impracticable, as it consisted of a bridge with a narrow causeway on the opposite end through a very deep marsh, a quarter of a mile in breadth, which terminated in a hill on which they were encamp'd. The river on that side also offer'd a very favourable bank for the defence of the bridge. We march'd at 4 in the afternoon with 250 rank and file and 2 three pounders, leaving Major Manson with the remainder to guard the town. A little after dark one of the light infantry with great spirit made himself master of one of the rebel light horse who was on the lookout, and from him we got such intelligence as determin'd us to attempt surprizing them. We accordingly mov'd on within about a mile of the bridge and there lay on our arms, meaning to attack them between 3 and 4 in the morning. Volunteers immediately turn'd out for the dangerous service of seizing the necessary centinels, every precaution taken for securing any patrole which might come near us, and I have not the smallest doubt of our having succeeded, had not an unlucky accident put an end to all our hopes. A serjeant and a private man found themselves so closely beset by six horsemen, before they were aware of it, that they had not time to throw themselves into the wood but were oblig'd to fire. As all idea of surprizing them was now over, we push'd forward directly and follow'd the patrole so closely that they had neither time to take up the bridge or use any other precaution. The light infantry (with a part of Major Manson's command attach'd to them) and the grenadiers form'd within 50 yards of the rebel party on this side the bridge, who challeng'd us and fir'd. They were immediately charg'd and run over the bridge. As I found they had not taken the bridge up and seem'd in a great panick, I determin'd to push them and, notwithstanding the strength of the ground, thought circumstances bid fair for succeeding in an attack on their post itself, which would at once secure their vessels and probably prevent their assembling again. Captains Nesbitt[11] and Pitcairne[12] were therefore order'd to pass the bridge and pursue the attack, which they did with the greatest spirit. I form'd the companies of the 82nd with the field pieces to cover the bridge in case of misfortune, which was done in a moment, and then advanc'd with the marines to support the flank companies. Every thing gave way. In a few minutes all was over and we in possession of the rebel camp, where we found a number of arms, canteens, some provisions etc. After waiting a sufficient time to be sure they were totally dispers'd, we return'd over the bridge, as I wish'd the men to rest in security after the fatigue of two days' march and laying five nights either on their arms or on the decks of sloops and boats without covering. I have since learn'd the rebels to have been between 250 and 300. As we did not extend our search far, we only found three dead, and the darkness of the night together with their precipitate flight prevented our making more than 7 or 8 prisoners. Many, however, were wounded who are since got home. On our side six private men were wounded, but I am sorry to add that Captain Nesbitt receiv'd two shots in his leg on the first discharge of the centinels, notwithstanding which he charg'd with his company to the enemy's camp and exerted himself so much that I did not perceive he was hurt till all

---

[11] Colebrook Nesbitt had entered the 32nd Regiment as an ensign on 7th June 1773 and been promoted to lieutenant on 25th October 1775. He transferred on 5th January 1778 to a captaincy in the 82nd, a regiment being newly formed by the Duke of Hamilton for service in North America. (*Army Lists*)

[12] Commissioned a lieutenant in the 14th Regiment on 13th January 1776, Thomas Pitcairn had been promoted to a captaincy in the 82nd on 7th January 1778. In the spring of 1779 he was on passage to New York with the flank companies when he was shipwrecked off the coast of New Jersey and was fortunate to escape being drowned. Taken prisoner and paroled to Reading, he was later exchanged. (*Army Lists*; Pitcairn to Congress, 27th May 1779 (ALS, DNA: PCC, 78, xviii, 223))

was over. He is, however, in a fair way of doing well and I hope only to have to lament the loss of his assistance, which I most sensibly feel. We took one iron three pounder, which we threw into the river after breaking off the trunnions. The capture of their vessells took place the next day as foreseen. The two largest, one of which was loaded with ammunition, were burnt and the remainder brought down here together with a brig, which was taken by a galley and two gun boats sent up the river by Captain Barkley. The following day we march'd 5 miles in front and destroy'd a considerable quantity of rum and stores, which might have been serviceable to an enemy, and, returning by another road, reach'd this on Friday evening.

In justice to the troops and marines under my command I cannot help mentioning that the town of Willmington was taken possession of and an extent of country of upwards of 45 miles march'd over with only one single instance of any article being touch'd or inhabitant injur'd in his property except as order'd by myself. This, I am sure, will entitle them to his Lordship's notice as much as the commendations I could bestow on their behaviour in the action.

I am preparing every thing for the further execution of my instructions, and am with the greatest respect, sir,

Your most obedient and most humble servant

JAMES HENRY CRAIG
Major, 82nd Regiment

Craig to Balfour, 10th February 1781   5(79): ACS

Willmington
10th February 1781

Sir

Captain Barkley has just inform'd me of his intentions of going down the river tomorrow morning to sail as soon after as possible for Charlestown. Since I wrote to you by the pilot boat nothing material has pass'd here. The rebels continue collecting, tho', from every information I can obtain, the people come in to them slowly, wish anxiously for tranquillity, and are only deterr'd by the apprehensions of my not being able to protect them from declaring so at least. The more sanguine affirm they would join me. The greatest body at present together are about four or five hundred near the bridge from whence we have drove them once already, but at present I can not get at them. Our unfortunate delays in the river gave them time to drive the country so compleatly before them that I have as yet been able to mount only 13 men. Tomorrow night, if the weather permits, I mean to make an attempt on about 100 or 150 mounted men who are at some distance from their main force. If we succeed, we shall probably get all mounted. I shall make my party as strong as possible, as from the situation it is not impossible but it may lead to some thing more serious. My whole safety in a manner consists in preventing their assembling in any very considerable force, at least till Lord Cornwallis gets nearer, and the best way of doing that is if possible to beat them as fast as they attempt it. The night before last I got intelligence of their intentions to carry off our patroles, for which they had pick'd out a select party. Captain Pitcairne with the light infantry and grenadiers way lay'd them, and our patroles drew them on very well, but they were so very cautious he could only get one volley at them, by which several were hurt but none killed. The light infantry attempted to follow them, but as they were all mounted, it was of course in vain.

I have already inform'd you that it is impracticable with our small force to keep possession of the town itself. We are therefore fortifying with redouts a situation just below the town, which will command it but is itself commanded almost all round, besides being still too extensive for our numbers, even including the marines. I was, however, determin'd not to abandon the town, as I think it would be attended with the worst effects, and was therefore oblig'd to take up with the best post we can find. We have borrow'd guns from the transports and are making the most of it. I pity the town because, if ever I am attack'd in force, I cannot prevent their burning it. I cannot help repeating a couple of hundred men more would make me master of the country and prevent, I think, every impediment to my communication with Cross Creek. As it is, I am at a loss how to accomplish it unless I can dissipate the collection in my front, which, while they keep on the other side the North East River, will be difficult, and they will not come on this side unless in great strength. They have got over the difficulty into which we threw them by destroying their ammunition vessel, having receiv'd a supply, tho' not equal to their wants, and they find plenty of provisions.

At length I have got some intelligence of Lord Cornwallis which I think may be relied on. The first instant he and Morgan were on the opposite sides of the Catabaw, 40 miles from Salisbury. The rains had swell'd the river so, he could not pass but was waiting till it fell. Morgan had sent to Salisbury to remove the stores etc, so was thinking of his retreat. A man set out last night for the second time to endeavour to reach Lord Cornwallis or General Leslie, who from the same information is somewhere on the Pedee (Hely's Ferry, I believe), where Green opposes his passage. Green has call'd every thing to him and there is at present only one company at Cross Creek, which is full of provisions. I have had serious thoughts of burning it as soon as my works are finish'd, but I am afraid I am too weak. A very little additional force would make me attempt it, however. Another difficulty which will attend the supplying the army from this place is the want of flatts and boats, being almost all up the river, chiefly at Cross Creek. Could I destroy them there, Green could never escape with General Leslie in his front and Lord Cornwallis above him. At present he must depend on them for passing the river. This would make an attempt on Cross Creek a noble stroke, but it is above my strength so much I can only think on it.

Captain Barkley has taken ten of his marines with him, so that I have only 60 left. By my returns this day I have 289, including the marines, fit for duty, exclusive of artillery and mounted men. I hope you will allow I have a difficult task to go through. However, I do not despair and found no small hopes on my confidence in your assistance as far as in your power. If I receive none from you, I shall attribute it to your inability only, being certain of your good wishes as well as confidence in my intentions.

I have as yet pursued the method of making the people prisoners on parole without requiring them to take the oaths of allegiance, as I cannot protect them from the troubles to which they would be expos'd in the latter case. We have paroled near 200, and as they look on it as a sanction for remaining quiet, which is all they desire, it answers my purpose better than alarming them by requiring what I could not compell them to.

I am, sir,
Your obedient and most humble servant

J H CRAIG

[*Subscribed*:]

I can get no accounts of Marion, tho' I have made several attempts. I hear of large parties of Tories in arms in different parts, with whom I have tried to open a communication but hitherto without effect.

JHC

Craig to Balfour, 10th February 1781　　　　　　　　　　　　　*5(81): ACS*

Private　　　　　　　　　　　　　　　　　　　　　　　　　　　　　　Willmington
　　　　　　　　　　　　　　　　　　　　　　　　　　　　　　　　　　10th February 1781

Dear Sir

Captain Barkley has given me so little notice that I must beg you to read my publick letter with an indulgent eye as I have hardly had time to give it a second perusal. May I beg, if you can ever turn the scales relative to his returning here, that it may be in the negative. He and I differ so much in our sentiments that I much fear we can never carry on service together with that cordiality so requisite to do it effectually. He talks of leaving only one sloop of war here by and by. If he does, our vessels will be constantly expos'd by sea as they cannot come within six miles of us. In short, pardon me if for your private information I warn you to receive with caution every thing he tells you. *Son interêt* will be his chief inducement. I had once thoughts of returning him his marines that he might have no reason for coming back, but I could not part with six and twenty fine fellows.

I beg to recommend to your notice Doctor Cobham[13], who goes with him. He is a man

---

[13] Dr Thomas Cobham was a highly respected citizen of Wilmington who had set himself up there as a 'practitioner in physics' in 1766. Five years later he saw service as a physican under Tryon during the campaign against the Regulators. A loyalist, he in March 1775 refused at first to subscribe to the Continental Association subversive of the Crown but was 'persuaded' to do so two days later. After the Battle of Moore's Creek Bridge in February 1776 he attended without pay the Scots Highlanders who had been wounded. With the onset of the war he had intended to take passage to England but was prevailed upon by the revolutionary authorities to remain. He later claimed that he had never sworn an oath of allegiance to the revolutionary state but obtained a certificate from a magistrate that he had done so. Now, in February 1781, he was repairing to Charlestown, where he would take up the post of surgeon to HM Naval Hospital, eventually moving on to occupy the same post at St Augustine. When East Florida was ceded to Spain in 1783, he and the hospital were removed to New Providence in the Bahama Islands, where he continued in service till March 1786. Six months later he returned to England, learning on arrival that his property in North Carolina, consisting mainly of one plantation and a half interest in another,

so universally well spoken of that he must be valuable. We have found him very usefull. I beg to trouble you with my compliments and thanks to Mr Cruden, whose information I have found equally just and usefull.

Captain Nesbitt continues mending, tho' I think slowly. He is a very great loss to me. However, with Major Manson's and Sutherland's assistance I make it out tolerably well. The rest of our wounded men are all mending, but the flux and fevers have got among us a little owing to bad weather and hard duty.

I am, dear sir,
Your most oblig'd servant

J H CRAIG

Craig to Balfour, 12th February 1781   5(87): ACS

Willmington
12th February 1781

Lt Colonel Balfour

Sir

Yesterday evening I received intelligence, which may be depended on, that Mr Nash (the rebel Governor of this province) was to arrive at the rebel camp at Heron's Bridge last night or this day. He brings a considerable force with him, tho' all militia. They have repair'd the bridge which I destroyed, and Tuesday night is fix'd on for their march towards me. They are in high spirits and say they will attack me either in the night or Wednesday morning. I cannot obtain their numbers but suppose it will not exceed 1,200. I think I can stand their attack and mean to try it, but if they take post near me, which I suspect, and bring canon, my situation will be more precarious and I must look for assistance from some quarter or other. I have no other accounts of Lord Cornwallis or General Leslie than what is contain'd in my letter of yesterday.

I am, sir,
Your most obedient and most humble servant

J H CRAIG

---

had been confiscated. He was still alive in 1797. (Janet Schaw, *Journal of a Lady of Quality*, 3rd edition (Yale University Press, 1939), 192, Appendix XII)

Balfour to Craig, 30th January 1781　　　　　　　　　　109(9): C

Charles Town
January 30th 1781

Major Craig
82nd Regiment

Dear Sir

The inclosed[14] will explain my motives for sending you this dispatch.

You may be assured of Arnold's being in the Chesapeak, where he has burnt the stores at Richmond and was proceeding to Petersburgh.

You will shew this to Captain Barclay and communicate with him. To him I beg my best compliments.

I request you will dispatch back the pilot boat that brings you this as soon as possible, as I shall be anxious to hear from you.

I am, dear sir,
Your most faithful and obedient servant

N BALFOUR

Craig to Balfour, 18th February 1781　　　　　　　　　　5(85): ACS

Willmington
18th February 1781

Lt Colonel Balfour

Sir

Yesterday I had the honour of your letters by the pilot boat. As Captain Barkley sails this day, I propose detaining Kane's boat[15] for four or five days in case any thing should happen which it may be necessary to inform you of, or that[16] I should obtain any information of Lord Cornwallis, when I shall dispatch her immediately.

---

[14] *The inclosed*: not extant.

[15] *Kanes's boat*: the pilot boat, perhaps commanded by a junior naval officer. If so, he may have been Charles Loder Carne (?-1819), who had been commissioned a lieutenant in the Royal Navy in January 1771. (Syrett and DiNardo, *The Commissioned Sea Officers*, 73)

[16] *that*: the meaning is 'in case'. As in modern French, a subordinate conjunction, if repeated in 18th-century English, was often replaced by 'that'.

We have now very nearly compleated our abbatis round the redouts, and tho' we have been under the necessity of occupying an extent of ground far beyond the proportion to our numbers, yet I think our situation too good to fear the whole *militia force* of the country were they to assemble. Mr Nash join'd the rebel camp according to the information contain'd in my last letter, but they have not yet, as I can learn, mov'd or come any ways nearer us. Their numbers I believe to be from six to eight hundred, but it is the only thing, almost, of which I cannot get any intelligence.

I have sent three people to Lord Cornwallis, one of which return'd, but as the other two have continued, I am in hopes one will reach him. The principal difficulty which I foresee in the further prosecution of my instructions will arise from the want of proper craft. I shall attempt to build some if possible. I have mention'd the circumstance to Lord Cornwallis, requesting he will take measures for securing those at Cross Creek, where they are almost all assembled.

I have the honor to be, sir,
Your most obedient and most humble servant

J H CRAIG

Craig to Balfour, 18th February 1781   5(89): ACS

Private   Willmington
18th February 1781

Dear Sir

Captain Barkley hurries me so that he will hardly allow me to add three lines in a more familiar stile than my publick letter. The information contain'd in my second letter was very exact, tho' they, from some reason which I am unacquainted with, did not chuse to come near us. I do not believe their numbers to be above 600, and as I do not fear them, I was in hopes they would have come nearer us so as to have given us an opportunity of dispersing them. For this purpose I have kept very close and given them every demonstration of fear which I thought could encourage them, but as yet in vain. In their present position they are inattackable.

I once more beg to recommend my *petites affaires* to your protection. You know my meaning.

Your very sincerely obedient servant

J H CRAIG

Balfour to Craig, 30th March 1781   5(186): ALS

Charles Town
30th March 1781

Dear Craig

Ere this reaches you, you must certainly have heard of Lord Cornwallis's success on the 15th instant, the only acount of which I send you a copy of by the inclosed note receved on the 23rd by Lord Rawdon[17].

The moment it came to me, I have forwarded a supply of those things I thought the most essentialy necessary for the use of the army and sent them off directly. Medicines, hospital stores and necessarys are the principal things wanted by an army after such a business, and the stores now sent are only hurried off to lose no time and get the advantage of the convoy of the *Loyalist*, who is just about to sail for New York. Dunloop[18] will tell you of all matters here and as much of the victory as we know.

But[19] this day a frigate arrived from the Chesapeak with acounts of an action at sea betwixt the French fleet and Admiral Arbuthnott in which the French got a trimming and were obliged to get out to sea pursued by our fleet, who could not get up with them, being so much dissabled. No shipps were taken on either side, although two French shipps are said to have struck to us but could not be taken posession of in time.

This business, although not decisive, yet prevents a plan taking place of transporting a French army (which was in the fleet) to attack Arnold, and which was to be mett by an American force of 1,500 men to be transported from the head of Elk across Chesapeak Bay to cooperate with the French troops.[20]

---

[17] *the inclosed note..*: see Cornwallis to Rawdon, 17th March, p 46.

[18] Although an Andrew Dunlap was serving as a captain in the 82nd, it is more likely that Balfour is referring to James Dunlop (?-1832), who had been commissioned a lieutenant in the regiment on 11th January 1778. He had only recently been exchanged, having been taken prisoner in the spring of 1779 when the vessel taking him and the flank companies to New York was shipwrecked off the coast of New Jersey. Four-fifths of his company were drowned. Paroled to Reading, he appears to have had a rather torrid time there, as recounted by Thomas Pitcairn to Congress: 'On Saturday last the 23rd instant Lieutenant Dunlop in company with some ladies of the place were walking the streets. He received several rotten eggs thrown by some boys standing a short distance from him. That was often repeated. He found it necessary to correct the offenders, whose fathers with a mob immediatly interfer'd and beat the said Lieutenant Dunlop in most inhuman manner, insomuch I find his life was in danger. Lieutenant Dunlop was in that condition committed to jail under the same rooff with the common felons... Lieutenant Dunlop is still confined and required to give bail and appear at the quarter sessions to answer just conduct..., the imposibility of his getting bail being totally unknown to any body here and every man being equally his enemy.' (*Army Lists*; Thomas Pitcairn to Congress, 27th May 1779, qv p 32)

[19] *But*: used in the sense of 'only'.

[20] The action between Arbuthnot and Destouches occurred off the Capes of Virginia on 16th March and had the effect which Balfour describes.

Admiral Arbuthnott being now in pursuit of the French after refitting four days in the Chesapeak, and a large reinforcement for the southward being at the Hook, I hope things may still go well.

Being in haste, I have only to add that your holding your post has been of very great consequence to Lord Cornwallis's operations and must gain you the reputation you wish. As to future plans, untill I hear from Lord Cornwallis, I cannot say positively, but my idea at present is for your corps to return here the moment you are relieved, and to give you the command here of the light corps, infantry and cavalry, which moves in this country against a very active enemy, and which, if not soon suppressed, may very materialy effect Lord Cornwallis. The regiments from England, when they arrive, will certainly come up your way and they must be got up to the army. I mean Sutherland to conduct them there and hope part of them will make the garrison of Willmington, of all which I shall communicate upon with his Lordship immediately and let you know. The mate and medicines you mention, if necessary, may be taken from those now sent for the army, but every thing will depend upon your intelligence from Lord Cornwallis and I can only say: tell us what to send that we have.

I do not think the *Blonde* will come near you. Barclay has wrote for one of the sloops to come here to convoy money, stores and provisions which I shall have all ready, but do not part with your force if it is absolutely necessary to keep it, but send us word how you are and how we shall manage for you.

Yours most sincerly

N BALFOUR

PS

I would have sent the money now, but that the *Loyalist* was not to go over the barr, which made it unsafe. You know *who* I have to deal with.

The bag of letters for Lord Cornwallis will be delivred by Dunlopp and I would not wish them sent but by a very careful and safe hand. The opening the communication is the first great object now, and every thing depends upon it. I shall with much anxiety expect to hear of it by return of the *Loyalist*.

I have paid your bill and shall honour any draft you may make upon me. I think we have no chance of communicating with you if one of the sloops does not come. I feel the dreadfull grievance you mentioned lye very heavy upon me.

I am about to buy a pilot boat for the purpose of expresses to you. Adieu. I expect you will have heared of Broderick by this time.

Barry to Craig, 30th March 1781   *5(189): ALS*

Charles Town
March 30th 81

Major Craig etc

My dear Sir

So little communication is there between us that I have now before me your letter of the 10th ultimo to answer. However, tho' late, I must beg you to accept those sincere thanks I now return you for it and also my congratulations for your success in North Carolina. The victory at Guildford will make it tell and force the good people with you to take an active part for Government, and that with security to themselves, for, tho' circumstanced as you were, I highly approve the mild line of conduct you followed, yet it has always been a principle of mine to force men to take that marked kind of part which should cut off from them a return to the other side and make them, tho' against their inclinations, and in all changes, ours. I hear all the armed world is in the Chesapeak and that great events are looked for from thence. I wish you had your eye on it. I should think essential information might be had there and that it is in your power to procure it. How are you off in this respect?

I will send some news papers to you. Those parts on the movements and successes of the army are mine and as true as such accounts usually are. Adieu!

Your most truly

H BARRY

§ - §

4 - From Cornwallis to Balfour

Cornwallis to Balfour, 21st February 1781   *85(3): CS*

Hillsborough
February 21st 1781

Lt Colonel Balfour etc etc etc

Dear Balfour

As I am informed that Greene expects reinforcements from Pensylvania and that the Virginia militia are turning out with great alacrity and in great numbers, I should wish the three regiments expected from Ireland to be sent to me as soon as possible by the way of Cape Fear with orders to proceed without loss of time to Cross Creek. As they will be all new, some proper conductor must be found for them. If, however, it should appear necessary to Lord Rawdon and yourself to keep one of those battalions in South Carolina, you will forward the other two and the flank companies of the three. If a cruiser could send them first into Cape Fear, much time would be saved.

I have written to Greene to threaten to send the prisoners of war to the West Indies in case he does not consent to an exchange. I would therefore have you make every publick demonstration of doing it and inform the principal officers that you cannot answer the delaying it longer than the first week in April. A convoy should likewise be required without letting the officers of the navy doubt my being in earnest.

Yours sincerely and affectionately

CORNWALLIS

Cornwallis to Balfour, 5th April 1781   85(21): ADfS

Camp on Cape Fear River, 16 miles from Wilmington
April 5th 1781

Lt Colonel Balfour
Commandant of Charlestown

Dear Balfour

On my arrival at Crosscreek I found that it would be impracticable to open the communication by water to Wilmington, the river being about an hundred yards wide with high banks on each side, the inhabitants chiefly hostile, and a considerable militia prepared to attack the boats, the distance above an hundred miles. It was impossible to live long at Crosscreek, there being but little provision and no forage; the army was barefooted and in the utmost want of necessaries of every kind; and I was embarrassed with about 400 sick and wounded[21]. These considerations made me determine to march down to Wilmington[22].

Now, my dear Balfour, send with all possible dispatch shoes and necessaries of all kinds, and some appointments and clothing for the Legion, who are quite naked, having lost every thing on the fatal 17th of January. Saddles are greatly wanted. Be as expeditious as possible, for should the enemy threaten South Carolina, I must not stay here. I do not think it probable, but this war has taught me to think nothing impossible. Arrange immediately with Berkeley some ship to carry Brodrick to England. I write to him on the subject. No reinforcement arrived. I had a letter from Lord Rawdon dated 24th of last month[23] and was happy to find that every thing had gone on so well in South Carolina. He thinks you should

---

[21] After 'wounded', the following is deleted: 'the latter suffering much by being moved, and rendering it'.

[22] 'to Wilmington' is substituted for 'untill the navigation can be secured'.

[23] *a letter..*: see p 51.

keep one of the regiments from Ireland at Charlestown. If you think it necessary, of course you will do it, but as those regiments must have many men unfit for the service I am at present engaged in, perhaps a detachment of about 300 of their worst marchers and weakest men under one of the brevet majors may answer your purpose. At all events send what you can spare to me as soon as they arrive. Many of the wounded which I shall send to you will soon be fit for garrison duty. I am in the utmost distress for money. It is likely, when I again move into the country, that I shall think it right to abandon Wilmington, in which case Craig's corps will return to you. I know you too well to think it necessary to say any thing to quicken you. I shall want medicines and some of the faculty to attend the sick and wounded to Charlestown. I cannot spare much assistance from hence, Mr Hill and two mates being left with the bad cases at the Quaker Meeting House about five miles from Guildford Courthouse. Captain Schutz died a few days after the action, and poor Webster on the 2nd of this month after suffering much pain. Maynard of the Guards and Captain Wilmousky of the Regiment of Bose are not likely to live. I hope the rest of the officers will do well, but Lord Dunglass's arm is in some danger.[24]

I am, dear Balfour, with the greatest regard
Most sincerely yours

CORNWALLIS

[*Subscribed*:]

Nothing could behave better than the 23rd. Peters wounded in the thigh, not dangerous, about 65 men kill'd and wounded.

Cornwallis to Balfour, 6th April 1781   *85(27): C*

Cape Fear River
6th April 1781

Lt Colonel Balfour
Commandant of Charlestown

Dear Balfour

I have just seen your letter to Craig of the 30th[25]. You have as usual in most of my wants prevented my wishes. We are, however, in the greatest distress for every thing, and

---

[24] William Home (1757-1781), Lord Dunglas, was the eldest son of the Earl of Home (pronounced 'Hume'). Entering the Coldstream Regiment of Foot Guards as an ensign in 1774, he was promoted four years later to lieutenant, a rank which carried with it a captaincy. Like Maynard, he would soon succumb to fever and die. (Valentine, *The British Establishment*, i, 461; Tarleton, *Campaigns*, 285) Von Wilmowsky, whose name Cornwallis has anglicised, was no doubt related to Ernst and Wilhelm von Wilmowsky, both of whom were majors, the first in the Regiment von Losberg and the second in the Regiment von Lengerke. He too would soon die. (WO 65/164(3), (20) and (22) (National Archives, Kew); Bernhard A Uhlendorf ed, *The Siege of Charleston* (University of Michigan Press, 1938), 12, 413, 421)

[25] *your letter..*: see p 39.

especially clothing and all sorts of appointments for the cavalry. I am very glad to find that we are masters at sea in the Chesapeake.

Greene has availed himself of our embarrassments to keep still a strong army and, I hear, has sent for more cannon. By my last accounts he was on Deep River at Ramsay's Mill near its junction with the Haw. I have taken every means in my power to procure intelligence of his movements and will run all hazards if he attempts any serious move towards South Carolina. I am very impatient for the reinforcement.

Yours very sincerely

CORNWALLIS

[*Subscribed*:]

Transmit the contents of my letters to Lord Rawdon, to whom I write a short private letter.

§ - §

5 - Between Cornwallis and Rawdon

Cornwallis to Rawdon, 4th February 1781[26]   *85(1): ADfS*

Salisbury
February 4th 1781

Rt Hon Lord Rawdon etc etc etc

My dear Lord

We passed the Catawba on the 1st at a private ford about four miles below Beatty's. The Guards behaved gallantly and, altho' they were fired upon during the whole time of their passing by some militia under General Davidson, never returned a shot untill they got out of the river and formed. General Davidson was killed and his militia routed. General Leslie's horse fell with him in the river and bruised him very much. On the same day Tarleton attacked a considerable body of militia under Pickens, killed several, took some prisoners, and dispersed the rest.

I am much distressed by the rivers and creeks being swelled but shall try to pass the Yadkin at the Shallow Ford as soon as possible.

---

[26] Extracts from this letter are published in Ross ed, *Cornwallis Correspondence*, i, 83.

As Greene is now removed from you, I hope your difficulties will be lessened, but they will not cease. Some Georgia refugees and other banditti are assembling at Gilbertown and Sumpter is again in the field. I have the utmost confidence in your abilities and discretion. Our friends must be so disheartened by the misfortune of the 17th that you will get but little good from them. You know the importance of Ninety Six. Let that place be your constant care. I long to hear from you.

I was alarmed at a rebel report of the surprize of Georgetown but have since been informed that the garrison was not taken. Your friends are all well. Colonel Hall was killed at the passage of the Catawba. No other officer hurt.

Yours most sincerely

CORNWALLIS

Cornwallis to Rawdon, 21st February 1781[27]   *85(9): DfS*

Hillsborough
February 21st 1781

Rt Hon Lord Rawdon etc etc etc

My dear Lord

I tried by a most rapid march to strike a blow either at Greene or Morgan before they got over the Dan, but could not effect it. The enemy, however, was too much hurried to be able to raise any militia in this province. The fatigue of our troops and hardships which they suffered were excessive. I receive strong assurances from our friends. Tomorrow the King's standard will be erected and I shall try every means to embody them and avail myself of their services. I cannot be sure when I shall be able to open the communication with Cross Creek. It must be done soon as the troops are in the greatest want of shoes and other necessaries.

As I am informed that...[28]

Lt Colonel Balfour will communicate all accounts from me to the Commander in Chief and to England. I am very impatient to hear from you.

Yours most sincerely and affectionately

CORNWALLIS

---

[27] The original and duplicate of this letter miscarried. Rawdon received the triplicate, to which were added the subscriptions of 5th and 8th March appearing in the triplicate of Cornwallis's letter of 21st February to Craig, p 25.

[28] Cornwallis goes on to repeat, with one or two inconsequential amendments, the wording of his letter of 21st February to Balfour, p 41.

Cornwallis to Rawdon, 17th March 1781 — 85(14): A(in part) Df

Camp at Guildford
March 17th 1781

Rt Hon Lord Rawdon etc etc etc

My dear Lord

General Greene, having been very considerably reinforced from Virginia by eighteen months' men and militia and having collected all the militia of this province, advanced with an army of about 5 or 6,000 men and four six pounders to this place. I attacked him on the 15th and after a very sharp action routed his army and took his cannon. The great fatigue of the troops, the number of wounded and the want of provision prevented our pursuing the enemy beyond the Reedy Fork. Lt Colonel Stewart and Captain Goodricke of the Guards, Lieutenant Robinson of the 23rd, Ensign Talbot of the 33rd, Ensign Grant of the 71st and Lieutenant O'Hara of the artillery are killed. Captain Schutz of the Guards is mortally wounded. No other officer in any danger. I shall send my aide de camp, Captain Brodrick, as soon as possible to England with the particulars. In the mean time I beg you will transmit the contents of this note thither and to the Commander in Chief.

[CORNWALLIS]

[*Added to the triplicate and quadruplicate:*]

If the reinforcement from Europe is arrived, send the whole or greatest part to Wilmington with orders to proceed without loss of time to Cross Creek.

Cornwallis to Rawdon, 2nd April 1781 — 85(18): ADfS

Camp near Elizabeth Town on Cape Fear River
2nd April 1781

Rt Hon Lord Rawdon etc etc etc

My dear Lord

Finding the communication by water from Wilmington to Crosscreek impracticable, I determined to march down the west side of the river. The total want of necessaries for my troops and the great incumbrance and sufferings of the wounded rendered this move absolutely necessary. In the mean time be on your guard lest Greene should detach.

Yours etc

CORNWALLIS

Rawdon to Cornwallis, 7th March 1781   69(7): ALS

Camden
March 7th 1781

Earl Cornwallis etc etc etc

My Lord

I have been in the field ever since I wrote the enclosed. I am grieved (altho' it is merely a gazette) that during my absence no means could be found of transmitting it to you, as I know how anxious your Lordship must be to hear frequently from us, but the savage cruelty of the enemy, who commit the most wanton murders in cold blood upon the friends of Government that fall into their hands, makes it very difficult to procure a messenger at any price.

A very daring effort has been made to excite revolt in this province, but as the project is I think entirely baffled, the circumstance will probably conduce to our future tranquillity by having exposed to those whose sentiments were wavering how little prospect of success can ever attend such an enterprize. I mentioned to your Lordship that I relinquished the pursuit of Marion upon intelligence that Sumter was assembling a considerable force near Fishing Creek and the higher fords of Broad River. Ninety Six I supposed to be his object. Notwithstanding my utmost pains to secure early information, Sumter had gained the banks of the Congaree before I received the least notice of his movement. Upon the first intimation of this step *I marched with six hundred, an hundred cavalry* and *two pieces of cannon*, hoping to get upon the enemy before they could learn that I was in the field. On the first day's march I got certain information that Sumter had crossed the Congaree at Friday's Ferry and had invested Major Maxwell's post, a square redoubt enclosing two or three storehouses. Wade Hampton was in contract to furnish a certain quantity of provision to this post on a fixed day. As he maintained a secret correspondence with Sumter, he delayed fulfilling his agreement till he thought the stores in the redoubt were all expended, of which circumstance he gave Sumter notice. Sumter therefore concluded that a blockade of a few days would reduce Major Maxwell to surrender. In the mean time he summoned by proclamation all the inhabitants to join him, offering to all such as would take part with him a full pardon for their former attachment to us and denouncing penalty of death to all who did not range themselves under his standard by the 23rd of February. To give weight to these threats several persons known to be friendly towards us were inhumanly murdered, tho' unarmed and remaining peaceably at their own houses. Either thro' fear or inclination many joined the enemy, and several parties were in movement for the same purpose when Sumter received the news of our approach. I had detached Major McLeroth with 260 infantry and a piece of cannon to bar the enemy's retreat at Friday's Ferry whilst I endeavored to get round them. We crossed Broad River at a ford deeper, wider and more rapid than Lands Ford on the Catawba. Above thirty of the infantry were carried away by the force of the stream, but fortunately they were all saved (excepting one man of my light company) by the exertions of some of the New York dragoons, who were stationed lower in the ford for that purpose. The Saluda was so swollen that it was not fordable, but we passed it securely at Weaver's Ferry on the 22nd of February under cover of our cannon. Here we learned that Sumter had retired down the Congaree the night before, having had information of our march from the fugitives of some parties which we had fallen in with and dispersed as they were on their way to join him. I was likewise informed that Major McLeroth, deceived by false intelligence, had crossed the Congaree at Friday's Ferry instead of moving down to meet the enemy at McCord's as had been intended. To prevent loss of time I sent Major McLeroth directions to follow the track of the enemy, and I detached the cavalry to join him. Advancing with the remainder of my force to Friday's Ferry, I crossed the Congaree at that place during the night of the 23rd and next morning struck across the fork by forced marches in expectation of falling in with the enemy between McCord's and Camden. I soon learned that the enemy had met and taken sixteen waggons laden with public stores near Buckhead's, the goods contained in which they had put into the boats at McCord's Ferry and sent them down the Santee, they themselves pursuing the route along that river with intent to cross it at Manigault's as the only means of escaping. Sumter had made an attempt upon the post at Thompson's but was repulsed by Captain Robinson[29] of the Provincial light infantry, who commanded there. This information I received from Major McLeroth with an intimation of his purpose to pursue Sumter immediately. I crossed the Wateree at Camden on the evening of the 25th, and on the 26th continued my march towards Neilson's, having sent forward instructions that Lt Colonel Watson, who was on the High Hills, should hasten before me to Manigault's and that the post at Wright's Bluff should be on the watch for the boats. Sumter had in the mean time ordered Marion to advance to Manigault's and cover the passage from being interrupted by Watson. Our movement, however, prevented Marion from attempting to interfere, and the boats (in which Sumter had hoped to pass the river) were retaken with all the baggage as they attempted to pass Wright's Bluff. Lt Colonel Small was advancing from Monk's Corner with the 84th and Fanning's regiment, so that Sumter's retreat appeared scarcely possible, but, upon a rumor that Marion had crossed the Santee and joined Sumter, Major McLeroth unfortunately discontinued the pursuit. Sumter, finding that his rear was not pressed, undertook to cross the Santee by swimming his horses and passing his men in two canoes which he found by accident at Fludd's Plantation. He effected his purpose on the 27th and the same evening fell in with Lt Colonel Watson. An action ensued, in which the enemy were forced to fly, leaving 18 dead on the field, several wounded and about forty horses. Our loss was only a subaltern and seven privates wounded. Harrison's people, mounted and armed with swords, behaved very gallantly, routing the enemy's cavalry regularly formed and thrice their number. Finding on my arrival at Neilson's Ferry that Sumter had gotten clear into the country and had ensured a junction with Marion, I thought it very probable that upon learning my distance from Camden the enemy might be tempted to make a joint effort against it. Therefore, ordering the infantry of Major McLeroth's detachment to cross the Santee and join Lt Colonel Watson, I returned hither as rapidly as possible with the infantry which had accompanied me and with the cavalry, which had just rejoined me by way of Neilson's Ferry. I arrived here about noon on the 5th instant, and on the same evening I detached Major Fraser towards Ratcliff's Bridge with the South Carolina Regiment, which had formed part of the garrison of Camden during our march. The cavalry were to have been of the party, but a considerable body of the enemy

---

[29] Morris Robinson (1759-1815) had since 7th October 1777 been a captain in the Loyal American Regiment, a corps raised on the Provincial establishment by his father Beverley, who was its Colonel. He was now serving on secondment to the Provincial light infantry commanded by John Watson Tadwell Watson. In April 1783 he would transfer as a captain to the cavalry of the Queen's Rangers, and when it was disbanded at the close of the war, he continued in service in the regular army. At his death in Gibraltar he was serving as a lt colonel and assistant barrack-master general. (Raymond, 'British American Corps'; Sabine, *Biographical Sketches*, ii, 228-9)

having appeared at a plantation not very wide of the route to be pursued by Major Fraser, I ordered that the cavalry should first attempt to strike at that corps and afterwards join the South Carolinians. These directions proved unfortunate. The corps at which the cavalry were to strike got information of their approach and escaped thro' the swamps; and on the 6th, before the cavalry had joined him, Major Fraser unexpectedly met Sumter near the head of Black River. Sumter, ignorant of our return, was advancing towards this post to attempt fulfilling a particular purpose, which, an intercepted letter informs me, was enjoined by Greene[30], and he was not a little surprised at finding himself opposed in the open field. When the parties first met, Sumter's men were all mounted and quickly gave way before the fire of the infantry. They soon, however, dismounted and advanced with tolerable countenance to attack Fraser. The South Carolinians soon repelled the attack and entirely dispersed the enemy, pursuing them for some distance, but for want of cavalry no decisive advantage could be taken of the rout. The enemy lost ten killed and about forty wounded. Fraser had only six wounded. Marion was not with Sumter in this affair, and I believe from every circumstance that, finding the country deterred by his ill success from joining him, Sumter is retiring towards his old haunt near the Catawba lands. Sumter's force, when he crossed the Congaree, passed current for at least a thousand, but I am convinced it scarcely exceeded four hundred. They were all mounted. About a fourth of them were armed with swords as cavalry and had excellent horses. Of those who joined Sumter at Congarees, none I believe passed the Santee with him. Marion's numbers certainly do not amount to three hundred. Lt Colonel Watson has orders to press him to the utmost. I should not, my Lord, have thought so long a detail of our petty operations worth sending to you, only that I know a variety of rumors must reach you, which could not be explained by a less minute account. I would say that we have had great fatigue, were I not ashamed to mention it after the wonderful exertions which you have been making. Lt Colonel Watson, Major Fraser and Major Maxwell have all acquitted themselves very handsomely. The New York dragoons have distinguished themselves in many successful skirmishes; Captain Coffin particularly merits applause. I have not heard from your Lordship since you left Salisbury, but some intercepted letters from the enemy give me an idea of your purposes. *Campbell with the Back Mountain men* and *Pickens are gone to join Greene*. The fatigue of our little excursion has given me a cough and something of a feverish complaint. *I fear your Lordship must look out for some one to relieve me. I hope to leave the district in a state of tolerable quiet. Whilst I am wanted I will do my utmost, but I doubt my strength*.

I have the honor to be, my Lord, with equal respect and affection
Your Lordship's very faithful servant

RAWDON

[*Subscribed*:]

I have taken the liberty of permitting Major McLeroth to go to New York. *It was become too necessary*.

---

[30] In a letter of 21st February Greene had invited Sumter to destroy a mill near Camden as a means of forcing the garrison to leave the post through lack of supplies. (*The Greene Papers*, vii, 328)

Enclosure
Rawdon to Cornwallis, 15th February 1781   69(16): L

<u>Camden</u>
<u>February 15th</u>

I am just returned, my dear Lord, from my excursion after Marion. I found that his numbers did not much exceed three hundred, all mounted. By forced marches we got below him but he got off (tho' narrowly) across Scape Whore. We forced him over Lynches Creek and should have driven him across Pedee had not Ninety Six[31] recalled me. I find since from Cruger that the enemy are not in greater force than what Cunningham thinks himself equal to, but I take it for granted some effort will be made in that quarter. I therefore remain ready to march at one hour's warning. In the mean time I have taken measures which I hope will prevent Marion from troubling us much more.

A pacquet is arrived from England — sailed 14th December. Howard, Webster, Norton[32] are colonels by brevet. The thanks of the House of Commons are voted to your Lordship, opposed by Sir J Mawbey[33], who could not see much merit in the victory, and by Charles Fox[34], who thought Gates's defeat ruinous to Great Britain. The additional companies are stricken off and regimented in England. Both fleets in port. Empress Queen said to be dead.[35] No arrival from New York. Hood is in the West Indies. Our Sandwich got in distress to Antigua. The news about St Vincent's was premature.[36]

---

[31] A copy of this letter (69(23)) inserts 'news of a corps advancing against' before 'Ninety Six'.

[32] The third son of Lord Grantley, the Hon Chapple Norton (1746-1818) had been serving since 1774 as a captain in the Coldstream Regiment of Foot Guards, a rank which carried with it a lt colonelcy. In February 1780 he had distinguished himself by the capture of Young's House near White Plains. His promotion to colonel by brevet came into effect nine months later. After the war he served in the Commons for many years as the Member for Guildford and in 1802 was promoted to full general. Noted for his amiableness, he became a close friend of the Duke of York. (*ODNB*)

[33] Sir Joseph Mawbey Bt (1730-1798) was a radical MP who had been re-elected for the County of Surrey at the general election of 1780. A wealthy man, he had prospered as joint owner of a vinegar distillery at Vauxhall and gone on to inherit considerable property from his uncle and brother-in-law. Having first entered Parliament in 1761, he became associated with the Rockingham Whigs but increasingly gave his support to the radical cause of reform. He was a frequent speaker in the Commons, but because he professed to be above party, he was ridiculed by speakers and writers on both sides. Walpole called him 'vain, noisy, and foolish'. Wraxhall was more charitable, remarking that Mawbey 'could never obtain a patient... hearing in Parliament', yet 'spoke, nevertheless, with great good sense though not with brilliancy'. He left politics in 1790, feeling betrayed by Pitt's administration, which had failed to support his unsuccessful election campaign of that year. (*ODNB*)

[34] One of the most gifted men of the late 18th century, Charles James Fox (1749-1806) has been the subject of several biographies and numerous other writings. Currently MP for the populous and prestigious constituency of Westminster, which he would represent with only a brief interruption till his death, he had emerged as a leading critic of the North ministry, particularly with respect to America.

[35] A mistaken report about Catherine the Great (1729-96).

[36] Rodney and Vaughan had failed in an attempt to take St Vincent from the French three months earlier. The defenses were found to be too strong.

Craig has dispersed three hundred militia collected near Wilmington under Colonel Young. Captain Nesbit was wounded but not badly.

Innes wants some Provincial promotions published. Shall it be done? Coffin's majority? McLeroth wants to go to New York and hopes Bowes[37] will command the regiment.

Major Barclay[38] wants to join his regiment with Arnold.

If you have too many brigadiers, do not hesitate to send one hither if communication offers. I should wish for Webster that I might return the kind manner in which he served under me. A man has just been with me who says he left you beyond Salem. May you reap, my dear Lord, the success which such exertion deserves.

[RAWDON]

Rawdon to Cornwallis, 24th March 1781   69(21): ALS

Camden
March 24th 1781

Earl Cornwallis

You will believe me, my dear Lord, when I say that your note of the 17th by Lancaster did not give me more joy on the public account than what arose from so full a gratification of my private wishes for your personal credit and satisfaction. Your exertions have at length been repaid, and the various disappointments which have preceded this victory only serve to prove that you are indebted for the success to your own perseverance and not to the blind favor of fortune. I should have sighed at not having been a partaker in your triumph did I not think that in filling my present station I have rendered you the best service in my power; and that reflection, let me assure you, my dear Lord, has smoothed an anxious application to

---

[37] Frederick Bowes (1746-?) was a Scot who had spent his entire service in the 64th Regiment. Commissioned an ensign on 11th November 1761, he was promoted to lieutenant on 1st January 1766 and to captain on 17th August 1774. He was presently serving with Leslie as a brigade major and would be with him in Virginia. (*Army Lists*; Major H G Purdon, 'An Historical Sketch of the 64th Regiment' (Internet, 13th February 2006); *The Cornwallis Papers*)

[38] Thomas Barclay (1753-1830) was the son of Dr Henry Barclay, Rector of Trinity Church, New York. A graduate of Columbus College and a student of law, he entered the Loyal American Regiment as a captain on 10th April 1777 and was promoted to its majority six months later. He was now serving in South Carolina on secondment to the Provincial light infantry commanded by John Watson Tadwell Watson, whereas the Loyal American Regiment had accompanied Arnold to Virginia in December 1780. Having seen his estate in New York confiscated by the revolutionaries, he was placed on the Provincial half-pay list at the close of the war and settled in Nova Scotia, where he was elected to the lower house of the legislature and served for a time as Speaker. Between 1796 and 1828 he occupied several high offices under the Crown, among which were those of commissioner under Jay's Treaty and commissioner under articles 4 and 5 of the Treaty of Ghent. He was also for a time British consul general in the eastern and northern states of the USA. He eventually retired with an annual pension of £1,200 and died at New York. (Sabine, *Biographical Sketches*, i, 207-8; Raymond, 'British American Corps'; Treasury 64/23(3), WO 65/164(37), and WO 65/165(3) (National Archives, Kew))

the very teazing tho inglorious warfare which we have been waging in this quarter. Immediately upon the receipt of your Lordship's note yesterday, I wrote to Lord George Germain and to the Commander in Chief.

I wrote to your Lordship some time ago, detailing the efforts made by Sumter and Marion to excite revolt in this province. Lest that letter should miscarry, I will here mention that the enemy have failed in every attempt. Sumter was twice defeated by our detachments, once by Lt Colonel Watson and the second time by Major Fraser. Several other skirmishes have been fought, in which the enemy have suffered considerably with very little loss on our part.

Lt Colonels Watson and Doyle with separate corps are now pursuing Marion. Sumter has a small corps in the Indian land.

War with the Dutch! Rodney and Vaughan have taken St Eustatia with above a hundred sail of Dutch ships and thirty American vessels. Many Dutch prizes have been made at sea, one of them a ship of the line aboard which an admiral was killed.

A French 64 and two frigates from Rhode Island have been blocking up General Arnold in the Chesapeak. A squadron has sailed from Charlestown in quest of them and I hope they will soon wear British colors.

I believe Pensacola is attacked by the Spaniards and *Augustine is threatened.*

I received your Lordship's letters of the 21st February, 5th March and 8th March. I told Lt Colonel Balfour that *I did not want more men but I thought he needed one of the battalions from Ireland.*

I have cured my cough and am tolerably well but not perfectly stout.

I have the honor to be with great respect
Your Lordship's very faithful and affectionate servant

RAWDON

§ - §

6 - From Colonel Phillips of the South Carolina royal militia

Phillips to Cornwallis, 23rd February 1781   **67(85): LS**

> Biggars's Ferry on the Cataba
> February 23rd 1781

The Rt Hon Earl Cornwallis
Commander in Chief of His Majesty's forces in the Southern District

My Lord

Permit me to request your Lordship's attention to my situation. I was taken prisoner on my way to Camden as I was escorting some wounded officers and men to that place and still remain a prisoner, but as I understand that Lt Colonel Hopkins[39] is in your camp a prisoner[40], I could wish an exchange would take place between us if it meets with your approbation. General Sumter has made a proposeal for an exchange which Mr Spillard[41] will present you. Mr Spillard was taken on his way to join the army and has General Sumter's permission to go in with a flag to effect his own exchange as well as those mention[ed] in the list[42]. I am also to sollicit your Lordship for those poor people; they were taken at the same time with me and are sent to Virginia, where they are confined in gaol. The person who goes on the part of General Sumter with the flag has his instructions to set these men at liberty if

---

[39] Born in Virginia, David Hopkins (1739-1816) had settled north of Winnsborough between the Broad and Catawba Rivers in what was later to become Chester County, South Carolina. When the Provincial Congress raised a regiment of rangers in June 1775, he was commissioned a lieutenant, and after the regiment was transferred to the Continental establishment, he was promoted to captain in October 1776. By December 1780, when he was occupying the redoubt raised by Edward Lacey Jr on Turkey Creek, he had transferred to the South Carolina revolutionary militia and was serving as a lt colonel, probably in Colonel Richard Winn's regiment. How he came to be captured is uncertain, but it would have occurred in mid January when the redoubt, which lay close to William Hillhouse's plantation, was on the line of Cornwallis's advance into North Carolina. He would be exchanged – and John Phillips too – and go on to serve in Orangeburg District, succeeding to the colonelcy of Winn's regiment when the latter was promoted to brigadier general in late 1783. (Salley Jr, *Orangeburg County*, 386-7; Lyman C Draper Manuscripts (The State Historical Society of Wisconsin), 12VV276-8, SVV36-12; Revolutionary pension application S. 31626 made by John Combs of Wilkes County, Georgia, on 19th January 1830; Revolutionary pension application made by Hezekiah West of Johnson County, Illinois, on 3rd December 1832; Moss, *SC Patriots*, 461)

[40] Certain Continental, militia and other prisoners confined or paroled during the winter campaign are listed in 5(17), (92), (94), (96), (101), (111), (115), (119), (121), (122), (125), (127) and (288).

[41] Maurice Spillard also called at Greene's headquarters, where he was suspected of being a spy. Greene wrote to Sumter on 6th March that he did not wish to make an exchange unless Sumter was under some obligations; that all future exchanges had to be negotiated by Greene's Commissary of Prisoners, Major Edmund Hyrne, to whom Sumter should send a list of all unexchanged prisoners; and that a cartel for a general exchange was in the offing. Spillard would be detained in Caswell County, North Carolina, where he still remained at the end of June. (*The Greene Papers*, vii, viii, *passim*)

[42] *the list*: see the following document.

his proposeals meets your Lordship's approbation.

I am, my Lord, with parfect respect and attachment
Your Lordship's most obedient and most humble servant

JOHN PHILLIPS

Pass to set at liberty certain prisoners in Virginia, 23rd February 1781   5(91): DS

Biggars's Ferry on the Cataba River
February 23rd 1781

TO ALL OFFICERS and others in the service of the United States of America, and more particularly to the officer commanding where the underwriten are confined or paroled or to the gaoler or gaoler where the said prisoners or any of them is confined:

WHEREAS I have received instructions from Brigadier General Sumter commanding the forces of the United States in the State of South Carolina to set at liberty the undermentioned prisoners provided that his Excellency the Earl of Cornwallis do set at liberty certain person[s] proposed for an exchange for them by General Sumter, I DO therefor request that Mr Nicho[s] Curry[43] has a free passage to where ever those prisoners are. And I also certify that he is impower'd to set the said prisoners at liberty, he producing Lord Cornwallis' certificate of their exchange.

By the General's command

W[M] HILL

PRISONERS' NAMES

Captain Ross	Alex Robertson, private
Will[m] Young, private	Jam[s] Russell, ditto
Jam[s] Young, ditto	—— Hoffman, ditto
M—— Hanna, ditto	Geo Hesser, ditto
Rob[t] Phillips, ditto	

§ - §

---

[43] Nicholas Curry (?-c. 1852) had been serving as a commissary to the South Carolina revolutionary militia since 1779. After the war he would move, first to Lincoln County, Tennessee, and then to Coles and Scott Counties, Illinois. He is buried in the McAlebs graveyard one and a half miles north of the town of Bluffs. (Moss, *SC Patriots*, 227; Kim Torp ed, 'Revolutionary War Soldiers buried in Illinois' (Internet, 19th November 2005))

7 - Proclamations, warrants, and summons to arms

Proclamation, 20th February 1781[44] 5(83): C

By the Rt Hon Charles Earl Cornwallis,
Lt General of His Majesty's forces etc etc etc

A PROCLAMATION

WHEREAS it has pleased the divine providence to prosper the operations of His Majesty's arms in driving the rebel army out of this province, and whereas it is His Majesty's most gracious wish to rescue His faithful and loyal subjects from the cruel tyranny under which they have groaned for several years, I have thought proper to issue this proclamation to invite all such faithful and loyal subjects to repair without loss of time, with their arms and ten days' provisions, to the royal standard now erected at Hillsborough, where they will meet with the most friendly reception, AND I do hereby assure them that I am ready to concur with them in effectual measures for suppressing the remains of rebellion in this province and for the re-establishment of good order and constitutional government.

Given under my hand at head quarters at Hillsborough this 20th day of February in the year of our Lord 1781 and in the 21st year of His Majesty's reign

CORNWALLIS

By his Lordship's command
H BRODRICK
Aid de camp

GOD SAVE THE KING

Warrant to raise men for the Royal North Carolina Regiment, 22nd February 1781 101(7): CS

To William Chandler Esq

Confiding in your loyalty and ability to serve His Majesty, and by the power and authority to me vested, I do hereby authorise and impower you to recruit able bodied men (not less in number than fifty) to serve for eighteen months or during the rebellion in the Royal North Carolina Regiment under the command of Lt General Earl Cornwallis or any other commander His Majesty may think proper to appoint, and you shall be recommended for a captain's commission in said regiment.

And this shall be your sufficient warrant.

---

[44] Published in Tarleton, *Campaigns*, 256-7.

Given under my hand at Hillsborough the 22nd day of February 1781
and in the 21st year of His Majesty's reign

JN° HAMILTON
Lt Colonel commanding the Royal North Carolina Regiment

Draft warrant to raise a Provincial company[45]   *101(8): Df*

By Charles Earl Cornwallis,
Lt General of His Majesty's forces etc etc etc

To [*blank*]

Reposing special confidence in your loyalty, courage and abilities, I do hereby authorize and empower you the said [*blank*] to raise a company in the province of North Carolina on the Provincial establishment, of which you are to be captain, which company is to be afterwards incorporated in a battalion and is to consist of one captain, one lieutenant, one ensign, three serjeants, three corporals, one drummer and fifty three privates. Your men are to be engaged to serve during the rebellion and in the province of North Carolina only. They will be entitled to one guinea and a half bounty, the same clothing and provisions as the other Provincial troops, pay from the date of their attestations, and, when discharged, to a grant of half the quantity of land promised by His Majesty's proclamation to the Provincial troops who have engaged to serve in all parts of America. No man will be received under seventeen, nor above fifty years of age, nor under five feet five inches high, and they must be free from distempers that render them unable to undergo military service. You will be allowed to recommend your subalterns provided they are duly qualified, and you and your officers will receive half pay when your company is half raised, and, when it is mustered compleat, commissions will be issued to you and your subalterns of this date and full pay will commence from the date of the compleat muster. You are allowed ninety days from the date of this warrant to raise your company, but, if not effected within that period, the men that may have been inlisted will be turned over to other companies or regiments raised upon the same terms, and neither you nor your officers will be entitled to any allowance or advantage for raising such men, except the bounty and pay actually advanced to them.

Given under my hand at head quarters this [*blank*] day of [*blank*] AD 1781
and in the 21st year of His Majesty's reign

[CORNWALLIS]

---

[45] According to a list in 101(19), warrants were issued to Rigdon Brice on 26th February; James Munroe, Thomas Brazier and James Osborne on 1st March; and Eli Branston, Stephen Lewis, Michael Robins and Abraham Williams on 5th March. Munroe's warrant (101(17)) was in the form of this draft, and it is to be assumed the others were too.

NB

All non commissioned officers and soldiers to be attested and sworn, as soon as convenient after being inlisted, before a Justice of the Peace appointed by His Majesty's Governor, and the attestation to be signed by the Justice of the Peace and the soldier.

Draft form of attestation *101(12): Df*

We whose names are hereunto subscribed do swear to be true to our Sovereign Lord King George and to serve Him honestly and faithfully in the defence of His person, crown and dignity against all His enemies or opposers whatsoever, in the Provincial company commanded by [*blank*][46] to be hereafter embodied in a battalion during the rebellion and in the province of North Carolina only, and to observe and obey His Majesty's orders and the orders of the generals and officers set over me by His Majesty.

Sworn before the subscribing Justices of the Peace	*The [blank] day of the month*	*Men's names*

Summons to arms, 17th March 1781 *101(24): Df*

Guildford
March 17th 1781

The royal army having by the blessing of God totally defeated the rebel army commanded by General Greene on the 15th instant, who was obliged to abandon all his canon and fly with the utmost precipitation towards Virginia, all friends to Great Britain are now most earnestly called on to take a vigorous part. As we place the utmost confidence in the loyalty and bravery of the Highlanders in Cumberland, Bladen and Anson Counties, their utmost exertion is now requested, and we give them the most solemn assurance that we desire their services no longer than during the continuance of the rebellion and that they will never be called on

---

[46] *[blank]*: an otherwise identical form of attestation (101(21)) inserts here 'Captain James Munro'. The form was no doubt for the use of all persons mentioned in note 45 above.

to go out of the southern colonies. Our friends are desired to pay attention to the message delivered to them by the bearer, Captain Duncan Ray[47].

Summons to arms, 18th March 1781   101(26): Df

Camp at Guildford
March 18th 1781

His Majesty's troops having by the blessing of God totally defeated the rebel army under General Greene on the 15th instant and taken all his cannon, the friends to the true constitution of their country are now called on to stand forth and assist in securing their ancient rights and liberties.

The loyal subjects on Little River Pedee are earnestly requested to attend to the message delivered to them from us by Captain Fincannon[48].

Proclamation, 18th March 1781[49]   5(124): C

North Carolina

By Charles Earl Cornwallis, Lt General of His Majesty's forces etc etc etc

PROCLAMATION

WHEREAS by the blessing of almighty God His Majesty's arms have been crowned with signal success by the compleat victory obtained over the rebel forces on the 15th instant, I have thought proper to issue this proclamation to call upon all loyal subjects to stand forth and take an active part in restoring good order and government, and whereas it has been represented to me that many persons in this province who have taken a share in this unnatural rebellion, but having experienced the oppression and injustice of the rebel Government and having seen the errors into which they have been deluded by falsehoods and misrepresentations, are sincerely desirous of returning to their duty and allegiance, I do hereby notify and promise to all such persons (murderers excepted) that if they will surrender themselves with their arms and ammunition at head quarters or to the officer commanding in the district contiguous to their respective places of residence on or before the 20th day of April next, they will be permitted to return to their homes upon giving a military parole and

---

[47] Duncan Ray was a captain in the loyalist irregular militia of Anson County commanded by his namesake. He had fled to Charlestown by January 1782, at which time he is recorded as receiving pay for part of his service. (Clark, *Loyalists in the Southern Campaign*, i, 352; DeMond, *Loyalists in NC*, 220)

[48] Born in North Carolina, William Fincannon (*c.* 1755-*c.* 1831) was now serving as a captain in the loyalist irregular militia there. A settler near Connellys Springs, he remained in North Carolina after the war. (Robert Leahy, 'Fincannon Family Tree' (Internet, 23rd December 2005))

[49] Published in Tarleton, *Campaigns*, 312-3.

shall be protected in their persons and properties from all sort of violence from the British troops and will be restored as soon as possible to all the privileges of legal and constitutional government.

Given under my hand at head quarters this 18th day of March AD 1781
and in the 21st year of His Majesty's reign

CORNWALLIS

By his Lordship's command
HENRY BRODRICK
Aide de camp

GOD SAVE THE KING[50]

Sketch of a summons to arms — 101(23): Df

That the want of forage in the neighbourhood of Cross Creek renders it impossible for the army to remain there; that it is also necessary to open a communication with Wilmington to obtain necessary supplies for the army to prosecute the reduction of the province; and that the friends to His Majesty's Government are invited to join the army on its route to receive the equipments and arms of which they stand in need that no time may be lost in returning up the country.

Highlanders to Cornwallis, undated — 5(18): D

To his Excellency Charles Earl Cornwallis, Commander in Chief
    of His Majesty's [forces] in the Southern Department of America etc etc

It is with the greatest pleasure we learn that His Majesty's forces (under your Excellency's command) has reach'd these parts to the great joy of many of His Majesty's loyal subjects in this settlement, who has for many years laboured under the greatest distresses while deprived from the protection of their lawfull Sovereign. It is with gratitude we return our thanks to your Excellency for your particular attention to the Highlanders and your seasonable advice to those that has familys to stay at home without dread or fear for a certain time. We are glad to understand (by certain intelligence sent to this settlement by his Excellency Governor Martin) that your Excellency's intention is to render us your protection when your Excellency's army is supply'd with necessarys, and we are certain, whenever the Scotch in this country (and many others) finds themselves out of the reach of their nighest enemies and unmercifull tyrants, they will readily join their force and interest with those under your Excellency's command. We also render our just acknowledgement to his Excellency Governor Martin, by whose means we know your Excellency's attention to our countrymen,

---

[50] This formulaic expression is taken from another copy of the proclamation: 101(28).

in particular, we have his proclamation of October last[51], likewise Sir Henry Clinton's[52], and it is with pleasure we make known to you that there is great hopes it will have the desired effect.

§ - §

---

[51] *his proclamation..*: while at Charlotte, Josiah Martin had issued a proclamation on 3rd October 1780 presaging the restoration in North Carolina of government under the Crown. (R D W Connor, *History Of North Carolina* (Lewis Publishing Co, Chicago, 1919), i, 469)

[52] *Sir Henry Clinton's*: see vol I, p 49.

CHAPTER 42

Returns of troops etc and Care of wounded

1 - Returns of British etc troops, casualties and captured weaponry

State of troops fit for duty, 15th January to 1st April 1781[1]   5(134): D

State of the Troops that marched with the Army under the Command of Lt General Earl Cornwallis				
	Rank and File present and fit for duty			
	Jan 15 1781	*Feb 1 1781*	*Mar 1 1781*	*Apr 1 1781*
British				
Brigade of Guards	690	690	605	411
7th Regiment	167	-	-	-
16th Regiment, 3rd Company	41	-	-	-
23rd Regiment	286	279	258	182
33rd Regiment	328	334	322	229
71st Regiment, 1st Battalion	249	-	-	-
71st Regiment, 2nd Battalion	237	234	212	161
71st Regiment, Light Company	69	-	-	-

---

[1] Published in Stevens, *Clinton-Cornwallis Controversy*, i, 376.

German				
Regiment of Bose	347	345	313	245
Jagers	103	97	97	97
Provincial				
British Legion	451	174	174	174
North Carolina Volunteers	256	287	232	224
TOTAL	3,224	2,440	2,213	1,723

Return of casualties in North Carolina prior to the Battle of Guilford 103(17): DS

RETURN of the KILLED and WOUNDED on the March through NORTH CAROLINA in the various ACTIONS preceding the BATTLE of GUILFORD						
	REGIMENTS OR CORPS					
	Brigade of Guards	23rd	33rd	British Legion	Total	
KILLED					
Lt Colonels	1				1
Majors					
Captains					
Lieutenants					
Ensigns					
Serjeants					
Drummers					
Rank and file	7	1	2	1	11
WOUNDED					
Lt Colonels					
Majors					
Captains			1		1
Lieutenants		1			1
Ensigns					
Serjeants	6			1	7

Drummers					
Rank and file	57	8	10	4	79
TOTAL	71	10	13	6	100

Brigade of Guards: Lt Colonel Hall killed

23rd Regiment: Lieutenant Chapman wounded

33rd Regiment: Captain Ingram ditto

J DESPARD
Deputy Adjutant General

Return of troops at the Battle of Guilford   *103(19): DS*

FIELD RETURN of the TROOPS under the Command of LT GENERAL EARL CORNWALLIS in the Action at Guilford, 15th March 1781									
REGIMENTS OR CORPS									
	R Art	Guards	23rd	33rd	71st	Bose	Jagers	B Legion	Total
Br Generals		2							2
Lt Colonels		3		1				1	5
Majors						1			1
Captains		9	3	3	3	4	1	6	29
Lieutenants	3		8	4	6	4	1	8	34
Ensigns		1		4	5	2		3	15
Staff		4	1	1	1	1		6	14
Serjeants	7	27	12	8	25	35	1	20	135
Drummers		13	2		10	18	3	5	51
Rank & file	40	422	212	213	194	256	78	223	1,638

J DESPARD
Deputy Adjutant General

Return of casualties in the Battle of Guilford

RETURN of the KILLED, WOUNDED and MISSING of the TROOPS under the Command of LT GENERAL EARL CORNWALLIS in the ACTION at GUILFORD, 15th March 1781

	\multicolumn{9}{c}{REGIMENTS OR CORPS}
	R Art	Guards	23rd	33rd	71st	Bose	Jagers	B Legion	Total
KILLED									
Lt Colonels		1							1
Majors									
Captains									
Lieutenants	1		1						2
Ensigns				1	1				2
Serjeants		8		1	1	3			13
Drummers									
Rank & file	1	28	12	9	11	7	4	3	75
WOUNDED									
Br Generals		2							2
Lt Colonels				1				1	2
Majors									
Captains		6	1			2			9
Lieutenants				2		2			4
Ensigns		1		3		1			5
Staff		1		1					2
Serjeants		2	1	1	4	6		1	15
Drummers		2				3			5
Rank & file	4	143	53	55	46	53	3	12	369
MISSING									
Serjeants						1			1
Drummers									
Rank & file		22				2	1		25
TOTAL	6	216	68	74	63	80	8	17	532

_____	_____	_____
Officers' Names killed and wounded in the above Return		
REGIMENTS	KILLED	WOUNDED
Royal Artillery	Lieutenant O'Hara	
Brigade of Guards	Hon Lt Colonel Stuart	Brigadier General O'Hara Brigadier General Howard Captains (Swanton (Schutz (since dead) (Maynard (since dead) (Goodricke (since dead) (Lord Dunglass (Maitland Ensign Stuart Adjutant Colquhoun
23rd	2nd Lieutenant Robinson	Captain Peter
33rd	Ensign Talbot	Lt Colonel Webster (since dead) Lieutenant Salvin Lieutenant Wynyard Ensigns (Kelly (Gore (Hughes Adjutant Fox
71st	Ensign Grant	
Regiment of Bose		Captain Wilmousky (since dead) Captain Eichenbrodt Lieutenant Schwaner Lieutenant Geise Ensign de Trott (since dead)
British Legion		Lt Colonel Tarleton

J DESPARD
Deputy Adjutant General

Return of weaponry captured at the Battle of Guilford   103(23): DS

RETURN of Ordnance, Ammunition and Arms taken at the Battle of Guilford, 15th March 1781			
Ordnance brass	Mounted on travelling carriages with limbers and boxes complete	6 pounders	4
Shot	Round fixt with powder	6 pounders	160
	Case fixt..................ditto................................		50
Ammunition waggons			2
Stands of arms	Distributed among the militia and destroyed on the field		1,300

Wilmington
17th April 1781

J MACLEOD
Lieutenant and Commanding Officer of Artillery

Return of the wounded left at New Garden Meeting House   5(117): DS

A Return of the Number of Wounded of the different Regiments left at New Garden Meeting House, March 17th 1781			
Men's names	Where wounded	Died	Remaining state
Guards:			
Captain Schutz	Through the bowels	March 21st	
Thomas Sleaford, private	Body		Doing well
John Dawson	Thigh fractured		Doing well
Duncan McNorton	Eyes		Ditto
Wm Irwin	Leg		Ditto
Thomas Mitchell	Back		Ditto
John Chamberlain	Thigh		Ditto
John Lee	Knee		Bad case. Amp.
John McCoy	Compound fracture of the leg	Died of mortification, 21st March	
Thomas Williams	Thro' the body	Died March 25th	
James Ball	One the head and each arm, with fracture	Died March 21st	
Thomas Stoakes	Through the intestines		Very bad
Thomas Howard	The thigh and testicle		Recovered

Richd Lambourn	Ditto		Ditto
James Clarke	The arm, shoulder and breast		Dangerous
Serjeant Davis	Clavicle fractured		Ditto
Serjeant Major [German]	Upper part of the hip, iliac artery wounded	Died April 4th of an haemorrhage	
Corporal Tasker	Fractured leg		Better
Thomas Sturton	Thro' the knee. Amputated March 31st		Recovering
Thomas Robinson	The body	Died March 26th	
James Clarke	The breast	Died March 24th	
John Hudson	The head of the humerus and scapula		Very bad case
Edwd Rawley	The breast		Bad
James Pritchard	The head and body		Recovering
Wm Walford	Arm and body		Ditto
John Lawson	Shoulder and back		Ditto
John Careless	The body	Died March 22nd	
Benjⁿ Sutherland	The back - badly		Recovering
7th:			
Thomas Avory	Both eyes		Ditto
17th Light Dragoons:			
Richd Ripine	The right side		
23rd:			
Wm Jones	The radius and oleccran[2] fractured. Amputated March 23rd	Died March 27th	
James Elleban	Femur fractured		Badly
John Yewell	Thro' the thigh. Fractured		Ditto
Robt Butler	Thro' the knee. Amputated March 24th		Recovering
Wm Henley	The breast		Ditto
Charles Hunt	The body		Ditto

---

[2] *oleccran*: an abbreviation of 'olecranon', the projection of the ulna at the elbow, forming the bony protuberance there.

Hugh Murphy	The knee		Ditto
Gilbert	The body	Died March 26th	
Shacle	Leg fractured and wound thro' the body	Died March 22nd	
William Deacon	Ilium fractured		Recovering

British Legion:

Jessey Philpot	Head, arm and shoulder	Died March 23rd	
Rich[d] Baker	Arm and body		Recovering

33rd:

Joseph Bates	Compound fracture of the leg. Amputated 23rd March		Recovering
Rob[t] Yeald	Through the thigh		Ditto
John Bateman	Fractured thigh - bad	Died March 30th	
John Martin	Through the arm and back		Recovered
W[m] Hoyd	Through the chest		Ditto
John Yeald	Through the thigh		Ditto
Thomas Needham	Through the lungs	Died March 20th	

2nd Batt, 71st:

John Wallace	The leg fractured		Mending
Dan[l] McCallam	The thigh		Recovering
Alex[r] Campbell	The thigh and side		Ditto
Rory McKenzie	The left side and breast		Doubtful
John McKuhan	The body and lungs	Died March 25th	
John McCoy	The arm and side		Doubtful

Regiment of Bose:

Saze	The thigh and thro' the scrotum	Died March 28th	
Hoofe	The thigh fractured		Doubtful
Schaeler	Head of the arm and shoulder		Very bad case
Smith	The body		Doubtful
Tapneer	Ditto	Died March 29th	
Packer	Each thigh		Recovered
Datrick	Arm fractured badly		Dangerous case

| Ezertan | Right side | | Recovered |
| Fiefear | Ditto | | Ditto |

Wounded N°................................ 64	Brigade of Guards officer	1	Died
of which 17 have died from the 17th of	Ditto non commissioned and private	27	
March to the 8th April............................. 17	7th Regiment ditto	1	
Remains 47	17th Light Dragoons ditto	1	
	23rd Regiment	10	
of which number upwards of 20 will	British Legion	2	
require waggons to remove them. The	33rd Regiment	7	
others are able to walk as soon as	2nd Battalion, 71st Regiment	6	
exchanged.	Regiment of Bose	9	
		64	

WEST HILL
Surgeon, General Hospital

Return of dead and deserters, New Garden Meeting House 5(180): D

Men who have died at New Garden Meeting House from the 19th of March 1781 to the 6th April 1781		
Brigade of Guards	Geo McKoy	March 21st
	James Ball	March 21st
	John Careless	March 22nd
	James Clarke	March 23rd
	Thomas Williams	March 25th
	Thomas Robinson	March 26th
	Serjeant Major German	April 3rd
23rd Regiment	John Hill	March 19th
	Franc^s Schaile	March 22nd
	Franc^s Gilbert	March 26th
	Wm Jones	March 27th
33rd Regiment	Thos Needham	March 20th
	John Bateman	March 30th
2nd Battalion, 71st Regiment	John McKuhan	March 25th

British Legion	Jossey Philpot	March 23rd
Regiment of Bose	Christopher Saze	March 29th
	Tepneer	March 30th
Deserters		
23rd Regiment	Wm Warren, orderly	Deserted March 26th
Combined Regiment, Guards	Jeremiah Putney, the late Captain Shutz' servant, with his master's portmanteau	Deserted 4th April

§ - §

2 - Care of certain British etc troops seriously wounded at Guilford and left at New Garden Meeting House

Ross to whom it may concern, 19th March 1781　　　　　　*5(123): ACS*

Head Quarters
19th March 1781

Mr West Hill, surgeon, and Mr Teare, mate, of the General Hospital being sent by Earl Cornwallis to the assistance of the British wounded at New Garden Meeting with a waggon containing a supply of necessaries and medicines for them, it is hoped by his Lordship that the surgeons and waggon will not meet with any interruption from the troops under the command of General Greene or from the militia or inhabitants of the country and that the surgeons will be permitted to return to the army when their attendance upon the wounded can be dispensed with.

A ROSS
Aide de camp

Hill to Pierce, 21st March 1781 — 5(128): C

New Garden Meeting House
March 21st 1781

To Captain Pierce
Aid de camp to Major General Greene

Received of the army commanded by the Hon Major General Greene in the service of the United States of America one sergeant major, one corporal and fifty nine private British soldiers as wounded prisoners to be accounted for in the general or future exchanges.

W HILL
Surgeon, General Hospital

Pierce to the inhabitants of New Garden settlement — 5(128): C

The inhabitants within 4 miles west and south of New Garden Meeting House are desired to furnish the British prisoners with provisions according to their applications.

By order of Major General Greene

WILLIAM PIERCE J^{R3}
Aid de camp

[*Subscribed*:]

The persons authorised to procure provisions are Thos Dart, John Reid, Wm Robinson, Wm Ring and John Bowdler.

W^M PIERCE J^R
ADC

---

[3] William Pierce Jr (*c.* 1740-1789) was a Virginian who had entered the Continental Army in November 1776 as a captain of artillery. Later on he served as General John Sullivan's aide-de-camp before returning to Virginia when Sullivan resigned in November 1779. Thirteen months later he was invited by Nathanael Greene to be his aide and joined him in January 1781. Promoted to brevet major in 1783, he left the army in the same year and began to engage in business at Savannah as head of the house of William Pierce & Company. In 1786 he was elected to the Continental Congress, and in 1787 he became one of Georgia's delegates to the Federal Convention, where he wrote his well-known notes and character sketches. His last years were blighted by business misfortunes and the subsequent failure of his firm. (*The Greene Papers*, vi, 522-3n, 608; *DAB*; Heitman, *Historical Register*, 441)

Provisions for the wounded[4]

	The Account of Articles received at New Garden Meeting House for the Use of the Wounded Prisoners		
March 21st	Wm Coffin Junior	One beef	100$^\#$ wt
March 23rd	Wm Coffin Senior	Ditto	165
March 25th	Thos Thornberrry	Ditto	140
March 27th	Silas Williams	Ditto	120
March 29th	Henry Safewright	Ditto	120
March 31st	John Cannady	Ditto	74
April 3rd	Allen Unthanks	Ditto	140
April 6th	[Isiah?] Hunt	Ditto	80
	Wm Coffin Senior	Flour - 6 bushels	
	Thos Thornberry	2 fowls, 2 dozen eggs	
	John Cannady	One sheep, 2 fowls and milk	
	Howell	One bushell meal and milk	
	Perkins	Ditto, 2 fowls	
	Pritchard	—— 2 fowls and milk	
April 4th	Wm Coffin Senior	4$^\#$ hogs, lard - paid for Hh[5]	
April 6th	George Eddings	½ c^t flour	
	Thos Kendall	1 pound candles	
	Geo Hyatt	2 bushels meal	
	Thos Pearce	2 fowls, 1 pound candles	
	John Ballinger	1 bushel meal, 2 fowls	
	Enoch Macy	2 fowls, eggs and milk	
	Jeremiah Hume at the Widow Hussey's, Deep River	2 bushels of indian meal	

---

[4] According to an annotation, supplied by the Quakers of New Garden settlement.

[5] *Hh*: hogshead?

Pierce to Hill, 31st March 1781 5(136): ALS

Head Quarters
March 31st '81

Doctor Hill

Sir

Every thing conducted under the sanction of a flag is considered as sacred, and whenever you may think proper to return, General Greene gives his consent to your carrying with you all or any part of your attendance, as your convenience may make it suitable.

The route necessary for you to take is by Coxes Iron Works on Lick Creek to Cross Creek and so on to Wilmington.

The representation you give of the wounded at New Garden is distressing and painful. I will interest myself in it, and send on a commissary, for the purpose of supplying them with every necessary, immediately. This you had a promise of before, and till this moment I never knew but a commissary was with you.

I am, sir, with great personal respect
Your very obedient and very humble servant

WILL PIERCE JUN[R]
Aid de camp

§ - §

CHAPTER 43

Other papers

1 - Cartel for the exchange and relief of prisoners etc[1]

Cornwallis to Greene, 4th February 1781[2]   *91(29): ADfS*

Head Quarters
February 4th 1781

Major General Greene etc etc etc

Sir

[3]I forbear mentioning at present the prisoners taken by General Morgan but shall wait untill facts are better authenticated, as I think the reports which I have heard of the cruelties exercised on them are almost incredible. But I must remark that the appearance of our prisoners found in Salisbury Jail shocked me extremely, as it was evident that they had been denied common sustenance. This, however, I do not impute to you, as by your distance from them you may have been unacquainted with their sufferings.

---

[1] For the sake of continuity and completeness these papers extend to 3rd May 1781.

[2] Summarised in *The Greene Papers*, vii, 250.

[3] At the beginning of this paragraph the following words are deleted: 'On my arrival at Salisbury I was much shocked to find several of our prisoners almost starved to death. I conclude you was unacquainted with their sufferings, as you have been for some time at a considerable distance from this'.

As the situation of prisoners of war, even without studied insult and barbarity, is liable to many inconveniences and hardships, I think it proper from motives of humanity to propose to you an exchange of prisoners beginning with those at present in possession of this army[4], at the same time agreeing on an equitable and convenient mode of exchanging the prisoners at Charlestown. I must desire that you will please to send your answer to this proposal as soon as you conveniently can, for the close manner in which we are obliged to confine the prisoners in Charlestown to prevent their escape must prove fatal to many of them when the warm weather commences if they are not removed. I have therefore (unless an exchange is finally settled) determined to send them in the course of next month to His Majesty's islands in the West Indies, where they will be more commodiously confined or, if they chuse it, be permitted to serve in the British regiments employed there or on the Spanish Main.

I am, sir,
Your most obedient humble servant

CORNWALLIS

Greene to Cornwallis, 24th February 1781[5]

91(31): LS

Head Quarters
February 24th 1781

Lt General the Earl Cornwallis etc etc etc

My Lord

Your Lordship's letter of the 4th instant I had the honor to receive on the 19th.

Whatever information may have been received respecting the ill treatment of the prisoners taken by General Morgan, I persuade myself it was groundless. I would appeal to the officers that were taken with the party for the extraordinary degree of humanity exercised upon the day of action, and I believe too great indulgence was shewn them afterwards as it gave many an opportunity to make their escape. The greater part, however, from a sense of their kind treatment chose to continue in captivity rather than avail themselves of the opportunities afforded them.

I cannot say any thing respecting the sick at Salisbury, but as the situation of the army interrupted the regular channel of supplies, it is not improbable the prisoners might feel an inconvenience for a day or two. I believe they had no reason to complain at any other time.

---

[4] The following words are deleted after 'army': 'whom I would immediately release for an equal number of men of similar descriptions who may either be with or in the neighbourhood of your army,'.

[5] Published in *The Greene Papers*, vii, 342.

I agree with your Lordship that prisoners of war are subject to many inconveniences without studied insult and barbarity, and on that account it has been my wish to effect an exchange of prisoners as soon as it could be made convenient. For this purpose I will direct the commissary of prisoners to have a conference with your commissary to agree upon an exchange.

I must beg your Lordship to believe that no cruelties which our prisoners may be subjected to will induce me to make an exchange but upon just and equal terms, and that I shall be under the necessity fully to exercise the law of retaliation agreeable to the Acts of Congress.

I am, my Lord,
Your Lordship's most obedient humble servant

NATH GREENE

Cornwallis to Greene, 4th March 1781[6]   91(33): C

[4th March 1781]

Sir

I was favoured with your letter of the 24th of February on the 1st instant.

I now inclose the affidavits[7] of some of the prisoners who made their escape since they were taken by General Morgan, from which you will observe that the accounts I had received of the treatment of those prisoners were not groundless, and I trust that you will order a strict enquiry to be made and punishment to be inflicted on those who have been guilty of the barbarities complained of. Circumstanced as General Morgan then was, I make many allowances for the prisoners being hurried on their march and for their being irregularly supplied with provisions, but shedding their blood can admit of no apology.

The number and quality of the guard put upon the prisoners after passing the Yadkin will sufficiently account for a number of them making their escape; and the miserable situation of the remainder, having almost stripped themselves to purchase provisions and in a country with which they were totally unacquainted, will (if I am not misinformed) better account for any of them crossing the Dan than by ascribing it to their gratitude or dependance upon the humanity of their conductors.

I think that upon revising my letter you will see that it was not necessary upon this occasion to threaten retaliation of harsh treatment of prisoners. It is as far from my intention to give just cause for it as it is to suffer cruel usage to ours to pass with impunity.

---

[6]   Summarised in *The Greene Papers*, vii, 388.

[7]   *the affidavits*: no extant copies.

You cannot suppose me unacquainted with the means that have been taken in different forms to delay the exchange of an equal number of our prisoners for those of yours now confined at Charlestown, particularly the opposition made to it by the delegates of North Carolina and their motives for it.[8] If by a continuance of those measures I am forced to send the prisoners to the West Indies, I mean it as a convenience for them as well as for ourselves; but if the measure of exchanging them is sincerely adopted, the mode may be soon settled, for I have not the smallest wish to insist upon unequal conditions. Those that at present appear equal to me are that, after exchanging in this country those now in my possession, the exchange of the others shall take place either in James River in Virginia, at Wilmington upon the Delaware, or at Elizabeth Town in New Jersey, beginning with those in confinement at Charlestown, as the most pressing case, against an equal number of those taken at different times in the Southern District, going on with them against the Convention army, and then proceeding to those on parole from both sides. And that those terms or any others that may appear mutually convenient and reasonable may be settled without loss of time I have named the Hon Captain Brodrick, my aide de camp, to meet a proper person named by you. I shall give full powers to Captain Brodrick to conclude this business, and I hope you will think proper to furnish the person employed by you with similar powers, that there may be as little delay as possible. And I propose the ninth day of this month as the time and Butler's house near Armstrong's Ford on the Haw as the place of meeting.

Having a sincere compassion for the sufferings of the prisoners on both sides, I own it will give me great satisfaction if by some reasonable agreement they can be relieved.

[CORNWALLIS]

Greene to Cornwallis, 8th March 1781[9]   *91(35): LS*

Head Quarters
March 8th 1781

Lt General the Earl Cornwallis etc etc etc

My Lord

Your Lordship's letter of the 4th instant I have been favoured with.

My wishes to relieve the suffering prisoners on both sides have induced me to appoint Lt Colonel Carrington[10] of the First Regiment of Artillery as a commissioner with full powers to settle the terms of an exchange of prisoners who have been taken in this department.

---

[8] See Sharpe to Davidson, 9th November 1780, p 91.

[9] Summarised in *The Greene Papers*, vii, 410.

[10] Born in Charlotte County, Virginia, Edward Carrington (1749-1810) had been commissioned lt colonel of the 1st Continental Artillery Regiment in November 1776. He was now acting ably and resourcefully as Nathanael Greene's quartermaster. Reverting to the artillery, he would soon take part in the siege of Yorktown. In 1785-6 he was a delegate from Virginia to the Continental Congress. (*Appletons'*; Heitman, *Historical Register*, 146; *The Greene Papers*, vi, 517n, ix, 455)

I am unhappy that circumstances oblige me to request the time may be postponed untill the 12th instant, when Lt Colonel Carrington will expect to see the Hon Captain Broderick at Butler's house unless your Lordship should think proper to alter the time of their meeting.

I am, my Lord,
Your Lordship's most obedient very humble servant

NATH GREENE

Cornwallis to Brodrick, undated[11]   91(43): C

Memorandums from Lord Cornwallis to Captain Broderick

I proposed in my letter to General Greene, first to exchange on the spot the prisoners in my possession, then an equal number of those now confined at Charlestown for those of ours taken in the Southern Department, proceeding to exchange the remainder against the Convention army, and then to go on with the prisoners on parole from both sides. I likewise said that it appeared to me to be *equal* that the exchange should take place either in James River in Virginia, at Wilmington in the Delaware, or at Elizabeth Town in New Jersey. The substance of those proposals you are of course at liberty to agree to, and if any other place is proposed by Colonel Carrington which appears evidently to you to be equal to both sides, you may readily agree to it, but if you are doubtfull of the equality, you must take time to consider untill you can receive my directions.

I have no objection to take the first steps in the exchange by sending a certain number of the prisoners from Charlestown to the place appointed to meet ours, the flag of truce being sacred going with the American prisoners, and with ours in exchange for them, to the port where they are to be landed; and a safe conduct to Charlestown will be wanted from General Greene for an express to carry the order for the embarkation of the American prisoners, engaging that this express shall not be charged with any other business.

The exchange need not be delayed by waiting for correct lists of prisoners as they can be made up while the first division of prisoners is upon the way.

Militia taken in arms by either side must be looked upon as soldiers.

As a mode for the exchange of officers was under consideration some time ago and perhaps is now settled between General Moultrie and the Commandant of Charlestown, I wish to leave that branch of the business to them. However, I have no material objection to settle a reasonable general plan here, only I cannot agree to their officers being picked for exchange by name.

---

[11] The terms of this document suggest it was written before Brodrick's first meeting with Carrington on 12th March. For Greene's instructions to Carrington, see *The Greene Papers*, vii, 425.

I expect that it will be explicitly declared by General Greene whether he *will* or *will not* exchange the prisoners of the militia taken at Charlestown that are now upon parole at St Augustine and in the two Carolinas, because that declaration will in some measure affect the future treatment of them.

The expence of maintaining prisoners must have been greatest on our side by the number taken at Charlestown and may be a point for future discussion.

Cornwallis to Greene, 16th March 1781[12] 90(3): C

Head Quarters
16th March 1781

Major General Greene etc etc etc

Sir

I have given orders to collect the wounded of your army at Guildford Court House, where every possible attention shall be paid to them, but as it is not in my power to give them sufficient assistance, I must recommend it to you to send immediately surgeons to take care of them and a supply of necessaries and provisions.

I am, sir,
Your most obedient and most humble servant

CORNWALLIS

Greene to Cornwallis, 16th March 1781 90(5): ALS

Flagg of truce

Head Quarters
March 16th 1781

Lt General Earl Cornwallis etc etc etc

My Lord

As I suppose we have some wounded men in your possession, who may be unhappily situated, I must request that you will permit Doctor Wallace[13], a surgeon in the American army, to attend them. He has instructions to govern his conduct agreable to the custom of officers on parole during his stay with your army.

---

[12] This and the following three letters are summarised in *The Greene Papers*, 433 and 444-5.

[13] James Wallace was a Virginian who had entered the Continental service as a surgeon in June 1777. (Heitman, *Historical Register*) His will may be found among the Wallace Family Papers. (Manuscript Collection of the Filson Club Historical Society, A/W194)

I have the honor to be
Your Lordship's most obedient humble servant

NATH GREENE

Greene to Cornwallis, 17th March 1781 — *90(7): ALS*

Head Quarters
March 17th 1781

My Lord

Your letter of yesterday arrived last evening. Doctor Wallace, one of the surgeons in this army, was previously dispatched to answer the purposes of your recommendation.

I am much obliged to you for the attention you have paid the unfortunate wounded of my army, and as it meets with your permission, I shall send on immediate supplies of provisions and other necessaries for the hospital.

I am
Your Lordship's most obedient and most humble servant

NATH GREENE

Greene to Cornwallis, 18th March 1781 — *91(37): LS*

Head Quarters
March 18th 1781

Lt General Earl Cornwallis

My Lord

Lt Colonel Carrington and the Hon Captain Broderick had a meeting at General Butler's on the 12th instant for the purpose of settleing a cartel for the exchange of prisoners of war, as proposed by your Lordship and agreed to by me. Captain Broderick's powers being incompetent to the business of the meeting, it was agreed on between the parties to meet again on the 16th. Lt Colonel Carrington attended but had not the honor of meeting Captain Broderick. Your Lordship will please to explain the cause and inform me whether the negotiation is to be discontinued or otherwise.

I have the honor to be, my Lord,
Your Lordship's most obedient humble servant

NATH GREENE

Warrant to Brodrick, 22nd March 1781　　　　　　　　　　　91(39): CS

By Charles Earl Cornwallis, Lt General of His Majesty's forces etc etc etc

To the Hon Captain Brodrick

　　Whereas in consequence of my proposal Major General Greene, commanding the troops acting under the authority of the Congress in the Southern District, has appointed Lt Colonel Carrington commissioner to meet you at General Butler's house near Armstrong's Ford on Haw River on the 12th instant for the purpose of settling an exchange of prisoners that have been taken in the Southern District on terms mutually convenient and reasonable, I do therefore constitute and appoint you the said Captain Brodrick a commissioner to meet the said Lt Colonel Carrington on the 24th instant at Major O'Neale's house for the above purpose and, which being settled, to negotiate a cartel for the exchange and relief of prisoners that may be left in captivity or may hereafter be taken in the said district, hereby declaring whatever you shall agree to conclusive and confirmed.

　　　　　　　　　　In testimony whereof I have hereunto set my hand and seal at head quarters
　　　　　　　　　　　　　　　　　　　　　　　this 22nd day of March AD 1781

　　　　　　　　　　　　　　　　　　　　　　　　　　　　　　　　CORNWALLIS ○

Carrington's proposals and Brodrick's answers,　　　　　　91(45): C
　　28th March 1781

Proposals made by Lt Colonel Carrington for the exchange and relief of the prisoners of war taken in the Southern Department	Answered by Captain Brodrick
1st, that regular troops be exchanged for regular troops and militia for militia.	Agreed to.
2nd, that the mode of exchange be rank for rank as far as similar ranks shall apply.	Agreed to.
3rd, that there be a reciprocal option as to the subjects of exchange, and that option exercised by naming particular corps or particular persons adapted to the characters proposed to be exchanged.	Cannot be admitted. The reasonable and common mode is according to the dates of capture.
4th, that no non commissioned officer or private soldier admitted to parole shall be considered as a prisoner of war, but finally liberated, unless paroled on the faith of a commissioned officer.	Agreed, to take place in future.

5th, that officers who cannot be exchanged for want of proper ranks to apply be immediately admitted to parole till exchanged, and the same indulgence extended to those captured in future.

Lord Cornwallis has often indulged and probably will continue to give paroles to many officers while the balance is in his possession, but he cannot agree to the general proposal because it is unequal in many respects and has never been practised between the armies under the respective Commanders in Chief.

6th, that passports be allowed for such supplies as may be sent from either side to prisoners in captivity.

Agreed.

7th, that commissaries of prisoners be permitted to pass into the respective lines for the purpose of a free communication with the prisoners and representing their situations.

Agreed to pass and reside, but removeable at the pleasure of the respective commanding officers.

8th, that prisoners shall not be sent from the Continent or compelled to enlist into either service.

Lord Cornwallis cannot agree to the first part of this proposal. The latter is never practised by the British troops.

9th, that such officers be permitted to remain with the prisoners in captivity as may be requested by the party to whom they belong.

Cannot be admitted.

10th, that the commissaries of prisoners shall immediately put into practice exchanges on the above principles, as far as the subjects on each side will go, and continue them in future as characters shall apply.

Agreed to on the principles settled by the commissioners.

11th, that a certain time be fixed on for the first delivery of prisoners on both sides, by which time correct lists of the prisoners may be made up.

Agreed to.

Carrington to Brodrick, 31st March 1781 91(41): ALS

Head Quarters
March 31st 1781

The Hon Captain Brodrick

Sir

Yours of the 28th inclosing Lord Cornwallis's answers to my proposals for the exchange and relief of prisoners I received.

I now do myself the pleasure to inclose yours with General Greene's answers thereupon.

In forming the proposals made on the part of General Greene the most extensive relief to those in captivity was had in view, and they were calculated on general principles so equally advantageous that the General cannot think of receding from them except as to the commissaries of prisoners being permitted to pass into the respective lines. This proposal he is willing to adapt to Lord Cornwallis's wish expressed in his answer.

Should you be willing to close with me in the negotiation upon the footing I now set it, I shall be happy to meet you on the third of April, but as the present situation of the two armies will necessarily prevent its taking place at Ramsey's Mill, I beg leave to propose the house of Henry Caster on or near Upper Little as the place of meeting. It will be necessary for me to hear from you before the time of meeting. Should the flag not be dispatched in time for that purpose, you will oblige me by naming any other time or place you may think proper.

You will be pleased to observe a necessary alteration in your powers so as to comprehend those officers, now in captivity and who cannot be exchanged, in whatever may be agreed on for the relief of prisoners.

I am with much respect
Your most obedient servant

ED CARRINGTON

Enclosure
Brodrick's proposals and Carrington's answers 91(48): D

Proposals made by the Hon Captain Brodrick for the exchange of prisoners	Answered by Lt Colonel Carrington
That an immediate exchange should take place on the spot of the prisoners in our possession for an equal number of ours	This would be drawing the commissioners into a series of business very unnecessarily. It will be much better to lay down general

taken in the Southern Department, afterwards an equal number of those now confined in Charles Town for those of ours taken in this district, and then to proceed to the exchange of those on parole from both sides.	principles for exchanges on which the respective commissaries of prisoners will regularly proceed.
That if a balance of prisoners is left in the hands of either party, any officer belonging to that party that may be taken hereafter shall be immediately sent in and an officer of equal rank belonging to that party released.	Such balance of officers as may be left on either side to be immediately paroled to return home 'till exchanged, and the commissaries to continue the exchanges as characters from time to time shall apply.
Regulars will be exchanged for regulars, and militia for militia, but the subjects for exchange are not to be picked.	Agreed as to the first part of this proposal, but a reciprocal choice of subjects must be insisted on.
Eighteen months' men and State troops to be looked upon as regulars.	Agreed.
That a certain time shall be fixed for the first delivery of prisoners on both sides, by which time correct lists of the prisoners may be made up.	Agreed.
That the exchange shall take place either in James River, Virginia, Wilmington in the Delaware, or Elizabeth Town in New Jersey.	One of those places will be agreed upon.
That the flag of truce should be sacred going with the American prisoners, and returning with ours in exchange, to the port where they are to be landed.	Agreed to under proper restrictions.
That a safe conduct shall be given by General Greene for an express to carry the order to Charles Town for the embarkation of the American prisoners, engaging that the express shall be charged with no other business.	Agreed.

Cornwallis to Greene, 3rd April 1781[14]

91(50): C

Head Quarters
3rd April 1781

Major General Greene etc etc etc

Sir

Captain Brodrick has communicated to me the conversations and the correspondence that have passed between Lt Colonel Carrington and him on the subject of the exchange of prisoners. I confess I should be much concerned at the failure of a plan which my feelings for the captives of both sides had induced me to propose. My anxiety for its success would lead me to acquiesce under some disadvantages, but I consider several of the articles on which you insist to be so manifestly unreasonable in their present form that I should think myself criminal in agreeing to them, and indeed if you continue to insist on them I must conclude that you do not seriously wish the exchange to take place.

I particularly allude to four articles which I shall answer after mentioning them.

1st, your desiring 'that there may be a mutual choice of the subjects of exchange adapted to the characters proposed to be exchanged'.

This mode would, as I conceive, be not only unprecedented but most evidently unequal to us because, the balance of officers being at present greatly in our favour, it would enable you to select your most usefull officers in exchange for ours and to leave the remainder in our hands of those that you value least. I cannot see any reasonable objection to this exchange taking place by the dates of captivity.

2nd, 'that officers who cannot be exchanged for want of proper ranks to apply be immediately admitted to parole till exchanged'.

Although it has not been the practice during this war to permit the officers taken by either side to go upon parole as a right, and tho' the advantage of this article will be almost entirely on your side, I will agree to its becoming the practice in this district during our respective commands after an exchange has taken place as far as the number of prisoners in your possession will admit of. Those officers giving their parole in the usual form to surrender when required.

3rd, 'that prisoners shall not be sent from the Continent'.

The feeding and guarding our prisoners is no great expence or trouble on your side but the case is different to us with respect to your prisoners confined at Charlestown. However, it never was, nor is it now, my intention to send any of your prisoners from the Continent while there are the least hopes of your chusing to exchange them, and therefore I will agree to keep

---

[14] Summarised in *The Greene Papers*, viii, 39.

at Charlestown the balance of your prisoners that may remain in our hands whilst the articles of the cartel continue to be observ'd.

4th, 'that such officers be permitted to remain with the prisoners in captivity as may be requested by the party to whom they belong'.

This proposal would subject both sides to much inconvenience and occasion many disputes. It is likewise without precedent unless in consequence of previous capitulations. I cannot therefore think myself at liberty to agree to any innovation on that head.

Having acted openly and very far from any design of gaining an advantage over you in this transaction, I trust that it will be apparent to the prisoners of both sides, as well as to all candid persons, that I do not wish to prolong the distresses of the unfortunate. If you are inclined to close the negociation by removing the obstacles that I have mentioned, I propose that it may be done by the commissioners on the 16th instant at Crosscreek or at any other place more convenient for you on the Cape Fear River.

I am, sir,
Your most obedient and most humble servant

[CORNWALLIS]

Greene to Cornwallis, 9th April 1781[15]   *91(54): LS*

Head Quarters
April 9th 1781

Lt General Earl Cornwallis etc etc etc

My Lord

I had the honor to receive your Lordship's letter of the 3rd of this instant on the evening of the 6th.

I cannot conceive myself justly chargeable with either proposing or insisting upon any unreasonable terms. My object was to procure the most speedy and effectual relief to the unfortunate captives in the hands of both parties. I have not insisted upon any conditions but what are mutual, and in settling the principles of a cartel I should suppose accidental circumstances should have no influence. It is true the advantage with respect to officers at present is on our side, but that may not always be the case. In the exchange of privates it is evidently on your side upon the conditions which were proposed and which I shall continue to insist upon, but to convince your Lordship that I am not less desireous of effecting an exchange than you can be, tho' I am sensible of the political inconvenience that will attend the measure, I agree to the officers being exchanged according to the dates of their captivity,

---

[15] Summarised in *The Greene Papers*, viii, 73.

the remainder being admitted to paroles, not subject to be recalled unless for a breach thereof or for a violation of the conditions of the cartel by the party to whom the officers belong.

If a just and equal treatment are meant towards the prisoners remaining in captivity, I cannot conceive how any inconvenience or disputes can arise by officers residing with the men, and if a benefit will result to the unfortunate and there is no political reason opposed to it, I cannot persuade myself that the want of a precedent is a sufficient objection, and therefore I hope your Lordship on further consideration will agree to the measure, but if you should not, my desire is so great to relieve those in captivity that I shall not insist upon it.

Your Lordship agreeing to the conditions here proposed and insisted upon in addition to those already agreed to, I beg leave to propose Mr Pegee's on the Pedee opposite to the Cheraws on the 24th of this instant for the meeting of the commissioners to compleat this business.

I am, my Lord,
Your Lordship's most obedient and most humble servant

NATH GREENE

Cornwallis to Greene, 15th April 1781[16]

91(56): C

Head Quarters
15th April 1781

Major General Greene

Sir

I have just received the favour of your letter of the 9th of this instant.

As I have now the greatest hopes that the very desirable object of a cartel upon fair and equal terms may take place, I will send a commissioner with full powers to conclude the business to the place and on the day proposed by you, but as it will be inconvenient for Captain Brodrick to attend, I presume you will have no objection to my substituting Captain Cornwallis[17] of the 33rd Regiment in his room.

I am etc

[CORNWALLIS]

---

[16] Summarised in *The Greene Papers*, viii, 102.

[17] Having spent his entire service in the 33rd Regiment, of which Lord Cornwallis was Colonel, and sharing his name, Frederick Cornwallis may have been related. Commissioned an ensign on 9th December 1768, he was promoted to lieutenant on 15th January 1772 and to captain on 2nd February 1776. (*Army Lists*)

Articles of the cartel, 3rd May 1781

Articles of a Cartel for the Exchange and Relief of Prisoners of War taken in the Southern Department, agreed to at the House of Mr Claudius Pegee on Pedee the third of May 1781 between Captain Cornwallis on the part of Lt General Earl Cornwallis and Lt Colonel Carrington on the part of Major General Green

1st, that regular troops be exchanged for regulars, and militia for militia.

2nd, that men enlisted for six months and upwards in Continental or State service be look'd upon as regulars.

3rd, that the mode of exchange be rank for rank as far as similar ranks shall apply.

4th, that officers be exchanged by rotation according to the dates of capture, but a reciprocal option to be exercised as to subjects in non commission'd and privates by naming particular corps or particular persons.

5th, that no non commission'd officer or private soldier admitted to parole shall be considered as a prisoner of war, but finally liberated, unless paroled on the faith of a commission'd officer.

6th, that officers who cannot be exchanged for want of similar ranks to apply be immediately paroled to their respective homes till exchanged, subject to be recall'd upon a breach thereof or for a violation of the cartel by the party to whom they belong.

7th, that passports be allow'd for such supplies as may be sent from either side to prisoners in captivity.

8th, that commissaries of prisoners be permitted to pass from each side into the opposite lines and reside there for the purpose of viewing and representing the situations of the prisoners, but removable by the respective commanding officers.

9th, that the prisoners shall not be sent from the Continent whilst the articles of the cartel continue to be observed.

10th, that commissaries of prisoners shall immediately put in practice exchanges on the above principles as far as the subjects on each side will go, and continue them in future as characters shall apply.

11th, that the first delivery of American prisoners shall embark at Charles Town on or before the 15th of June and sail immediately for James Town in James River, where the first delivery of British prisoners shall embark on or about the first week in July and sail immediately for the nearest British port.

12th, that the flag of truce shall be sacred going with the American prisoners, and returning with the British, to the port where they are to be delivered.

FRED^K CORNWALLIS
ED CARRINGTON

§ - §

2 - Extracts from the Davidson Papers

Regimental return, North Carolina militia, 27th October 1780   106(10): DS

	Captain Forbes	Captain Pierce	Captain Wilson	Captain Morgan	Lieut Vernon	Lieut Clapp	Total
Weekly Return of Colonel Peasley's Regiment of North Carolina Militia[18], Camp Providence, October 27th 1780							
Officers present fit for duty							
Field:							
Colonel							
Lt Colonel	1						1
Major							
Commission'd:							
Captains	1	1	1	1			4
Capt Lieutenants					1	1	2
Lieutenants	1	1	1	1			4
Ensigns	1		1		1		3
Staff:							
Adjutant		1					1
Pay Master							
Quarter Master	1						1
Surgeon							
Surgeon's Mate							
Non commission'd:							
Serjeant Major		1					1
Qr Master Serjeant		1					1
Drum Major							
Fife Major							

---

[18] It was the 3rd Regiment.

Serjeants	3	3	1	1	2	1	11
Drums and Fifes							
Rank and File							
Present fit for duty	42	32	36	26	16	12	164
Sick present	1				1	2	4
Sick absent[19]	5	8	2		6		21
On command	4			21		1	26
On furlough	4	1	5	4	3		17
Total	64	48	48	54	30	17	261
Wanting to compleat							
Serjeants						1	1
Drums and Fifes	2	2	2	2	2	2	12
Rank and File		11			25	37	73
Alterations since last return							
Dead							
Discharged							
Deserted	9	5	1		1	1	17
Promoted							
Transferred							
Joined:							
Serjeants							
Drums and Fifes							
Rank and File							

The above commenced service August 15th 1780

	On command, Surrey County	Waggon Master	Forage Master	Waggoners	Total
On command	21	1	1	9	32
Captain Peay	Sick at Guilford				
Captain Whitsail	On furlough				
Ensign Mosley	On command, Surrey County				

JOHN HARVEY, adjutant   JOHN PEASLEY

---

[19] According to the return, absent sick were lodged at 'Salsberry' (Salisbury).

Postscript, Sharpe to Davidson, 9th November 1780[20]   *106(12): DS*

November 9th

PS

I forgot to inform you that General Lincoln with upwards of an hundred officers are lately exchanged and that the Commanders in Chief are about to negociate a general exchange, including the Convention troops and our militia. General Washington is instructed to endeavour to obtain a condition that the Convention and other British prisoners shall not take the field nor bear arms before the first of May.

However humanity dictated an immediate exchange, yet our critical situation to the southward made it a great question in policy. Was the exchange to take place immediately and the enemy at liberty to arm and send forth their liberated troops, it might be a fatal stroke to the State of North Carolina, because in that State we have not arms, stores etc at present to put into the hands of our liberated troops and militia in order to make a vigorous defence. Therefore the delegates of North Carolina have been the means of keeping back the exchange a few weeks past and of quallifying the measure as above mentioned with a view to get General Greene in command, get forward some arms, stores etc, and get time to draw out and organize a little army that may promise us some defence, all which I hope will sufficiently justify our conduct to our brave and virtuous officers and soldiers who are in a distressing captivity. We have been so opposed in this business of delaying the exchange by some of our neighbouring delegates, who has a passionate fondness for their friends, that we have been threatned with the displeasure of those in captivity. These things have but little effect on the minds of men determined to do what appears to be *right*. We are so well assured of the patriotism of our officers and soldiers that they would at the risk of their lives endure six months' or perhaps twenty months' longer confinement rather than obtain liberty at the risque of a whole State.

W^M SHARPE[21]

General Davidson

---

[20] The rest of this letter is not extant.

[21] Born in Cecil County, Maryland, William Sharpe (1742-1818) studied classics and law before being admitted to the bar and commencing practice in Mecklenburg County, North Carolina, in 1763. He also engaged in surveying. Moving on to Rowan, he became a member of the Provincial Congress in 1775-6 and helped to frame the North Carolina revolutionary constitution. In the latter year he also served as aide to Rutherford during the Cherokee campaign. Since 1779 he had been sitting in the Continental Congress and was currently a member of its committee for corresponding with the commanding officer of the southern forces. Completing his term in Congress in 1781, he would go on to serve in the lower house of the North Carolina revolutionary legislature in 1781-2. He died near Statesville in Iredell County, North Carolina, and was interred in Snow Creek Graveyard. (Joel D Treese and Dorthy J Countryman, *Biographical Directory of the United States Congress 1774-1996* (Cq Pr, 1996))

Butler to Giles, 19th January 1781
106(13): ALS

January 19th 1781

Major Edward Giles[22]
   with General Morgan

Dear Sir

Your letters of the 12th and 14th by express was handed me last night. The letter of the 5th came to hand this day. The express returns immediately, which prevents my giving you so much of my chatt as I could wish. A detachment of 400 Virginians, Colonel Lee's corps of 250 and your[23] regiment have arrived with some recruits for the Maryland line, and I expect 400 more Virginians are on the route. We daily expect large quantities of stores from the northward. The Spaniards have certainly attacked Pensacola and an expedition against St Augustine will take place this month.

General Phillips is in the neighbourhood of Petersburg with 2,500 men, which I hope will arouse the great knife[24].

Nothing can be undertaken against Lord Cornwallis that will alarm him so much or prevent his attempting to penetrate so effectually as maintaining your position beyond Broad River. General Davidson has called out half the militia of Mecklenburg and Roan Counties and has 300 Hillsbro' militia. They are under the orders of General Morgan.

General Sumter is, I believe, a man of great ambition, a good officer and very well informed and decided in his measures. I think General Morgan will receive great advantage from him if they could see each other.

A few weeks, I hope, will put us in a situation to oppose his Lordship in a very respectable manner.

I shall take pleasure in transmitting your letters to Miss ——.

Adieu. Present my respectfull compliments to General Morgan and all friends.

---

[22] Edward Giles was a major in the Maryland state regiment. Having declined in mid December the offer of an appointment as a commissary of prisoners, he had gone on to serve as a volunteer aide-de-camp to Daniel Morgan. After the Battle of Cowpens he had the honour of carrying the dispatches announcing the victory. As a reward for his services Congress brevetted him a major in the Continental line. He then returned to Maryland, where he served as William Smallwood's aide-de-camp for the rest of the war. (*The Greene Papers*, vi, 591n)

[23] 'your' is substituted for 'the State'.

[24] *the great knife*: perhaps a paraphrase of 'war to the knife' (after the Spanish *guerra al cuchillo*). If so, the meaning is 'relentless warfare'.

Yours

JB[25]

Whitlock to Davidson, 20th January 1781   *106(15): ALS*

Duchmancreek
January 20th 1781

His Excellency William Davidson BG

Sir

I am the unfortunate woman that is wife or otherwise widow to Ja^s Whitlock, who went with Colonel Brian's. I have eight children to provide for and am at present in a condition very unable either for that or to ride to you in order to lay my case before you. A great deal of my property has been taken for the use of the public or under that pretence, but there is a Negro boy of mine at Mr Fortune's, not returned to any commissioner, that might help me greatly that I beg to have returned at least for some time. And also there is 20 bushels of corn demanded of me for the use of the public, which, if taken, will distress.

Yours

SYLVIAS WHITLOCK

Scheer to whom it may concern, 26th January 1781   *106(18): ALS*

Head Quarters
26th of Jenuary 1781

Martin Frytag has permission to pass and repas whit horses in the camp of the Regement of Bosa.

SCHEER Captain[26]

---

[25] Brigadier General John Butler, North Carolina revolutionary militia.

[26] Scheer and Frytag were obviously German immigrants or persons of German extraction, which is why they were interested in gaining intelligence from the Regiment von Bose. Apart from no doubt being members of Davidson's brigade, they have not otherwise been identified.

Sumter to Davidson, 28th January 1781 — 106(19): ALS

28th January 1781

The Hon Brigadier General Davidson

Favour by Mr Price

Dear Sir

I have received undoubted intelegence of the strength and find that their regular force do not exceed 1,600. The number of field peaces they have no doubt you are informed of. Lord Cornwallis had 680 men with him before he was join'd by General Leslie. General Leslie had 578 with him. Total 1,258. Since join'd a detachment from Camden, near 100. These, together [with] which survived Tarlton's defeat and has fell in, are what I alow to make up the above number, which is certainly making the most unfavourable computation. I am convinced, if our force was collected, that they never would gain even their nearest post, provided any exertions was made. Some have doubts that they may send a party or the whole [to] cross at the Tuckey Segee. However, this you are the best judge of by the advices you may receve.

I am, dear sir,
Your most obedient humble servant

THOS SUMTER

Greene to Hagens, 31st January 1781 — 106(20): ALS

Camp at Beatty's Ford
January 31st 1781

Lt Colonel Hagens[27]

Sir

The enemy are laying on the opposite side of the river and from every appearance seem determined to penetrate the country. General Davidson informs he has called again and again for the people to turn out and defend their country. The inattention to his call and the backwardness among the people is unaccountable. Providence has blessed the American arms with signal success in the defeat of Tarlton and the surprise of George Town by Colonel Lee with his Legion. If after these advantages you neglect to take the field and suffer the enemy

---

[27] Probably William Heaggins, but a John Haggans is on record as serving in the revolutionary militia of Salisbury District. (vol III, p 192, note 89; Hay ed, *Soldiers from NC*, 390) In Tarleton, *Campaigns*, 252-3, there is a letter couched in the same terms but written from Greene to Francis Locke, Colonel of the Rowan County revolutionary militia.

to over run the country, you will deserve the miseries ever inseparable from slavery. Let me conjure you, my country men, to fly to arms and to repair to head quarters without loss of time and bring with you ten days' provision. You have every thing that is dear and valuable at stake. If you will not face the approaching danger, your country is inevitably lost. On the contrary, if you repair to arms and confine yourselves to the duties of the field, Lord Cornwallis must be inevitably ruined. The Continental army is marching with all possible dispatch from the Pedee to this place, but without your aid their arrival will be of no consequence.

I am, sir,
Your humble servant

NATH GREENE

Intelligence, undated — *106(6): D*

3rd[28]	700
Hessian	300
Yaugers	100
23rd	300
33rd	300
North Carolina Volunteers	200
71st	200
Tarlton	200
	2,100[29]

§ - §

---

[28] *3rd*: a reference to the Brigade of Guards.

[29] The total should be 2,300.

3 - Intercepted letters

Extract, Greene to Locke, 4th December 1780[30]   *2(406): LS*

... [for] the confinement of the prisoners of war now in our possession and for the reception of such as may hereafter fall into our hands induces me to wish that a place may be made at Salisbury for the purpose. I have instructed Captain Marberry[31] to superintend the building of it and directed him to have it compleated as speedily as possible. The public stores are so destitute of the articles necessary for the purpose that he must rely in a great measure on the inhabitants for axes, spades and some other tools which will be wanted, and perhaps for labourers.

   I... materials that he may want.

I am, sir, with regard
Your most obedient humble servant

NATH GREENE

General Lock

Murphey to his wife, 8th February 1781   *5(77): ALS*

Guilford Court House
8th February 1781

Mrs Jane Murphey

Dear Spouse

   I wrote you yesterday of my marching towards the Yadkin and this evening have returned to this place. We have now joyned General Green's troops and shall be under the command of General Morgan. We hear that the British army hath crossed the Shallow Ford, and expect they will march this road. The militia of the different countys are collecting, so that we shall have a strong army in a few days.

   It is said that General Wayne and 1,500 troops are to joyn us in a day or two. I hope you'l make your self as easy as possible about me, and in case the enemy should advance near you, you'l send my Negroes and best property over Dan. I don't expect to be home as my duty in camp is very close unless the army should lay encamped some time in a place, which I don't expect.

---

[30] Summarised in *The Greene Papers*, vi, 522. The rest of the letter is not extant. Francis Locke was a colonel commanding the revolutionary militia of Rowan County, North Carolina. In addressing him as 'General', Greene anticipated his promotion to brigadier general in 1781.

[31] Joseph Marbury was an acting deputy quartermaster with Greene's army.

Should be glad that Mr Harralson will take care of my office, and in case of danger to remove the records. Our army has had three schirmishes with the British since I have been in camp, and I have been in two of them. My brother James was with me in the last. Have heard that he escaped without being hurt. It is impossible to give you a naritive of the situation of all the armys as I am confined to one, yet you may rest assured that I yet hope to see something done in honour to the American arms before I return. When I have any opportunity, I will write you any thing which is new to us. Expect you'l send me a letter first oppertunity. Give my best wishes to Mr Williams and inform him that I much depend on his industry for the wellfare of my plantation.

My love to you and my children, and am sincearly, madam,

Your loving husband

A[D] MURPHEY[32]

§ - §

---

[32] According to 2(409), Archibald Murphey (?-1817) had been a prominent revolutionary in the Richmond District of Orange County, North Carolina. He was at this time captain of a militia company, a list of which is given in 2(408). His son, Archibald De Bow Murphey, went on to become a noted lawyer, State Senator for Orange County, and Judge of the Superior Court. (Wheeler, *Reminiscences*, 333-4)

PART EIGHT

Refitment at Wilmington

8th to 24th April 1781

CHAPTER 44

Introduction to the rest of Part Eight

In this chapter we address the absurdity of Cornwallis's decision to march into Virginia and the light thrown on it by these Papers. A central enigma of the southern campaigns, it has until now never been satisfactorily explained.

As early as 5th and 6th April[1] Cornwallis was advising Balfour that he would not remain at Wilmington but run all hazards if Greene attempted any serious move towards South Carolina. As interpreted by Balfour[2], the letters indicated Cornwallis's intention of coming after Greene in case of his movement that way. Indeed, they are capable of no other interpretation. And as late as the 22nd[3] Cornwallis reaffirmed to Balfour his intention to return, stating that he could not positively ascertain whether he would keep as low as Georgetown or pass by the head of the Waccamaw. He went on to direct that supplies coming from Charlestown had better be detained, so that sufficient appear to have been available at Wilmington for his march, a fact borne out by the ample provisions he took with him to Virginia and by Craig's assessment[4] that on 5th May the following were in store for 1,500 men: 'flour 150 days, rum the same, salt meat 60 days'. So much, then, for Cornwallis's protestations elsewhere that he found it impracticable to return overland to South Carolina, for clearly by these letters he is damned with his own pen. Therefore we must look to other reasons for his failure to keep his word.

Cornwallis was, in fact, in two minds as to what he should do. Not revealed to Balfour during this period but disclosed on the 10th to Phillips, who was commanding a diversionary

---

[1] See pp 42-4.

[2] See pp 171 and 177.

[3] See p 122.

[4] See p 168.

force in the Chesapeake, was Cornwallis's preference to forsake South Carolina and Georgia in favour of desultory operations in Virginia. Matters came to a head on the 23rd, perhaps at a council of war, at which Cornwallis's views would have been decisive. On that day he advised Germain and Clinton of his decision to march northward. Why?

If we are to take Cornwallis's words at face value[5], he did not expect any considerable corps left by him in South Carolina to be lost by Greene's movement, so high was his opinion of Rawdon's abilities and the precautions taken by him and Balfour. Yet, contradictorily, he went on to fear the worst and cite it as a reason for his not marching southward. Yes, he could have provided no immediate assistance, but fulfilling his expectations, Rawdon maintained his post at Camden and would have remained there if Cornwallis had marched promptly to relieve him, sending messengers ahead. As to Cornwallis's protestation that he would have had to return by sea, it is controverted by his letters to Balfour. All in all, Cornwallis's words are not those of an officer desiring in a perfectly feasible way to retrieve the situation in South Carolina, but rather those of one who was seeking any excuse to shore up his preference to swan around the highways and byways of Virginia – a preference which, as he readily admitted to Phillips[6], was very unlikely 'to overturn the rebel government [*there*] and to establish a militia and some kind of mixed authority of our own'. At the end of the day it does not take an accomplished strategist to see that desultory operations which did not involve the possession of Virginia would in no way compensate for the loss of South Carolina and incidentally Georgia. Nor, contrary to Cornwallis's protestations, is it unreasonable to assume that, in line with Clinton's instructions, they could have continued to be held defensively, albeit tenuously. So, if Cornwallis's stated reasons for his decision do not make sense, were there others propelling him on? Almost certainly, yes.

A dynamic officer best suited to offensive action, Cornwallis was, as stated elsewhere in these Papers[7], temperamentally ill at ease with defensive warfare, a prospect now facing him in his immediate sphere of operations. A humane, cultivated man, he was moreover sickened by the murderous barbarity with which the war was waged by the revolutionary irregulars and state troops of the Carolinas and Georgia. Deterrence was essential, but in keeping with his character he had no stomach for the disagreeable measures involved, a point also made elsewhere[8]. In short, as the Wickwires make clear, 'Cornwallis had no place in a civil war.' Also contributing to his malaise was the mental and physical fatigue of commanding a whole year's hard and solid campaigning, fatigue which can be glimpsed later in this Part. Writing to Phillips[9], he remarked in a jocular but nevertheless sincere way, 'I am quite tired of marching about the country in quest of adventures,' to which there need to be subjoined a few

---

[5] See pp 107-8.

[6] See p 115.

[7] See vol I, p 5.

[8] See vol I, p 156.

[9] See p 114-5.

revealing words in the draft of his letter to Amherst[10]: 'I can with great truth assure your Lordship that I have experienced as much care, anxiety and responsibility as ever fell to the share of any commanding officer.' Altogether, it is fairly clear that the weight of his command was bearing down heavily on him. Against this background it is not entirely surprising that Cornwallis should have cast around, perhaps subconsciously, for reasons to release him from the predicament of dealing with a situation which he had come to detest. Always keen to act offensively, he simply opted for the more congenial alternative of doing so in Virginia, well way from the distasteful nature of the war farther south – an alternative, incidentally, which pricked his pride less than the perceived ignominy of conducting a defensive war to the southward after another unsuccessful campaign. These, then, were more likely the real reasons why Cornwallis took the absurd and fateful decision that he did.

It ill became Cornwallis to advise Balfour of his determination in such an offhand way.[11] Not only Balfour but Rawdon, Cruger, Brown and countless other officers and men, many at the expense or risk of their lives, had been valiantly involved in maintaining the British position in South Carolina and Georgia at a vast outlay to the exchequer. All was now to come to nought. However much we may sympathise with Cornwallis's reasons for not wishing to return southward, more weighty considerations were involved. That he chose to discount them or rationalise them away, and incidentally contravene Clinton's instructions, was at best a serious flaw in his character and at worst a gross dereliction of duty.

Tarleton is not free of blame for placing Cornwallis in the situation in which he found himself. If the light troops had not been lost at Cowpens, then, as previously explained, there might well have been a favourable outcome to the disastrous winter campaign.[12] In that event Cornwallis would not have felt impelled to march into Virginia and the catastrophe at Yorktown would have been averted.

Intuitively convinced that Clinton would not approve of his march northward, Cornwallis quite simply presented him with a *fait accompli*. Greene, meanwhile, arrived on the 19th within two or three miles of Camden.

§ - §

Papers consulted in the writing of this chapter

The Cornwallis Papers (UK National Archives, Kew)

§ - §

---

[10] See p 117, note 30.

[11] See pp 122-3.

[12] See ch 39.

CHAPTER 45

Letters to or from England, New York or Virginia

1 - To Germain

Cornwallis to Germain, 18th April 1781[1]   *5(254): C*

Nº 9   Wilmington
April 18th 1781

Rt Hon Lord George Germain etc etc etc

My Lord

I marched from Guildford on the morning of the 18th of March and next day arrived at Bell's Mill, where I gave the troops two days' rest and procured a small supply of provisions. From thence I proceeded slowly towards Cross Creek, attending to the convenience of subsistence and the movement of our wounded. On my way I issued the inclosed proclamation[2] and took every other means in my power to reconcile enemies and to encourage our friends to join us.

From all my information I intended to have halted at Cross Creek as a proper place to refresh and refit the troops, and I was much disappointed on my arrival there to find it totally impossible. Provisions were scarce, not four days' forage within 20 miles, and to us the navigation of the Cape Fear River to Wilmington impracticable, for the distance by water is upwards of a hundred miles, the breadth seldom above a hundred yards, the banks high, and

---

[1] Published in Stevens, *Clinton-Cornwallis Controversy*, i. 414. The only material difference is the omission of the final sentence in the fourth paragraph.

[2] *the inclosed proclamation*: see p 58.

the inhabitants on each side generally hostile. Under these circumstances I was obliged to continue my march to this place, in the neighbourhood of which I arrived on the 7th instant.

I have been busy since my arrival in disposing of our sick and wounded and in procuring the necessary supplies to put the troops in a proper state to take the field. I am in daily expectation of seeing the reinforcement from Europe and of receiving the Commander in Chief's directions for the further operations of the campaign.

Captain Schutz died a few days after the action as we expected, but I am sorry to inform your Lordship that, notwithstanding the flattering appearances and the assurances of the surgeons, Colonel Webster (whose loss is severely felt by me and the whole army), Captain Maynard of the Guards, and Captain Wilmousky and Ensign de Trott of the Regiment of Bose are since dead. The rest of the officers are recovering fast and many of the wounded soldiers have already joined their regiments.

Major Craig, who took possession of this place in the latter end of January, has conducted himself with great zeal and capacity, having with a very small force not only secured the post from all insults but made himself respectable in this part of the country by several successful excursions.

I shall not trouble your Lordship on the subject of South Carolina[3], having directed Lord Rawdon, who commands on the frontiers, and Lt Colonel Balfour, Commandant of Charlestown, to take every opportunity of communicating to your Lordship as well as to the Commander in Chief the state of affairs in that province. As they are both officers of capacity and great merit, I trust that their conduct will have given satisfaction.

I have the honour to be with great respect, my Lord,
Your Lordship's most obedient and most humble servant

CORNWALLIS

Cornwallis to Germain, 18th April 1781[4]   *5(270): C*

N° 10   Wilmington
April 18th 1781

Rt Hon Lord George Germain etc etc etc

My Lord

As Governor Martin returns to England by this opportunity, I shall beg leave to refer your Lordship to him for many particulars relating to this province, but I think it incumbent on me to be explicit to your Lordship, as His Majesty's Minister, on one or two capital points.

---

[3] In the draft (76(45)) of this dispatch, the clause ending in 'South Carolina' is substituted for 'My communication with South Carolina has been so uncertain and imperfect'.

[4] Published in Stevens, op cit, i, 416. There are no differences.

The principal reasons for undertaking the winter's campaign were the difficulty of a defensive war in South Carolina and the hopes that our friends in North Carolina, who were said to be very numerous, would make good their promises of assembling and taking an active part with us in endeavouring to reestablish His Majesty's Government. Our experience has shewn that their numbers are not so great as had been represented and that their friendship was only passive, for we have received little assistance from them since our arrival in the province, and although I gave the strongest and most publick assurances that after refitting and depositing our sick and wounded I should return to the Upper Country, not above two hundred have been prevailed upon to follow us, either as Provincials or militia.

This being the case, the immense extent of this country, cut with numberless rivers and creeks, and the total want of internal navigation, which renders it impossible for our army to remain long in the heart of the country, will make it very difficult to reduce this province to obedience by a direct attack upon it.

If therefore it should appear to be the interest of Great Britain to maintain what she already possesses and to push the war[5] in the southern provinces, I take the liberty of giving it as my opinion that a serious attempt upon Virginia would be the most solid plan, because successfull operations might not only be attended with important consequences there but would tend to the security of South Carolina and ultimately to the submission of North Carolina. The great reinforcements sent by Virginia to General Greene whilst General Arnold was in the Chesapeak are convincing proofs that small expeditions do not frighten that powerfull province.

I have the honor to be, my Lord,
Your Lordship's most obedient and most humble servant

CORNWALLIS

Cornwallis to Germain, 18th April 1781[6]

Private

76(49): ADf

Wilmington
April 18th 1781

Rt Hon Lord George Germain etc etc etc

My Lord

I feel myself much indebted to your Lordship for your kind assistance in procuring the rank of major for my aide de camp, Major Ross. As I am at present engaged in a most difficult service, where I have as many cares and as much responsibility as usually fall to the share of a Commander in Chief, I feel the distress of having no power to gratify those whose zealous services, courage, and abilities have often relieved me in my most anxious moments.

---

[5] The draft (76(51)) of this dispatch inserts a comma after 'possesses' and another after 'war'.

[6] Extracts from this letter are published in Ross ed, *Cornwallis Correspondence*, i, 90.

I hope therefore that your Lordship will forgive my troubling you to request your kind interference to obtain some favours for those whose services have been most meritorious, and whose interest I have particularly at heart. I was much disappointed to find that His Majesty did not think Lt Colonel Tarleton's services deserved to be rewarded with the rank of lt colonel in the army, and it will give me the most sensible mortification if it should be now withheld from him. He was once, it is true, unfortunate, but the affair of the 17th of January must be classed amongst the extraordinary events of war, as his disposition and conduct of the action were as unexceptionable as his previous manœvres were able to force General Morgan to fight. Lieutenant Macleod, who has always commanded my artillery, is an officer of the greatest merit. He stands so high in the list of lieutenants that it is probable he may have succeeded to the rank of captain in his regimental turn before your Lordship receives this letter. If that should not have happened, I should be very desirous that he might receive it by brevet as a mark of His Majesty's approbation of his services. Your Lordship must know so well how agreeable any favour conferred upon my near relation and aide de camp, Captain Brodrick, must be to me that I think it unnecessary to trouble you on that subject, but I must take the liberty of adding one more request in favour of Lieutenant Haldane, to whose good services I am greatly indebted and for whose prosperity I am very particularly interested. He wishes much to quit the Corps of Engineers, and as many vacancies have unfortunately fallen in the Guards, and as only one ensign has been serving with the southern army, I beg to recommend him for a lieutenantcy in that corps, or if that does not meet with His Majesty's approbation, I should hope that he might obtain a brevet of captain.

[I have the honour to be etc

CORNWALLIS]

Cornwallis to Germain, 23rd April 1781[7] 5(268): C

Nº 11

Wilmington
23rd April 1781

Rt Hon Lord George Germain etc etc etc

My Lord

I yesterday received an express by a small vessel from Charlestown informing me that a frigate was there but not then able to get over the bar with dispatches from Sir Henry Clinton notifying to me that Major General Phillips had been detached into the Chesapeake with a considerable force with instructions to co-operate with this army and to put himself under my orders. This express likewise brought me the disagreeable accounts that the upper posts of South Carolina were in the most imminent danger from an alarming spirit of revolt among many of the people and by a movement of General Greene's army. Although the expresses that I sent from Cross Creek to inform Lord Rawdon of the necessity I was under of coming to this place and to warn him of the possibility of such an attempt of the enemy had all miscarried, yet his Lordship was lucky enough to be apprized of General Greene's approach at least six days before he possibly could reach Camden, and I am therefore still induced to

---

[7] Published in Stevens, op cit, i, 420. There are no differences.

hope from my opinion of his Lordship's abilities and the precautions taken by him and Lt Colonel Balfour that we shall not be so unfortunate as to lose any considerable corps.

The distance from hence to Camden, the want of forage and subsistence on the greatest part of the road, and the difficulty of passing the Pedee when opposed by an enemy render it utterly impossible for me to give immediate assistance, and I apprehend a possibility of the utmost hazard to this little corps, without the chance of a benefit, in the attempt, for if we are so unlucky as to suffer a severe blow in South Carolina, the spirit of revolt in that province would become very general and the numerous rebels in this province be encouraged to be more than ever active and violent. This might enable General Greene to hem me in among the great rivers and by cutting off our subsistence render our arms useless. And to remain here for transports to carry us off would be a work of time, would lose our cavalry, and be otherways as ruinous and disgracefull to Britain as most events could be. I have therefore under so many embarrassing circumstances (but looking upon Charlestown as safe from any immediate attack from the rebels) resolved to take advantage of General Greene's having left the back part of Virginia open and march immediately into that province to attempt a junction with General Phillips.

I have more readily decided upon this measure because, if General Greene fails in the object of his march, his retreat will relieve South Carolina, and my force, being very insufficient for offensive operations in this province, may be employed usefully in Virginia in conjunction with the corps under the command of General Phillips.

I have the honour to be with great respect, my Lord,
Your Lordship's most obedient and most humble servant

CORNWALLIS

Cornwallis to Germain, 24th April 1781[8]   *76(55): C*

N° 12

Wilmington
April 24th 1781

Rt Hon Lord George Germain etc etc etc

My Lord

[9]I have reflected very seriously on the subject of my attempt to march into Virginia and have in consequence written a letter to Major General Phillips[10] of which I have the honour to inclose a copy to your Lordship. I have likewise directed Lt Colonel Balfour to send

---

[8] A dispatch couched in the same terms was written on the same date to Clinton. See p 113.

[9] In the draft (76(53)) of this dispatch the following words are deleted at the beginning: 'Since I wrote my dispatch of yesterday,'.

[10] *a letter..*: of 24th April, p 116.

transports and provisions to this port in case I should find the junction with Major General Phillips inexpedient or impracticable and that[11] I should have the mortification of seeing that there is no other method of conveying His Majesty's troops to South Carolina without exposing them to the most evident danger of being lost.

I have the honour to be with great respect, my Lord,
Your Lordship's most obedient and most humble servant

CORNWALLIS

§ - §

2 - To Clinton

Cornwallis to Clinton, 10th April 1781[12]   5(209): C

Camp near Wilmington
10th April 1781

His Excellency Sir Henry Clinton KB etc etc etc

Sir

I am just informed that I have a chance of sending a few lines to New York by the *Amphitrite*, but as it depends upon my being expeditious, I cannot attempt to give your Excellency a particular account of the winter's campaign or the Battle of Guildford. I have, however, the satisfaction of informing you that our military operations were uniformly successfull and the victory of Guildford, altho' one of the bloodiest of this war, was very complete. The enemy gave themselves out for nine or ten and undoubtedly had seven thousand men in the field, upwards of two thousand of which were eighteen months' men or Continentals.

Our force was 1,360 infantry, rank and file, and about 200 cavalry. General Greene retreated the night of the action to the iron works on Troublesome Creek eighteen miles from Guildford, leaving us four six pounders, being all the cannon he had in the field. The fatigue of the troops and the great number of wounded put it out of my power to pursue beyond the Reedy Fork in the afternoon of the action, and the want of provisions and all kinds of necessaries for the soldiers made it equally impossible to follow the blow the next day. I

---

[11] *that*: the meaning is 'in case'. See p 37, note 16.

[12] Published in Stevens, op cit, i, 395. There are no differences.

therefore issued the inclosed proclamation[13] and, having remained two days on the field of battle, marched to Bell's Mill on Deep River near part of the country where the greatest number of our friends were supposed to reside. Many of the inhabitants rode into camp, shook me by the hand, said they were glad to see us and to hear that we had beat Greene, and then rode home again, for I could not get 100 men in all the Regulators' country to stay with us even as militia.

With a third of my army sick and wounded, which I was obliged to carry in waggons or on horseback, the remainder without shoes and worn down with fatigue, I thought it was time to look for some place of rest and refitment. I therefore by easy marches, taking care to pass through all the settlements that had been described to me as most friendly, proceeded to Cross Creek. On my arrival there I found to my great mortification, and contrary to all former accounts, that it was impossible to procure any considerable quantity of provisions and that there was not four days' forage within 20 miles. The navigation of Cape Fear[14], with the hopes of which I had been flattered, was totally impracticable, the distance from Wilmington by water being 150 miles, the breadth of the river seldom exceeding one hundred yards, the banks generally high, and the inhabitants on each side almost universally hostile. Under these circumstances I determined to move immediately to Wilmington. By this measure the Highlanders have not had so much time as the people of the Upper Country to prove the sincerity of their former professions of friendship, but tho' appearances are rather more favourable among them, I confess they are not equal to my expectations.

General Greene marched down as low as the mouth of Deep River, where he remained four days ago. He never came within our reach after the action, nor has a shot been since fired except at Ramsey's Mill on Deep River, where Colonel Malmedy with about 20 of a gang of plunderers that are attached to him galloped in among the centries and carried off three Yagers.

I cannot sufficiently commend the behaviour of both officers and men under my command. They not only shewed the most persevering intrepidity in action but underwent with chearfullness such fatigues and hardships as have seldom been experienced by a British army, and justly merit every mark of favour and reward. The great assistance which I received from Generals Leslie and O'Hara and Lt Colonel Tarleton deserves my warmest acknowledgements and highest commendations.

I am now employed in disposing of the sick and wounded and in procuring supplies of all kinds to put the troops into a proper state to take the field. I am likewise impatiently looking out for the expected reinforcement from Europe, part of which will be indispensably necessary to enable me either to act offensively or even to maintain myself in the upper parts of the country, where alone I can hope to preserve the troops from the fatal sickness which so nearly ruined the army last autumn.

---

[13] *proclamation*: see p 58.

[14] *Cape Fear*: the draft (5(207)) of this dispatch has 'Cape Fear River'.

I am very anxious to receive your Excellency's commands, being as yet totally in the dark as to the intended operations of the summer. I cannot help expressing my wishes that the Chesapeake may become the seat of war, even (if necessary) at the expence of abandoning New York. Untill Virginia is in a manner subdued, our hold of the Carolinas must be difficult if not precarious. The rivers of Virginia are advantageous to an invading army, but North Carolina is of all the provinces in America the most difficult to attack (unless material assistance could be got from the inhabitants, the contrary of which I have sufficiently experienced) on account of its great extent, of the numberless rivers and creeks, and the total want of interior navigation.

In compliance with your Excellency's general directions I shall dispatch my aide-de-camp, Captain Brodrick, to England with the particular accounts of the Battle of Guildford, of the winter's campaign and the present state of the province, copies of which I shall have the honour of transmitting to your Excellency with my next dispatch.

I have the honour to be with great respect, sir,
Your most obedient and most humble servant

CORNWALLIS

Cornwallis to Clinton, 10th April 1781   72(78): ADf

Camp near Wilmington
April 10th 1781

Sir

The lt colonelcy of the 33rd Regiment being vacant by the death of my much lamented friend Colonel Webster, I should take it as a favour if your Excellency would please to remove Lt Colonel Yorke[15] from the 22nd to the 33rd, and I believe that I can answer that the removal will be very acceptable to Lt Colonel Yorke.

As Colonel Webster was to my knowledge indebted to his family for part of the money with which he purchased his promotion, I conclude[16] that if the blank commission was not already sent to him, your Excellency will still permit his father to reap the advantage of it. I took the liberty of recommending Adjutant Fox for one of the vacant ensigncys in a former

---

[15] Clinton would accept and promptly implement Cornwallis's recommendation. On 4th May John Yorke would set sail from New York with Lord Chewton in the *Richmond* and join Cornwallis in mid June, having vainly called at Charlestown and Wilmington. Commissioned a lieutenant in the 33rd Regiment on 3rd December 1762, he had been promoted there to captain on 10th June 1768 and to major on 8th August 1776. Some two years later he transferred to the lt colonelcy of the 22nd. Now to command the 33rd, he would be taken prisoner with it at Yorktown. (*The Cornwallis Papers*; *Army Lists*)

[16] After 'conclude' the following is deleted: 'that the money arising from the sale of the blank commission which your Excellency was so kind as give him to dispose of will be applied towards the disbursement of it.'

letter[17]. Volunteer Talbot, whom I had appointed to act as ensign untill your pleasure was known, was killed in the late action. Lieutenant and Quarter Master Ward, who purchased the latter commission and is a very old soldier and is now totally unfit for service, wishes much to retire. It is difficult to settle it for him unless you would be so kind as to allow him a blank commission to indemnify him for quarter mastercy, which has been very much the practice of late years in the army and is the only means of preventing that usefull commission from being improperly disposed of. In justice to merit I must mention Adjutant Watson of the 23rd, who is really very deserving of a 2nd lieutenant's commission in that regiment. I must likewise observe that Captain Campbell[18] of the 33rd has commanded the regiment in two important actions and that on both occasions he behaved with the greatest bravery and distinguished himself very much. He is an old captain and very deserving of a share in the promotion occasioned by the death of his late lt colonel.

I have the honour to be etc

[CORNWALLIS]

Cornwallis to Clinton, 23rd April 1781[19]

5(249): C

Wilmington
23rd April 1781

His Excellency Sir Henry Clinton KB etc etc etc

Sir

I have the honour to inclose to you a duplicate of my letter of the 10th sent by the *Amphitrite* and copies of all my letters to the Secretary of State. As they contain the most exact account of every transaction of the campaign, of the present state of things in this district, of my great apprehensions from the movement of General Greene towards Camden, and my resolutions in consequence of it, I have nothing to add to it for your Excellency's satisfaction. Neither my cavalry nor infantry are in readiness to move. The former are in want of every thing, the latter of every necessary but shoes, of which we have received an ample supply. I must, however, begin my march tomorrow. It is very disagreeable to me to decide upon measures so very important and of such consequence to the general conduct of the war without an opportunity of procuring your Excellency's directions or approbation, but the delay and difficulty of conveying letters and the impossibility of waiting for answers render it indispensably necessary. My present undertaking sits heavy on my mind. I have

---

[17] *former letter*: Cornwallis to Clinton, 3rd January, vol III, p 30.

[18] James Campbell had entered the 33rd Regiment as a lieutenant on 26th October 1764, having been commissioned a lieutenant in the army four years earlier. He was promoted to captain in the 33rd on 25th May 1772 and was now the most senior captain in the regiment. Probably a Scot, he would soon be promoted to major in the 71st (Highland) Regiment. (*Army Lists*; *The Cornwallis Papers*)

[19] Published in Stevens, op cit, i, 424. There are no differences.

experienced the distresses and dangers of marching some hundreds of miles, in a country chiefly hostile, without one active or usefull friend, without intelligence, and without communication with any part of the country. The situation in which I leave South Carolina adds much to my anxiety, yet I am under the necessity of adopting this hazardous enterprize hastily and with the appearance of precipitation, as I find there is no prospect of speedy reinforcement from Europe, and that[20] the return of General Greene to North Carolina either with or without success would put a junction with General Phillips out of my power.

I have the honour to be with great respect
Your Excellency's most obedient and most humble servant

CORNWALLIS

Cornwallis to Clinton, 24th April 1781[21]   *74(1): C*

Wilmington
April 24th 1781

His Excellency Sir Henry Clinton KB etc etc etc

Sir

I have reflected very seriously on the subject of my attempt to march into Virginia and have in consequence written a letter to Major General Phillips[22] of which I have the honour to inclose a copy to your Excellency. I have likewise directed Lt Colonel Balfour to send transports and provisions to this port in case I should find the junction with Major General Phillips inexpedient or impracticable and that[23] I should have the mortification of seeing that there is no other method of conveying His Majesty's troops to South Carolina without exposing them to the most evident danger of being lost.

I have the honour to be
Your Excellency's most obedient and most humble servant

CORNWALLIS

§ - §

---

[20] *that*: the meaning may be 'as'. See p 37, note 16.

[21] Published, with no differences, in Stevens, op cit, i, 426. A dispatch couched in the same terms was written on the same date to Germain. See p 108.

[22] *a letter..*: of 24th April, p 116.

[23] *that*: The meaning is 'in case'. See p 37, note 16.

3 - To Major General Phillips

Cornwallis to Phillips, 10th April 1781   *85(29): C*

Camp near Wilmington
April 10th 1781

Major General Phillips

Dear Phillips

I enclose to you a copy of my letter to Sir Henry Clinton[24], which contains as full an account of our past and present situation as I have time to send by the *Amphitrite*. I have only to add that I shall be glad to hear from you as soon and as frequently as possible, and am with great regard

Your most obedient and faithfull servant

CORNWALLIS

Cornwallis to Phillips, 10th April 1781[25]   85(31): C

Private

Camp near Wilmington
April 10th 1781

Major General Phillips

My dear Phillips

I have had a most difficult and dangerous campaign and was obliged to fight a battle two hundred miles from any communication against an enemy seven times my number. The fate of it was long doubtfull; we had not a regiment or corps that did not at some time give way. It ended, however, happily in our compleatly routing the enemy and taking their cannon. The idea of our friends rising in any number and to any purpose totally failed, as I expected; and here I am, getting rid of my wounded and refitting my troops at Wilmington. I last night heard of the naval action[26] and your arrival in the Chesapeak. Now, my dear friend, what is our plan? Without one we cannot succeed and I assure you that I am quite tired of

---

[24] *my letter..*: of 10th April, p 109.

[25] The bulk of this letter is published with minor inaccuracies in Ross ed, *Cornwallis Correspondence*, i, 87.

[26] *the naval action*: occurring on 16th March between Arbuthnot and Destouches off the Capes of Virginia, it frustrated the French attempt to support Lafayette against Arnold.

marching about the country in quest of adventures. If we mean an offensive war in America, we must abandon New York, bring our whole force into Virginia. We then have a stake to fight for and a successfull battle may give us America. If our plan is defensive, mixed with desultory expeditions, let us quit the Carolinas (which cannot be held defensively whilst Virginia can be so easily armed against us) and stick to our salt pork at New York, sending now and then a detachment to steal tobacco etc.

I daily expect three regiments from Ireland. Leaving one of them at Charlestown, with the addition of the other two and the flank companies I can come by land to you, but whether after we have joined we shall have sufficient force for a war of conquest, I should think very doubtfull. By a war of conquest, I mean to possess the country sufficiently to overturn the rebel government and to establish a militia and some kind of mixed authority of our own. If no reinforcement comes, and that[27] I am obliged to march with my present force to the upper frontiers of South Carolina, my situation will be truly distressing. If I was to embark from hence, the loss of the upper posts in South Carolina would be inevitable. I have as yet received no orders. If the reinforcement arrives, I must move from hence, where the men will be sickly and the horses starve. If I am sure that you are to remain in the Chesapeak, perhaps I may come directly to you. Pray let me hear from you as soon and as often as you can. I send you a good cypher, but it is very difficult to get any letters conveyed by land on account of the vigilance and severity of the rebel government. I believe all mine to General Arnold miscarried and I did not receive one from him. I have lost poor Webster. O'Hara is recovering fast and will soon be fit for duty. I cannot sufficiently commend him; he is a new man. His whole attention is paid to the care of his brigade, which under his auspices is become the pattern of good order, attention and subordination to the rest of the army. My best wishes for your honor and welfare will constantly attend you. It will give me the greatest pleasure if we can meet. I trust you will forgive my superseding you.

I am with great truth
Most sincerely yours

CORNWALLIS

[*Subscribed*:]

Take the first opportunity of telling O'Hara what I say of him.

---

[27] *that*: the meaning is 'if'. See p 37, note 16.

Cornwallis to Phillips, 24th April 1781[28]

74(2): CS

Wilmington
April 24th 1781

Major General Phillips

Dear Phillips

My situation here is very distressing. Greene took the advantage of my being obliged to come to this place and has marched to South Carolina. My expresses to Lord Rawdon on my leaving Cross Creek, warning him of the possibility of such a movement, have all failed. Mountaineers and militia have poured into the back part of that province and I much fear that Lord Rawdon's posts will be so distant from each other and his troops so scattered as to put him into the greatest danger of being beat in detail, and that the worst of consequences may happen to most of the troops out of Charlestown. By a direct move towards Camden I cannot get time enough to relieve Lord Rawdon, and should he have fallen, my army would be exposed to the utmost danger from the great rivers I should have to pass, the exhausted state of the country, the numerous militia, the almost universal spirit of revolt which prevails in South Carolina, and the strength of Greene's army, whose Continentals alone are at least as numerous as I am, and I could be of no use on my arrival at Charlestown, there being nothing at present to apprehend for that post. I shall therefore immediately march up the country by Duplin Court House, pointing towards Hillsborough, in hopes to withdraw Greene. If that should not succeed, I should be much tempted to try to form a junction with you. The attempt is exceedingly hazardous and many unforeseen difficulties may render it totally impracticable, so that you must not take any steps that may expose your army to the danger of being ruined. I shall march to the lowest ford of the Roanoke, which I am informed is about 20 miles above Taylor's Ferry. Send every possible intelligence to me by the cypher I inclose, and make every movement in your power to facilitate our meeting (which must be somewhere near Petersburg), with safety to your own army. I mention *the lowest ford* because in a hostile country ferries cannot be depended upon, but if I should decide upon the measure of endeavouring to come to you, I shall try to surprize the boats at some of the ferries from Halifax upwards.

I am, dear Phillips,
Most sincerely yours

CORNWALLIS

§ - §

---

[28] Published in Stevens, op cit, i, 427. There are no material differences.

4 - To Amherst

Cornwallis to Amherst, 18th April 1781   85(36): C

Wilmington
18th April 1781[29]

Rt Hon Lord Amherst etc etc etc

My Lord

My aide de camp, Captain Brodrick, will have the honour of delivering this letter to your Lordship and will answer readily, and I trust intelligently, any questions that your Lordship may think proper to put to him relative to the campaign in North Carolina, the action of the 15th of March, and the state of the army which I have the honour to command.

I can with great truth assure your Lordship that I have experienced much care and anxiety in the course of this command[30], but if my services meet with His Majesty's approbation I shall think myself amply rewarded. Having no patronage, I must trust to your Lordship's kind interposition to obtain some marks of favour for those officers to whose assistance I think myself principally indebted.

Lt Colonel Tarleton's services have been throughout eminent and distinguished. It is true he was once unfortunate, but by no fault of his. He never shewed more ability than in the manœuvres which compelled General Morgan to fight him, and his disposition was unexceptionable. The fate of that unfortunate day was one of the extraordinary events to which war has been ever liable. It will give me the most sensible mortification if His Majesty should still think him unworthy of the rank of lt colonel.

Your Lordship already knows how much I am interested about Captain Brodrick. His carrying the account of the action at Guildford and the services he rendered me on that occasion will, I hope, procure for him the rank of major. As he is a young man of family and my near relation, I should feel it as a most flattering mark of His Majesty's favour if he should be allowed on a proper occasion to purchase a company in the Guards.

Lieutenant McLeod, who has on every occasion commanded my artillery with so much credit to himself and utility to the service, deserves my warmest recommendation. He is so old a lieutenant that at the time this letter arrives in England he may probably have the rank of captain. If that should not be the case, I am convinced that a brevet of captain would be highly acceptable to him as a mark of His Majesty's approbation of his services.

---

[29] The draft (85(42)) of this letter is dated the 19th.

[30] In the draft the words from 'much care' to 'command' are substituted for: 'as much care, anxiety and responsibility as ever fell to the share of any commanding officer'.

Lieutenant Haldane, altho' he has done his duty as an engineer, has been constantly employed in my family when it did not interfere with his other business. He is a young man of very great merit and whose interest and prosperity I have much at heart, and as he is desirous of quitting the Corps of Engineers, I should be much obliged to your Lordship if you would recommend him to His Majesty for a lieutenancy of the Guards, in which corps many vacancies have unfortunately happened and only one ensign has been serving with the southern army. If this request should not meet with His Majesty's approbation, I must then hope for your Lordship's assistance to procure for him the rank of captain.

I am much obliged to your Lordship for the part you took in procuring the brevet of major for my aide de camp, Major Ross, who will, I am convinced, prove himself worthy of your favour and patronage.[31]

I have the honour to be, my Lord,
Your Lordship's most obedient and most humble servant

CORNWALLIS

5 - From and to the Speaker of the House of Commons

Cornwall to Cornwallis, 30th November 1780[32]   66(13): ALS

Privy Garden
November the 30th 1780

Lt General Earl Cornwallis

My Lord

In obedience to the commands of the House of Commons I have the honour to transmit to your Lordship the enclosed resolution.

I have the highest satisfaction in this opportunity of expressing that I have the strongest sense of the merit and importance of the services which your Lordship has rendered to your country, and of assuring you that

---

[31] In the draft this paragraph is substituted for: 'I cannot conclude this letter without acknowledging in the strongest manner my great obligations to Major Ross, to whose able assistance I am greatly indebted and whose distinguished merit will, I hope, insure to him His Majesty's kind remembrance.'

[32] A version is published in Ross ed, *Cornwallis Correspondence*, i, 88. It omits the enclosure and otherwise contains an inconsequential inaccuracy.

I am with the greatest respect, my Lord,
Your Lordship's most obedient and most humble servant

C W CORNWALL[33]

Enclosure
Resolution of the House of Commons, 27th November 1780   66(15): DS

LUNÆ 27° DIE NOVEMBRIS 1780

RESOLVED

That the thanks of this House be given to Sir Henry Clinton, Knight of the Most Honourable Order of the Bath and Commander in Chief of His Majesty's forces in North America, and to Vice Admiral Arbuthnot, Commander in Chief of His Majesty's fleet in North America, and to the Rt Hon Lt General Charles Earl Cornwallis, for the eminent and very important services performed by them to His Majesty and this country, particularly by the reduction of Charles Town by the army and navy under the command of Sir Henry Clinton and Vice Admiral Arbuthnot, and by the late most glorious victory obtained by Lord Cornwallis at Camden.

ORDERED

That Mr Speaker do signify the said thanks to Sir Henry Clinton, Vice Admiral Arbuthnot and Earl Cornwallis.

J HATSELL
Cl Dom Com[34]

---

[33] Presently the Member for Rye, the Rt Hon Charles Wolfran Cornwall (1735-1789) had been chosen Speaker of the House of Commons in 1780, having until then served for six years as a Lord of the Treasury. 'As speaker he possessed a sonorous voice, a manly as well as an imposing figure, and a commanding deportment,' remarks Wraxall, who also points out his habit of relieving the weariness of his position during debates by frequent draughts of porter. Not a man of ability, he owed his political career to family influence and died while in his present office. He was buried at St Cross Church near Winchester. (*DNB*; Henry B Wheatley ed, *The historical and the posthumous memoirs of Sir Nathaniel William Wraxall 1772-1784* (New York, 1884), i, 259-261, iii, 385, iv, 269)

[34] *Cl Dom Com*: Clericus Domus Communium, Latin for Clerk of the House of Commons.

Cornwallis to Cornwall, 18th April 1781[35]

85(40): C

Wilmington
18th April 1781

Rt Hon Charles Wolfran Cornwall
Speaker of the House of Commons

Sir

I have received with the greatest satisfaction the favour of your letter of the 30th of November 1780 inclosing the resolution of the House of Commons of the 27th of that month so very favourable and flattering to me.

I must desire, sir, that you will be pleased to inform the House that I am truly sensible of the high honour they have conferred upon me and that it shall be my constant study, by the most earnest attention to the duties of my profession, to merit a continuance of their approbation.

I beg that you will accept my acknowledgements for the obliging manner in which you communicated to me the thanks of the House, and

I have the honour to be with great respect, sir,
Your most obedient and most humble servant

[CORNWALLIS]

§ - §

---

[35] Published in Ross ed, *Cornwallis Correspondence*, i, 89.

CHAPTER 46

Miscellaneous letters etc

1 - To Rawdon or Balfour

Cornwallis to Rawdon, 15th April 1781 *85(35): C*

Wilmington
15th April

Rt Hon Lord Rawdon etc etc etc

'Tis reported that Greene has marched or detached in force towards you. Be compact and on your guard.

CORNWALLIS

Cornwallis to Balfour, 21st April 1781 *85(44): C*

Wilmington
21st April 1781

Lt Colonel Balfour
Commandant of Charlestown

Dear Balfour

I wrote to you[1] by the *Pearl*, which sailed from this bar on the 9th, to say how much we wanted all kind of necessaries for the troops and appointments for the cavalry. I likewise mentioned the possibility of Greene's taking the opportunity of our being in this *cul de sac* to disturb South Carolina. I expressed the same in my private letter to Lord Rawdon. I have since heard that he has certainly marched towards Salisbury. I cannot conceive it likely that he would risque his army far down the country, but he may very possibly send his light troops

---

[1] Cornwallis to Balfour, 5th and 6th April, pp 42-4.

to assist Sumpter, Pickens etc and, whilst he remains in Mecklenburgh or Rowan, will always be in time to prevent my intercepting him. Put Lord Rawdon as much upon his guard as possible. I begin to despair of the reinforcement. We are all impatience to hear from you.

Yours ever most sincerely

[CORNWALLIS]

Extract, Cornwallis to Balfour, 22nd April 1781[2]   85(46): C

Wilmington
April 22nd 1781

I cannot positively ascertain whether I shall keep so low as George Town or pass by the head of the Waggamaw. Either will be attended with great difficulty.

If the supplies have not sailed from Charlestown, they had better be detained. Even if things should take a favorable turn in South Carolina, the want of reinforcement will prevent my undertaking any material offensive operations.

Cornwallis to Balfour, 24th April 1781   85(49): C

Wilmington
24th April 1781

Dear Balfour

You will easily conceive that for some time past the situation of South Carolina has employed much of my reflection. In fact I have hardly been able to think of any thing else.

The immense distance from hence to Camden, the difficulty of subsistence on the road, and the impracticability of the passage of the Pedee against an opposing enemy would render a direct movement totally useless to Lord Rawdon, and this corps might be lost in the attempt. I have therefore, after a number of intended plans, decided for this: to pass the North East River with all the cavalry and as much of the infantry as are able to march, taking the road which leads for some time either to Hillsborough and the Dan or to Taylor's Ferry on the Roanoke, by which measure I hope to force Greene to quit South Carolina, but failing that, I shall march on to join General Phillips in Virginia if I find it practicable, laying my account that, if we are so unfortunate as to lose some of the outposts and the country of South Carolina, that Charlestown is not in danger. But to be provided for the event of my deciding to return to Wilmington and from thence to South Carolina, as I look upon it as impracticable by land, with my present force, and in the present situation of affairs, I beg that you will with the utmost dispatch send to this place with a convoy as many transports and hired vessels as you can collect with a supply of provisions to bring off the troops, taking care not to reduce the stock of the town too low.

---

[2] The rest of this letter is not extant.

Craig remains here at present with a detachment of his own corps, the Yagers and convalescents, having in charge the sick and wounded and followers of the army, who must at all events go to Charlestown, and he will have directions to go off when in his power or wait for me according to circumstances which I shall describe.

Do every thing in your power to forward General Phillips's and the Commander in Chief's letters[3], and duplicates and triplicates of them (especially of the first), as it is so important that they should be acquainted with my situation and designs as soon as possible.

Surrounded as I am with embarrassments myself, I feel very much for yours and am highly sensible of your zeal for the service and friendship for me. Take every opportunity of writing to Craig, thro whom I may sometimes hear from you. God bless you, my dear Balfour, and believe me ever

Most faithfully yours

[CORNWALLIS]

§ - §

2 - To or from the Royal Navy[4]

Cornwallis to Barkley, 5th April 1781   85(23): ADfS

Camp near Livingston's Creek on Cape Fear River
near Wilmington
April 5th 1781

Captain Berkeley
Commanding His Majesty's ships on the Southern Station

Dear Sir

As I think it necessary to send my aid de camp, Captain Brodrick, with all possible dispatch to England with the account of my winter's campaign and the action of the 15th of March, I must beg that you will please to order one of His Majesty's ships for that service and send her to the bar of Cape Fear River. I refer you to Lt Colonel Balfour for all accounts of us, and am with great regard, dear sir,

Your most obedient and most humble servant

CORNWALLIS

---

[3] ...*letters*: Cornwallis's to Phillips and Clinton, pp 112-3 and 116.

[4] For the sake of continuity these papers commence on 5th April. Barkley's letter of the 14th (p 131) is included, although Cornwallis had not received it by the 24th and probably had not done so before he left Wilmington.

Cornwallis to Inglis, 5th April 1781 85(25): ADfS

Camp near Livingston's Creek
April 5th 1781

Captain Inglis
Commanding His Majesty's ships in Cape Fear River

Dear Sir

I have occasion to send a letter of the utmost importance to Lt Colonel Balfour[5]. As the *Delight* appears to be the only safe and expeditious conveyance, I shall be obliged if you will be kind enough to carry it and return with his answer. I beg you will accept my warmest acknowledgements for the attention and assistance which you have given to Major Craig and his detachment, and believe me to be with great truth

Your most obedient and faithfull servant

CORNWALLIS

Inglis to Cornwallis, 6th April 1781 5(175): ALS

My Lord

I had the honour of receiving your Lordship's letter by Major Craig of yesterday's date mentioning that you have occasion to send a letter of the utmost importance to Lt Colonel Balfour and request that I wou'd carry it in the *Delight* and return with his answer, in answer to which I have to assure your Lordship that I will chearfully proceed upon that service with the utmost expedition. As I apprehended there might be a call for the *Delight* for the service you have mention'd, I had her unmoor'd immediately upon hearing of your Lordship's arrival in this neighbourhood and intended to have dropt her down from her present station, where she has been laying for the protection of the transports, victuallers etc, to the mouth of the harbour. The wind being out of the way has prevented me doing it hitherto, but the moment it can be effect'd it shall be done. And if the *Delight* cannot be got down immediately, I will send your dispatches by the *Loyalist*, who is just arrived off the bar and can immediately proceed to Charles Town, particularly as I understand from Major Craig that it will be necessary to have them sent off immediately and he has recommend'd to me that if the *Delight* cannot get down, your Lordship wou'd rather chuse to have them sent off directly than wait for the uncertainty of a wind for the *Delight* geting down. Your Lordship has made me very happy in noticing me as being any way assistant to Major Craig and his detachment. I have only to assure your Lordship I wish it had been more in my power and that I ever shall be proud and happy to do my little mite for His Majesties Service and to convince your Lordship that I ever shall be

---

[5] *a letter..*: of 5th April, p 42.

Your Lordship's most respectful and most obedient servant

JOHN INGLIS[6]

PS

I have enclosed you a letter I had from Captain Creyk, which contains the only intelligence I have had by the *Loyalist* as no body is come up belonging to her. As there are some accounts of the French fleet being seen off Tybee, I thought it proper your Lordship should be acquainted immediately

JI

Enclosure
Creyk to Inglis, 6th April 1781   5(177): ALS

Otter, 1 am Friday morn

Captain Inglis
Commanding officer of the King's ships etc
Wilmington

Dear Sir

I thank you for your battle and heartily wish I could return the compliment with an equally glorious *sea* fight[7]. The men from Beaufort would give you a sketch of it, and Ardesoif, whose dispatches I forward to you, will, I dare say, fill up the outline. None sunk or taken, it's true, yet they've all *run* away. Well it might have been worse. Their design in coming to the Chesapeak was entirely frustrated, and they are gone, I fear, to attack Savannah whilst the Admiral thinks them in or off the Delaware. The *Assurance* (who arrived off Charles Town bar as the *Loyalist* came out) passed them off Tibee. I think the Admiral should have the earliest intelligence of their route.

When I saw it was a ship of war off the bar I sent Kennedy (as the wind was southerly and the *Delight* could not be moved) to bring her in, and Mr Hunter has left him there. You may be assured that I shall give all the assistance in getting the *Delight* where you wish her.

---

[6] John Inglis (pronounced 'Inguls') commanded the sloop of war *Delight* and was also the naval officer commanding at Wilmington. He had been commissioned a lieutenant in the Royal Navy in 1761 and promoted to commander some seventeen years later, a rank which carried with it the courtesy title of captain. As these Papers reveal, he was an active officer who was prepared to cooperate heartily with the army in forwarding the King's service. He would soon set sail in the *Delight* for England, charged with conveying Cornwallis's dispatches. He is not to be confused with his namesake who was also a naval officer. (Syrett and DiNardo eds, *Commissioned Sea Officers*, 238; *The Cornwallis Papers*)

[7] *sea fight*: the action of 16th March between Arbuthnot and Destouches off the Capes of Virginia. The French squadron, which had sailed to support Lafayette, retired to Rhode Island.

I hope when you see Lord Cornwallis you will be able to procure more than a week's provisions for the *Otter*. All the victuallers and transports are up in town. I wish you would hurry them down as the vessels cannot be moved without them. Mr Avery has sent the *Delight* and *Otter* a mouthful of beef. We ought to be thankful as I am persuaded 'twas all he had to send. I trust that the promised supply from Craig will satiate our appetites.

Tho' my boat's crew are heartily tired, yet I will not delay a moment forwarding the dispatches to Lord Cornwallis and Captain Inglis. I'll thank you to return the boat as soon as the service will admit and to send me some very good news in her. I have not yet read my own packet. If it contains any thing interesting or amusing to you, the next boat shall bring it.

I am, sir,
Your humble servant

R[D] CREYK

Inglis to Cornwallis, 9th April 1781 — 5(195): ALS

Delight
Monday morning, 2 o'clock

My Lord

Upon hearing in town that there were three large ships[8] seen off the harbour I push down to the *Delight* without delay and upon my arrival am informed that the largest of them appears not to be less than a 74 gun ship. It's at this time I write, 2 o'clock in the morning, so that in a few hours it will be day light and consequently, if they are for this place, I shall be able to make them out distinctly and will take the earliest opportunity of acquainting your Lordship further. Ardesoif in the *Loyalist* is still off Fort Johnston, where [he] has been from the first, as I was misinformed of his coming higher up. He waits a fair wind to carry him over the bar, as the wind has been quite different at the harbour's mouth to what it was at town. The wind is now fair for him and I fancy he will attempt going if it continues so when the day light makes and the tide answers. I shall either be with him or send to him that if the ships seen off do not answer the secret signal, [he is] to return, for in that case I think it must unquestionably be the French fleet, for there are no two deck vessels (which one of these are described to be) but what have the secret signals. I shall be anxious till day light.

In the meantime I am, my Lord,
Your Lordship's most respectful and most obedient humble servant

JOHN INGLIS

---

[8] *three large ships*: as would become apparent later in the day, HMS *Pearl* and HMS *Iris* bound for Charlestown, and HMS *Amphitrite* on her way from Charlestown to New York.

Inglis to Cornwallis, 9th April 1781   5(197): ALS

Delight
Monday, midday

The Rt Hon Lord Cornwallis etc etc etc

My Lord

The ships that were seen off the harbour yesterday have not been seen today. I cannot conjecture what ships they can be. Creyk insists on it that he cou'd distinguish a poop to one of them. If that fact is established, the ship spoke of must, I think, be either a ship larger than a forty gun ship or one of the old Indiamen.

I don't believe they were destined for this port or they wou'd have been in sight of this day (as the wind is) before the time of my writing. I think Admiral Arbuthnot wou'd not pass so near without sending a frigate to acquaint us. There is nothing to be apprehended from them here, even shou'd it be the whole French fleet, for no heavier ships can come into us than what the *Delight* and *Otter*, as they are now station'd, can keep off; nor can we be blocked up from sending expresses as the New Inlet is open and lies too exposed and dangerous to be blocked up. I shall stay down here for some days to see if I can learn any thing of them, and your Lordship shall be acquainted from time to time. Ardesoif made an attempt to sail out this morning but the wind was too light. He was obliged to come to an anchor. He will, I hope, get out next tide. I shall be able to know by the *Loyalist* whether they are lurking to the southward of the harbour as Ardesoif has orders, in case he shou'd meet them off the harbour and [they] hem him in between the Frying Pan and main and not answer his secret signal, to return (which they cannot prevent). And I shou'd judge, if they do not answer his secret signal, they must be enemies. This moment the man from our mast head has called out a sail. The other two are now called out, so that there they are. I shou'd be glad the marines of the *Delight, Otter* and *Blonde* cou'd be sent down, and a boat as an express boat.

I am, my Lord,
Your Lordship's most respectful and most obedient servant

JOHN INGLIS

PS

The ships mentioned above are all to an anchor. I will go down in a boat, reconnoiter them and send your Lordship my opinion.

Inglis to Cornwallis, 9th April 1781　　　　　　　　　　　　　　　　　　*5(199): ALS*

Loyalist off Bald Head
2 o'clock pm

The Rt Hon Lord Cornwallis etc etc etc

My Lord

I have this moment got on board the *Loyalist* and have at same time got the enclosed letter[9], which I thought for expedition I had best enclose your Lordship, and you can return it me at your leisure. I shall desire that the boat and officer that carries this to your Lordship express may wait and come down any hour day or night you shall please direct him. I am going off to Captain Montagu[10]. I shall take all your expresses with the gentlemen etc that were for Charles Town and put them on board the *Pearl*, as you'l observe she with *Iris* are for Charles Town and I dare say your Lordship will approve my giving dispatches the chance of two copper bottoms in preference to a pitch tub. I shall detain the *Loyalist* to convoy the ships carrying round the wounded, which I hope your Lordship will also approve of.

Excuse my haste and believe me
Your Lordship's most respectful faithful servant

JOHN INGLIS

Inglis to Cornwallis, 9th April 1781　　　　　　　　　　　　　　　　　　*5(201): L*

Delight
Cape Fear River
April 9th 1781

The Rt Hon Lord Cornwallis etc etc etc

My Lord

As His Majesty's Sloop *Otter* is entirely run out of provisions, and as there is no navy provissions here, I will be obliged to your Lordship if you will be pleased to cause an order to be given to the Commissary General of the army under your Lordship's command to supply the said sloop with two months' provissions of the different species.

---

[9] *enclosed letter*: not extant.

[10] After entering the Royal Navy in 1763, George Montagu (1750-1829) was commissioned a lieutenant on 14th January 1771. By now a post-captain, he was in command of the 32-gun frigate *Pearl*, which was making its way with the *Iris* from New York to Charlestown. He is chiefly remembered as being a very effective commander-in-chief at Portsmouth, a post which he held as a vice admiral of the red for five and a half years from 1803. Knighted (GCB) in January 1815, he died an admiral of the red. (*ODNB*; Log of the *Pearl* (National Archives, Kew); Syrett and DiNardo eds, *Commissioned Sea Officers*, 316)

I am, my Lord,
Your Lordship's most humble servant

[JOHN INGLIS]

Inglis to Cornwallis, 10th April 1781   5(213): ALS

HM Sloop *Delight*
2 am, April 10th 1781

The Rt Hon Lord Cornwallis etc etc etc
McLean's Bluff

My Lord

Your letter relative the *Amphitrite*[11] I have this moment had the honor of receiving and forwarding a copy to Captain Biggs[12]. When the boat returns with an answer from Captain Biggs, I will forward it with the utmost expedition to your Lordship, and am

Your Lordship's most respectful and most faithful servant

JOHN INGLIS

Cornwallis to Barkley, 23rd April 1781   85(48): C

Wilmington
23rd April 1781

Andrew Barclay Esq etc etc etc

Sir

Having occasion to write to Sir Henry Clinton and to General Phillips on business of great importance, I am under the necessity of requesting that you will be pleased to order a frigate

---

[11] *Your letter..*: no extant copy. The *Amphitrite* was requested to convey Cornwallis's dispatches of the 10th (pp 109-111 and 114) to Phillips and Clinton. She delivered the ones to Phillips on 18th April and the other to Clinton on the 22nd.

[12] Robert Biggs (?-1801) was captain of the 24-gun *Amphitrite*, a new frigate launched at Deptford in 1778. Commissioned a naval lieutenant on 7th August 1761, he was promoted to commander on 10th January 1771 and to post-captain some seven years later. He died a vice admiral of the white. The *Amphitrite* continued in service till 1794, when she was wrecked after striking an uncharted submerged rock while on passage between Elba and Livorno. (Syrett and DiNardo eds, *Commissioned Sea Officers*, 34; Michael Phillips, 'Ships of the Old Navy' (Internet, 22nd July 2006))

to carry my letter to General Phillips[13] in the Chesapeak, to proceed from thence with my letter to the Commander in Chief[14] at New York, if an equally expeditious and good opportunity does not otherways offer. But that the service of your district may suffer as little as possible, I have no objection (if you think it necessary) to my aide de camp, Captain Brodrick, calling at both places for the purposes mentioned in the frigate which I presume you have been so kind as allot to carry him with my dispatches to England.

I have the honour to be, sir,
Your most obedient and most humble servant

CORNWALLIS

Cornwallis to the officer commanding HMS Carysfort etc, 24th April 1781   85(51): C

Wilmington
April 24th 1781

To the officer commanding His Majesty's Ship *Carysfort*
   or any other of His Majesty's ships off the bar of Cape Fear

Sir

Having dispatches[15] of the utmost importance to send to Lt Colonel Balfour at Charlestown and to Major General Phillips in Virginia, I must desire that you will be pleased not to bring His Majesty's ship under your command of[16] the bar, but that you will be so kind as to take the letters to Lt Colonel Balfour to the bar of Charlestown and, after sending them in, proceed with the utmost dispatch to Major General Phillips in the Chesapeak. As this is a matter of the most serious importance to His Majesty's Service, I trust you will forgive my very earnest application. Should your ship be intended by Captain Barkley to carry Governor Martin and Captain Brodrick to England, I must still desire that both these services may be first performed.

I am, sir,
Your most obedient and most humble servant

CORNWALLIS

---

[13] *my letter to General Phillips*: presumably that of 24th April, p 116.

[14] *my letter to the Commander in Chief*: of 23rd April, p 112.

[15] *dispatches*: of 21st, 22nd and 24th April to Balfour, pp 121-3, and of the 24th to Phillips, p 116.

[16] *of*: off.

Barkley to Cornwallis, 14th April 1781

5(219): ACS

Blonde
Charles Town
14th April 1781

His Excellency Lord Cornwallis etc etc

My Lord

I had the honor of your Lordship's letter dated the 5th instant[17] requesting that a ship of war might be sent to England with your dispatches.

I must beg leave to acquaint your Lordship that Admiral Arbuthnot has sent me possitive orders not to send a ship to England without his possitive directions for so doing. I inclose a copy of his letter, but I firmly believe it was not the Admiral's intentions to refuse your Lordship a ship, which has induc'd me to appoint the *Delight* to perform the service your Lordship requests.

There is no ship on the southern service but the *Blonde*, the *Loyalist* being order'd to New York by the Admiral's particular desire. I am therefore preparing to come to Cape Fear to convoy a vessel or two with necessarys for your Lordship's army, but as the wind and weather may retard the *Blonde*'s getting out as soon I could wish, I have sent Captain Ingles his orders to proceed to England as soon as your Lordship pleases.

I most sincerely congratulate your Lordship on the vigorous and most extraordinary success of His Majesty's arms under your command, and it will afford me great happiness if I can be of the least use to your Lordship in any of your operations.

I have the honor to be
Your Lordship's most obedient humble servant

AND^W BARKLEY

---

[17] *your Lordship's letter..*: see p 123.

Enclosure (1)
Arbuthnot to the officer commanding the navy in Carolina,   *5(221): C*
  24th February 1781

Royal Oak in Gardner's Bay
February 24th 1781

Commanding officer of His Majesty's ships in Carolina

Sir

Haveing found many inconveniences to arise from the practice of detaching His Majesty's ships and vessels under various pretences to England or from off the station which has lately been adopted by officers in subordinate commands, it is therefor my positive directions that in future none of His Majesty's ships or vessels of war are to quit the stations by me assign'd to them without my particular orders, and I give you this information for your future guidance.

I am
Your most humble servant

M[T] ARBUTHNOT

Enclosure (2)
Barkley's instructions to Inglis, 14th April 1781   *5(223): C*

By Captain Andrew Barkley of His Majesty's Ship *Blonde*
and Senior Officer of His Majesty's ships and vessels
employ'd in the Carolinas

To Captain Ingles of His Majesty's Sloop *Delight*

The Rt Hon Earl Cornwallis having made a requisition for a ship of war to go with his aid d' camp to England with an account of his winter's campaign, you are hereby requir'd and directed to receive on board His Majesty's sloop under your command Captain Brodrick and proceed with the utmost dispatch to Spithead in Great Britain or the first port you can make there, acquainting the Rt Hon Lord Commissioners of the Admiralty on your arrival.

Given on board the *Blonde* in Charles Town Harbour
14th April 1781

AND[W] BARKLEY

§ - §

3 - From Craig

Craig to Cornwallis, 12th April 1781 *5(305): ALS*

Willmington
12th April 1781

My Lord

I beg your Lordship's permission to report in as short a manner as possible the proceedings of the detachment under my command since our arrival here.

On our taking possession of Willmington on the 29th of January, which in conjunction with the gallies we did without opposition, I found that a body of militia had retir'd to a very strong post about ten miles off and that several vessels loaded with provisions and other stores had gone up the river with them. The report of their number varied so much that I was at a loss to form any judgement of it. However, as Captain Barkley, senior officer of the navy, had at my request landed the marines of His Majesty's ships with us, I did not hesitate to march immediately to endeavour at best to make ourselves masters of the boats. The facility with which we drove the party of the enemy on this side the bridge encourag'd me, notwithstanding the peculiar strength of the ground, to attack their main body posted in the most advantageous manner on the opposite side. Captains Nesbitt and Pitcairne with their companies led the attack, supported by the marines, while the companies of the 82nd remain'd to cover the bridge. After a short resistance the enemy fled and left us masters of their camp, but, being favour'd by the darkness of the night, a few only were kill'd and seven or eight taken. Many were wounded and went to their homes, as did most of the remainder. On our side Captain Nesbitt and seven privates were wounded. The former, on the first discharge of the rebel centinels, receiv'd two wounds in his leg, notwithstanding which he charg'd with his company and exerted himself so much that I did not perceive he was hurt till the affair was over. The next day all the vessels fell into our hands. The two largest, loaded with ammunition, were burnt, and the remainder, together with a brig taken by a galley which Captain Barkley sent up the river, brought here. We then march'd between 40 and 50 miles thro' the country, destroying such stores as might be of use to the rebels, and arriv'd here without seeing any other enemy.

On my return I receiv'd a dispatch from Lt Colonel Balfour[18] informing me of your Lordship's being in pursuit of Morgan, which would probably retard your approach and leave us to ourselves a more considerable length of time than had been expected. I was also inform'd that the rebel Governor Nash was collecting the whole militia of the country and bringing down canon to oppose us. However, my Lord, on a serious consideration of the importance of Willmington for the execution of my instructions, and relying on the assistance of the navy, which has been at all times most readily given me, I determin'd to remain here

---

[18] *a dispatch..*: no copy.

at all events, only fortifying my post and resolving to act with such caution as not to risk any thing considerable, which might affect my small numbers and render the defence of the extent of ground we were oblig'd to occupy more precarious. On this general principle, which I hope will meet with your Lordship's approbation, I have conducted myself. The rebels have continued at the bridge the whole time, their numbers fluctuating between four and eight hundred in one body, besides detach'd parties and the militia of Brunswick and Bladen Counties, who to the number of about a hundred assembled at Hood's Creek and prevented a very necessary communication with that side of the country. I therefore determin'd to dislodge them, but being confin'd to my bed myself, I intrusted the execution to Major Manson, who with about eighty men fell on them at day light in the morning. A few were bayonetted and the rest so compleatly dispers'd that they have never since been able to collect above fifteen men. On this occasion we had a corporal kill'd and a private wounded. Lieutenant Winter, agent for the transports, who had the charge of the boats, was also badly wounded and I have suffer'd much from the loss of his assistance.

In the middle of March, finding the forage near us consum'd, and it being dangerous to procure it at any distance from the great numbers the rebels might oppose to the small parties I was able to send, I determin'd to march with two hundred men and two three pounders and take post opposite them at the end of the bridge. Their numbers were then at a low ebb, their main body not consisting of more than three hundred and fifty or four hundred with six canon. I intended by this to cover the country while with the assistance of Captain Inglis (who sent me a lieutenant and thirty seamen) I collected forage, and I was in hopes it would have encourag'd the country people to bring in fresh provisions of which the inhabitants were beginning to be in want. Our advanc'd guard surpriz'd a picquet of light horse, most of which were bayonetted or push'd into the river and drown'd, and by the prisoners taken I learnt that a party under a Colonel Brown consisting of 150 horse and foot were then on the sound. These I meant to have gone in quest of the next night, as I was well acquainted with their usual haunts and did not doubt but I should find them. However, they by good fortune prevented me and reduc'd our meeting to a certainty, for, deceiv'd by intelligence that we were only a party of fifty men, they came and attack'd us at four o'clock in the afternoon. Our picquet under Lieutenant Hovenden of the Legion, doing duty with the 82nd, and a small foraging party under Lieutenant Reeves[19] of the 82nd, who were coming in, receiv'd their attack and repuls'd them, and, the light company with the mounted men being order'd to their support, the rebels were pursued between four and five miles. The thickness of the swamps, the near approach of night and the attention I was oblig'd to pay to the enemy in my front, who canonaded us the whole time, by not allowing me to detach more men after them, prevented our doing greater execution. They left twenty dead and we took an officer and ten prisoners. Their number of wounded by accounts obtain'd since was very considerable, and among them Colonel Brown. Our loss was a serjeant and two men wounded, the former since dead, and one mounted man by engaging too far in the pursuit was taken. We had also two horses kill'd. We remain'd at the bridge four days, when, having collected a sufficiency of forage and finding the other purposes I expected from taking post there were not answer'd, we march'd at nine o'clock in the morning and return'd to this place, but without the enemy's accepting the fair invitation we gave them of following us.

---

[19] John Reeves had been commissioned a lieutenant in the 82nd Regiment on 6th January 1778. (*Army Lists*)

I have only to add to this report, my Lord, the capture of Mr Harnett[20], a man whose character Governor Martin will give your Lordship much better than I can, but it was on all hands represented to me in such a light that, together with his extensive influence in the country, which I was well assur'd he ever employ'd to the most traiterous purposes, it determin'd me to run any risk to seize him. On our arrival here he had fled the country, but trusting, I suppose, to the distance and to the rebels being in a manner between him and me, he had for some time come to live on the sound near forty miles off. I took every precaution I could to prevent being intercepted, and after riding with twenty of my mounted men seventy five miles without halting, I join'd my parties of infantry and lodg'd my prisoner safely in town. We also drove in a hundred head of cattle, and the advance guard of one of the parties which were posted to support me in case of need fell in with sixteen rebels in a house, mostly officers, who fir'd at them thro' the doors and windows, but, the former being immediately burst open, they all fell by the bayonet, having only slightly wounded one man.

I cannot close this report, my Lord, without endeavouring to do justice to the great readiness with which I have on every occasion been assisted by Captain Inglis of the *Delight* and the ships of war under his command. His personal assistance, or that of his men, or any other in his power has always been ready at the first request. I beg leave to add that the behaviour of the troops and marines has on all occasions been highly satisfactory to me and meriting your Lordship's approbation.

I have the honor to be with the greatest respect, my Lord,
Your Lordship's most obedient and most humble servant

J H CRAIG
Major, 82nd Regiment

§ - §

---

[20] A leading Wilmington merchant, Cornelius Harnett Jr (1723-1781) had served for many years in the colonial legislature before becoming a leader of the revolution in North Carolina. Not only had he been appointed President of the Provincial Council in 1775, a body which exercised the functions of government after Governor Martin had fled, but he had also been returned to the Provincial Congresses in 1776 and formed part of the committee which framed North Carolina's revolutionary constitution. From 1777 to 1780 he had gone on to serve in the Continental Congress. Castigated by Martin as unremitting in his 'labours to promote sedition and rebellion', he was imprisoned in an open blockhouse after his capture, where his health rapidly declined. Paroled, he would die on 28th April and be buried in St James' Churchyard, Wilmington. (William S Powell ed, *Dictionary of North Carolina Biography* (University of North Carolina Press, 1991); Wheeler, *Historical Sketches, passim*; Robinson, *NC Guide*, 260, 332)

4 - From officers of the 71st Regiment and the Brigade of Guards

Hutcheson to Cornwallis, 9th April 1781   5(203): DS

To the Rt Hon Lt General Earl Cornwallis etc etc etc

The memorial of Captain Robert Hutchieson commanding the 2nd Battalion, 71st Regiment,

Humbly sheweth

That as the want of the commissary's accounts of stoppages for rations prevents a real settlement taking place for the battalion's subsistence to the 24th of this month, the memorialist begs leave to request that your Lordship would be pleased to grant a temporary warrant upon the Deputy Paymaster General at Charlestown for two thousand pounds payable to Lieutenant Thomas Fraser, Paymaster to the 2nd Battalion, 71st Regiment, in order that the battalion may be supplied without loss of time with such necessaries as they want.

R HUTCHESON[21]
Captain commanding 2nd Battalion, 71st Regiment

Camp
9th April 1781

Lovelace to Cornwallis, 17th April 1781   5(225): ALS

Camp near Wilmington
April 17th 1781

My Lord

I beg leave to present to your Lordship the motives on which I ground my pretensions for requesting your Lordship's leave to return to England.

In consequence of a resolution I had taken of quitting the King's Service before I came to this country, I requested of Lt Colonel Hamilton of the Coldstream Regiment, who sail'd for England last autumn, to dispose of my commission, giving him by a certificate under my hand witness'd by Captain Corbett every ostensible authority for that purpose. I likewise at the same time urged in the strongest terms I cou'd to Lt Colonel Hamilton the extreme necessity of my return to Europe, begging his friendly assistance in the immediate dispatch

---

[21] Robert Hutcheson had been serving as a captain in the 71st (Highland) Regiment since 3rd August 1778. (WO 65/164(15) (National Archives, Kew))

of that business. Not having therefore the smallest doubt that my commission has been dispos'd of, I flatter myself your Lordship will dispense with the formality of being oficially acquainted of my having left the army and permit me to embrace the first opportunity of returning to England. I hope your Lordship will do me the justice to believe that no reasons whatever in the present critical situation of the Brigade of Guards cou'd have induc'd me to return to Europe if I consider'd myself in the service. I have only to add, my Lord, that I shall ever deem it the most fortunate event of my life in having had the honor of serving under your Lordship in the late glorious campaign.

I am, my Lord,
Your Lordship's obedient humble servant

R LOVELACE[22]

O'Hara to Cornwallis, 20th April 1781   5(229): DS

To the Rt Hon Lt General Earl Cornwallis etc etc etc

The memorial of Brigadier General O'Hara commanding the detachment of the Brigade of Guards

HUMBLY SHEWETH

That as the want of the commissary's accounts for provisions issued to the said brigade prevents a real settlement taking place for the brigade's subsistence, your memorialist begs leave to request that your Lordship would be pleased to grant a partial warrant upon the Deputy Paymaster General, payable to Captain Francis Richardson, Paymaster to the detachment of the Guards, for one thousand five hundred pounds sterling, being five hundred pounds on account of subsistence for each of the detachments from the First[23], Coldstream and Third[24] Regiments of Guards of which the said brigade is composed, in order that the said brigade may be supplied without loss of time with such necessaries as they want.

CHA^S O'HARA
Brigadier General

Wilmington
20th April 1781

§ - §

---

[22] Commissioned an ensign in the Coldstream Regiment of Foot Guards on 15th July 1768, Robert Lovelace had been promoted there to lieutenant on 6th May 1775 and to captain on 3rd May 1780, a rank which carried with it a lt colonelcy. As assumed in his letter, he had by now sold out. (*Army Lists*)

[23] *First*: Grenadier Guards.

[24] *Third*: Scots Guards.

5 - A proposed basis for offensive operations in North Carolina

MacAlester to Cornwallis, undated[25]   *2(224) ADS*

MEMORANDUM

The most apparent obstacle to the speedy reduction of the province of North Carolina to His Majesty's Government is its being destitute of any safe water communication into the heart of the country. From Cambden in South Carolina to James River in Virginia there is not one. All the rivers from thence to Cape Fear increase the difficulty of crossing the country without furnishing one single accommodation, and the town of Wilmington itself is so small a way up the river that it may with propriety (for the present purpose) be considered in no other light than as a port on the sea coast. The usual communication by water between that and Cross Creek cannot be kept open but by a considerable force in time of war. Albemarle Sound furnishes a large inland navigation by the dangerous inlett of Occracock and gives access some distance into the country up the River Roanoke, but the whole of this navigation is so intricate and tedious that it cannot be pointed out as imediately usefull to any regular operations.

If these premises are founded on fact, it justly follows that obstacles arise no less dangerous than unsurmountable in the operations of an army on the back parts of North Carolina.

A post cannot be left with any degree of safety in the heart of the country.

An army cannot remain in the country long without a communication with its posts for want of necessaries, and seldom above a few days in one place for want of subsistence.

In case of defeat it is liable to inextricable subsequent difficulties.

And as these circumstances make it impossible to protect the property of those who are invited to return to their alegiance, it is in vain to expect till then that they will take a decisive part in favour of His Majesty's Government.

Some other circumstances may be adduced which the enemy will impose upon *their own public* to the prejudice of His Majesty's arms.

My intention now is to shew that the point of communication from which the operations of war in North Carolina should originate is from Petersburg in Virginia. Without regarding the boundary lines of the different provinces, which are imaginary, James River is the nearest navigation to the back parts of North Carolina.

---

[25] Written sometime between Phillips' arrival in Virginia in late March 1781 and news of his death on 14th May 1781.

You will perceive by viewing the maps that James River and Roanoke with little variation run east and west, and that the rivers south of these run nearly south and north, so that James River and Roanoke, no great way up, run in a manner on the back of Carolina and cross the heads of its rivers, whereas in the south and north provinces of Carolina, to attain the heads of the rivers so as to ford them, the distance from any navigable post in some places is 300 miles and in all above 200. Now from Petersburg to Hallifax on Roanoke it is only 90 miles, from whence an army has in fact a higher station in the country with this short distance than that before mentioned. It requires very little marching from Hallifax to be high enough to ford all the transverse rivers of North Carolina. Consequently any part of the country is open (if the expression is proper) to a descent.

From all which it may be reasonably suggested that Hallifax is the most proper place to point to, providing the forces under the command of General Philips will act in conjunction. In this case the following consequences will result.

The troops on Roanoke will have plentifull subsistence, that being the best country in Carolina.

Having posession of both sides of the river, the armies may support a free communication across and either reinforce one another, move, or execute any plan in concert as circumstances will require. The advantage of this position is obvious. It will be difficult for the enemy to form a junction, and they are liable to be attacked separately.

Altho a communication from the south side of Roanoke with Petersburg is not very convenient, yet it is the best that can be afforded in Carolina. Occasionaly necessaries may be got from it, and posession of both banks will prevent any great misfortune to either army.

From Hallifax, it has been mentioned, the whole back of Carolina is open.

The other side of it is no less favorable to General Philips. The rebel magazines at Prince Edward Court House and at Chesterfield Court House are very little out of his route in prosecution of this plan, and from the very state of affairs at present he has no alternative but to act between James River and Roanoke.

With respect to the motions of General Green, if the movements that are proposed should take place, he must soon repair, or will be peremptorily called, to the frontiers of Virginia.

HECTOR MacALESTER[26]

§ - §

---

[26] Hector MacAlester was a Scottish loyalist who had migrated to Norfolk, Virginia, about 1760, where he established himself as a merchant with a large trade. In October 1775 he was appointed by Lord Dunmore, the deposed Governor, as Treasurer and Paymaster to HM forces in Virginia with the rank of captain. In January 1776 his stores and wharves at Norfolk went up in flames when the town was burned by Dunmore, and during the same month his sloop *Swallow* was seized by the revolutionaries. Now destitute, he would be appointed by Cornwallis as a commissary of prisoners at the beginning of June and fall prisoner at Yorktown. (Coldham, *Loyalist Claims*, 300; David Dobson, *Scots on the Chesapeake, 1607-1830* (Genealogical Publishing Co, 1992), 87; David Dobson, *Directory of Scottish Settlers in North America, 1625-1825* (Genealogical Publishing Co, 1985), v, 145; AO 13/31(205) and AO T/79/21(29) (National Archives, Kew); *The Cornwallis Papers*)

6 - Petition to become British subjects

Brice to Martin, 21st April 1781 *5(241): ALS*

Wilmington
April 21st 1781

His Excellency Josiah Martin Esq
Governor of North Carolina etc etc

Sir

At the request of sundry inhabitants of this town I do myself the honor to inclose to your Excellency an address which they have for several days pass'd wish'd to be presented to you, assuring themselves that you will be pleased to make use of your influence to have them placed in the situation of British subjects.

I have the honor to subscribe myself
Your Excellency's most obedient and most humble servant

F BRICE[27]

Enclosure
Petition, undated *5(243): DS*

TO his Excellency Josiah Martin Esquire, Governor
    and Commander in Chief of the Province of NORTH CAROLINA etc etc

THE HUMBLE PETITION AND ADDRESS of sundry inhabitants of the town of WILMINGTON

WE THE SUBSCRIBERS, having voluntarily surrendered ourselves prisoners at discretion to the detachment of His Majesty's troops under the command of Major Craig, and by him indulg'd with our paroles, DID previous to the arrival of your Excellency in this part of the province give Major Craig assurances of our attachment to His Majesty's person and Government and our sincere wishes to return to our allegiance, praying through his interposition to be restored to the blessings of previledges of British subjects, [and] REJOICE at the arrival of Lord Cornwallis and your Excellency as it affords us so favorable an opportunity of again avowing our loyalty and testifying our attachment to a government we have for a length of time considered superior to any other in the known world.

---

[27] Francis Brice was not a turncoat but a firm loyalist of Wilmington whose country seat, Mount Blake, lay near Cypress Creek in Duplin County. He had resided in the county since at least mid 1751. Mount Blake may have been destroyed by the revolutionaries in mid or late March 1781 after a party of Lillington's men were suddenly attacked and fired at from there by loyalists.

WE HUMBLY intreat your Excellency to receive our warmest assurances that we shall glory in every occasion of manifesting our zeal and contributing our assistance to suppress the REBELLION that has too long existed in this once happy country, AND we pray of your Excellency to represent us to his Lordship as earnestly wishing to be restored to the character and condition of British subjects that through the indulgence of his Lordship and your Excellency we may once more enjoy those inestimable previledges.

CHARLES JINKES	ALEXANDER HOSTLER	GEORGE MEEK
FRANCIS BRICE	JAMES RICHARD	W^M EWANS
ROB^T ELLIS	ARTHUR BENNING	HENRY GAMALIN
HENRY TOOMES	JAMES [MAICEFIELD?]	THOMAS KINGSWELL
T GRAHAM	JOHN SMITH	THO^S KELLY
AND^W THOMSON	FINGAL McKINNON	GEO SMITH
DANIEL McNEILL	JONA: DUNBIBIN	[IRONY?] JACOBS
JN^O KIRKWOOD	JO^N BLAND	MARK MABLING
JOHN HOPKINS	ARTHUR HARPER	JN^O JAMES WARD
RICHARD PLAYER	HENRY ROOKS	THO^S HENDERSON
THOMAS BROWN	ALEX^R CARMICHAELL	JA^S MORAN
JACOB [TRUIT?]	JOHN DRUMMOND	JOHN NUTT
WILLIAM NUTT	JONATHAN ROBESON	RICHARD HORTON

§ - §

7 - Troop return

State of the troops at Wilmington, 15th April 1781

103(28): D

State of the Army with Lt General Earl Cornwallis at Wilmington, North Carolina, 15th April 1781

Ranks	Guards	23rd	33rd	71st, 2nd Batt	82nd	Bose	B Legion	NCV[28]	Total
Officers present:									
Commissioned									
Colonels	-	-	-	-	-	-	-	-	-
Lt Colonels	3	-	-	-	-	-	1	1	5
Majors	-	-	-	-	1	1	-	-	2
Captains	6	3	3	3	3	2	5	5	30
Lieutenants	-	3	3	6	6	4	7	4	33
Ensigns	-	3	2	5	3	2	4	4	23
Staff									
Chaplains	-	-	-	-	1	-	-	-	1
Adjutants	2	1	-	1	1	1	1	1	8
Quarter Masters	1	-	-	1	1	1	3	1	8

---

[28] North Carolina Volunteers, that is to say, the Royal North Carolina Regiment.

Surgeons	1	1	1	1	1	-	1	2	1	8
Mates	2	-	-	-	1	1	5	-	-	9
Effective Serjeants, Drummers, Rank & File:										
Present and fit for duty										
Serjeants	20	16	15	22	17	43	14	13	160
Drummers	14	4	9	9	5	15	7	7	70
Rank & File	423	186	241	183	174	248	173	201	1,829
Absent on Command and Recruiting										
Within the District										
Serjeants	1	3	1	3	-	4	-	2	14
Drummers	-	11	-	-	-	2	-	-	13
Rank & File	23	45	8	24	-	28	4	36	168
Without the District										
Serjeants	2	1	1	-	8	8	1	4	25
Drummers	-	1	7	-	8	2	-	2	20
Rank & File	20	9	13	8	101	70	30	53	304
Prisoners with the Rebels										
Serjeants	3	-	1	2	-	2	17	2	27
Drummers	2	-	-	5	-	1	8	1	17
Rank & File	80	24	41	116	22	21	258	88	650
Sick										
Serjeants	2	3	4	6	5	2	1	-	23
Drummers	-	-	-	6	-	-	2	-	8

Rank & File	69	40	58	96	30	30	36	46	405
Wounded									
Serjeants	11	1	2	3	-	1	3	-	21
Drummers	1	-	-	-	-	2	1	-	4
Rank & File	160	57	60	34	4	22	34	1	372
Total effective									
Serjeants	40	24	24	36	30	60	36	21	271
Drummers	18	16	16	20	13	22	18	10	133
Rank & File	775	361	421	461	331	419	535	425	3,728
Wanting to compleat:									
Serjeants	-	-	-	-	-	-	-	9	9
Drummers	2	-	-	-	1	-	-	-	3
Rank & File	225	207	147	304	275	106	-	135	1,399
Alterations since last return:									
Inlisted or recovered	-	-	-	1	-	-	-	11	12
Transferred	-	-	-	-	-	-	-	-	-
Dead	6	-	3	1	-	1	26	2	39
Discharged	-	-	-	-	-	-	-	-	-
Deserted	1	-	-	-	-	-	16	6	23
Killed	-	-	-	-	-	-	10	-	10
Wounded	-	-	-	-	-	-	16	-	16

Detachments not included in the above				
	Royal Artillery	Jagers	Guides and Pioneers[29]	Total
Captains	-	1	-	1
Subalterns	3	1	1	7[30]
Staff	1	1	-	2
Serjeants	-	5	1	6
Drummers	-	2	-	2
Rank & File	69	90	37	196

§ - §

---

[29] The return for the Guides and Pioneers was taken on 1st February, those for the RA and Jägers on 15th April.

[30] 7: 5.

PART NINE

The March to Virginia

25th April to 19th May 1781

CHAPTER 47

Introduction to the rest of Part Nine

If, by using a factor of 17.5%[1], we extrapolate from the return[2] of rank and file who marched to Virginia, we arrive at a figure of about 1,680 for all ranks, to which must be added some 70 artillerymen and, say, 30 pioneers[3].

After a short delay while waggons were loaded with an ample supply of flour, rum and salt, Cornwallis quit Wilmington on 25th April. Tarleton with an advanced guard was directed to seize as many boats as possible on the north-east branch of Cape Fear River and collect them at a place about 15 miles above the town. A number were secured and Captain Inglis of the navy dispatched others to protect and expedite the passage of the troops, stores, waggons and cannon. Because many rivers and creeks intersected the country on the way to Virginia, two boats on carriages accompanied the corps.

Marching northward, Cornwallis reached Duplin Courthouse by the 30th, Dickson's Ford on the Neuse by 3rd May, and Nahunta Creek by the 5th. While there he gave Tarleton conditional authority to advance to Halifax with a detachment of 180 dragoons and 80 mounted light infantry. Tarleton reached there on the 7th. In the meantime Cornwallis arrived at Cobb's Mill on the 6th. It lay on Coteckney Creek 15 miles from Peacock's Bridge. He reached Tar River on the 8th and Halifax on the 10th. Five days later, having learnt that Phillips awaited him, he crossed the Roanoke to form a junction. Assuming overall command, he arrived in the vicinity of Petersburg on the 19th. By then Phillips was dead, having been succeeded by Arnold.

Meanwhile, fulfilling Cornwallis's expectations, Rawdon had defeated Greene on 25th April at Hobkirk's Hill but, finding it impractical to maintain his post at Camden, had begun

---

[1] To cater additionally for officers, staff, serjeants and drummers.

[2] See p 184.

[3] See p 145.

to retire within the Santee on 10th May. Throughout South Carolina the war was being waged with increasing and merciless barbarity by the revolutionary irregulars and state troops. 'They have,' related Balfour, 'adopted the system of murdering every militia officer of ours as well as every man (although unarmed) who is known to be a loyalist. The terror this mode of conduct has struck you will easily suppose. Some immediate stop must be put to it or the consequences will be very fatal and we shall not have one loyalist in the country, as they are crowding to town from all quarters.' Not surprisingly, 'the disaffection of the militia is... almost universal and they have joined the enemy wherever they have come.'

§ - §

Principal papers and works consulted in the writing of this chapter

The Cornwallis Papers (UK National Archives, Kew)

Banastre Tarleton, *A History of the Campaigns of 1780 and 1781 in the Southern Provinces of North America* (London, 1787)

§ - §

CHAPTER 48

Miscellaneous letters etc

1 - To or from Phillips or Arnold

Cornwallis to Phillips, 6th May 1781 — 86(13): C

6th May

Major General Phillips

Dear Phillips

I am on my march to join you. Come as near to Halifax as you possibly can without risque to your own army. Spare no pains to let me hear from you.

Yours most sincerely

CORNWALLIS

Cornwallis to Phillips, 8th May 1781[1] — 86(21): C

Camp on Tarr River
8th May 1781

General Phillips

Dear Phillips

I can learn no satisfactory accounts of you. Some say that you are embarked, others that you have passed James River. I have intelligence almost amounting to a certainty that Lord

---

[1] Published in Tarleton, *Campaigns*, 332.

Rawdon has beat Greene at Camden, and consequently South Carolina is safe. *Still I wish to join you, but* as many circumstances may happen which *may prevent my staying long enough* in this country *to get sufficient information of you, you must take no steps with* that view that may *hazard the safety of your own army. Let me hear from you by every possible opportunity*.

[CORNWALLIS]

Cornwallis to Phillips, 10th May 1781   86(25): ADf

Halifax
May 10th 1781

Major General Phillips

Dear Phillips

I have secured the passage of the Roanoke. Let me hear from you.

I wish to join you immediately and will endeavour to do it as soon as I can get any satisfactory information about you.

Yours sincerely

[CORNWALLIS]

Arnold to Cornwallis, 12th May 1781   6(64): L

Petersburgh
12th May 1781

General Phillips is here in force to cooperate agreeable to your Lordship's wishes. The Marquis La Fayette is on the opposite shore with, as is said, fifteen hundred Continental troops and some militia. General Phillips proposes waiting here five or six days in expectation of having your Lordship's orders or opportunity effectually to answer your purposes. From information received, we suppose your Lordship either at Halifax or on this side. Wayne has arrived or is on his way to Richmond with the Pennsylvania line, about [blank] *hundred men. A reinforcement has been requested by General Phillips and, it is said, was to sail from New York the 4th instant for Portsmouth.*

B ARNOLD

Cornwallis to Phillips, 14th May 1781[2]

86(29): C

Halifax
14th May 1781

Major General Phillips

I march tomorrow to join you.

[CORNWALLIS]

Arnold to Cornwallis, 16th May 1781

70(8): ALS

Petersburg
May 16th 1781
11 o'clock pm

Earl Cornwallis

My Lord

I am very sorry to inform your Lordship that Major General Phillips died the 14th instant after an illness of about a fortnight. His loss is greatly lamented as he was universally beloved and esteemed by the army.

I was this morning honoured with your Lordship's favor of the 14th instant dated at Halifax, and at three o'clock this afternoon I received a note from Lt Colonel Simcoe informing me that it is your Lordship's order that I march immediately to join your army at Bollen's Bridge on the Nottoway, where you expected to be on Friday evening. I conceive that when this order was given the security of this army was your Lordship's object and that you could not know our present situation, which is materially altered since Colonel Simcoe left us. The Marquis La Fayette the same day retreated by a forced march to Wilton on the other side of James River, eight miles from Richmond, where he still remained at 5 o'clock this evening. On the 14th late in the evening I received two letters from Sir Henry Clinton, copies[3] of which I do myself the honor to inclose, also an extract of a letter from Captain Valancey[4], by which your Lordship will observe that the post at Portsmouth is in a critical situation and will be in danger if the French fleet and troops arrive before the British, unless relieved by this army.

---

[2] Annotated: 'Written in cypher on a Congress note.'

[3] *copies*: of Clinton to Phillips, 30th April (99(32)), and of Clinton to Phillips, 30th April and 2nd and 3rd May (95(40)), vol V, ch 50.

[4] *extract...from Captain Valancey*: of 8th May (99(33)), vol V, ch 50. George Preston Vallancey had been serving since 18th August 1778 as a captain in the 62nd Regiment. After a period as Phillips' secretary in Virginia, he was now at Portsmouth acting on secondment as an assistant deputy quartermaster general and a deputy paymaster general, posts which he would occupy till the capitulation. He may have been related to Lieutenant Charles Vallancey (see vol III, p 201, note 103). (*Army Lists*; *The Cornwallis Papers*)

Two lines in cypher in my letter[5] I cannot explain as the key to the cypher is on board a ship at Brandon.

The army is under orders to march tomorrow morning towards the Nottoway. I have thought proper to transmit the inclosed copies of letters etc to your Lordship as the intelligence contained may induce your Lordship to alter your orders respecting the march of this army.

I have the honor to be with the greatest respect and esteem, my Lord,
Your Lordship's most obedient and most humble servant

B ARNOLD

Cornwallis to Arnold, 17th May 1781 — 86(35): C

May 17th, 9 am

Brigadier General Arnold etc etc etc

Sir

I have just received the favour of your letter of last night. The account of the death of my dear friend Phillips gives me the most sensible grief.

My reason for ordering you to march to the Nottoway was, as you supposed, to prevent the Marquis bringing you to action before I could join you. At present that consideration ceases. I am so unacquainted with the post at Portsmouth and the situation of your ships and boats that I cannot give immediate orders. I must therefore beg that you will let your corps remain where this letter finds you and that you will come yourself with the cavalry to meet me at Butler's Bridge early tomorrow morning. I must likewise desire that you will send to Portsmouth to assure the commanding officer that I will use every means in my power to succour him if there should be occasion.

I am, sir,
Your most obedient and most humble servant

CORNWALLIS

§ - §

---

[5] *my letter*: Clinton to Phillips of 30th April (99(32)), vol V, ch 50.

2 - To or from Tarleton

Tarleton to Cornwallis, 4th May 1781 *6(41): ALS*

Davis's Mill
May 4th, 7 pm

Lt General Earl Cornwallis etc etc etc etc

My Lord

I left Gray's Plantation at four this morning. The inhabitants in general at home except the rich and leading men, who are fled. Burk's Mill about 8 miles distant from Gray's is now employ'd. All the other mills between this place and the Nuse, except the two named last night, want water. Cobb's Mill, the best in the country and well supply'd with corn, I have dispatch'd a patrole to. It lyes on the Coteckney 15 miles above Peacock's Bridge and seven from hence.

The country is alarm'd but the militia will not turn out. They were very near securing their leaders. Many people have this day apply'd for paroles. They all mention a detachment of British troops being lately at Halifax. Some say that Philips and Arnold are pointing towards Roanoke. I have dispatch'd two good people to ascertain the news in that quarter, which I shall gladly communicate to your Lordship. No news this day from any place beside. I shall collect all the provisions to morrow and move, but not over the Coteckney till I receive your Lordship's instructions. I wish to hear from you, but if any account worth attending to occurs before that honor, I will instantly inform your Lordship. *If accounts are confirmed, no time is to be lost*.

I have the honor to be
Your Lordship's most devoted servant

BAN TARLETON

[*Subscribed*:]

To morrow to Cobb's Mill.

Cornwallis to Tarleton, 5th May 1781[6] *86(9): C*

Nahunty Creek
5th May 1781

Lt Colonel Tarleton

Dear Tarleton

If Cobb's Mill can grind 1,500 bushels in 24 hours and if it appears by your information that General Phillips is certainly within reach of joining, you may go on to Halifax to secure a passage, reporting to me the state of things to direct the movement of the infantry. Forward the inclosed by different hands.

Faithfully yours

CORNWALLIS

Tarleton to Cornwallis, 5th May 1781 *6(46): ALS*

Cobb's Mill
May 5th 1781, 2 pm

Lt General Earl Cornwallis etc etc etc etc etc

My Lord

I did myself the honor to write to your Lordship last night by a serjeant of the infantry of the Legion with an account of the occurrences of yesterday.

The people are directed to bring all their meal to this place from 5 mills.

The country people flock in with the news of a great defeat in Virginia of all the rebel forces and that the British troops are on Nottoway and Meherrin in their way from Petersburg, where the action happened. One Benjamin Vicars[7] of Tarrburg confirms the report and says

---

[6] Published in Tarleton, *Campaigns*, 330.

[7] Benjamin Vickers of Edgecombe County, North Carolina, was a planter who had amassed a land holding of some 1,000 acres on the south side of Town Creek. A covert loyalist, he was disinclined to take the test oath in 1778 and was summonsed to show just cause. Apparently 'persuaded' to repent, he attended two sessions of the county court as a juror in 1779, being a member of the grand jury in August. Now, as British troops marched through Edgecombe and Nash Counties, he threw caution to the winds and openly aided them. He would pay a heavy price for his recklessness. In 1785 he was banished and his estate confiscated, but not before he transferred some half of his holding to his father, John, who sold it on. (Weynette Parks Haun, *Edgecombe County, North Carolina, County Court minutes* (W P Haun, 1985), iii (1775-1785); Dr Stephen E Bradley Jr, *Edgecombe County, North Carolina, Deeds* (Bradley Publishing, Virginia Beach, 1995), iii (1778-1786), iv (1786-1794); The Court Records of Edgecombe County, North Carolina)

that the light horse militia of this district who were on their way with prisoners to Halifax from New Bern were order'd away to the mountains after Nash, Caswell etc etc by Colonel Long[8], who commands the militia of Halifax County. I have sent for a man from Little River who is come from Camden with an account that Lord Rawdon has made a succesful sally upon Greene and drove him with great loss. *I shall stay here for orders*. The road by *Lemond's is the best for Halifax*.

None of the people employ'd by your Lordship are yet come in. I have detained one Browne to day. He says nothing new but that Butler's militia have left him[9], all except 80 with arms at Ramsey's Mill. Browne is a suspicious fellow.

I have the honor to be with the greatest respect
Your Lordship's most devoted servant

BAN TARLETON

Cornwallis to Tarleton, 5th May 1781[10]   86(7): C

Nahunty Creek
May 5th 1781

Lt Colonel Tarleton

Dear Tarleton

You must be sensible that in the present instance I put the greatest confidence in you. I trust to your discretion my honour and future happiness. I am convinced you will be upon your guard against the sanguine opinions of friends and your own prejudices. Above all things attend to dates and distinguish between *is* and *has been*. You will read my letter. Send as many messages or notes as you can, but all conveyed in the same *cautious* language. *I confide in the correctness of your report as to the practicability of passing and the certainty of speedy communication with Phillips. If it won't do, take care not to stay too long*.

Yours very sincerely

CORNWALLIS

---

[8] Nicholas Long (1728-1798) was a wealthy planter whose plantation, 'Quanky Place', lay on Quanky Creek in the south-west part of Halifax. A delegate to the Provincial Congress which met at Hillsborough in August 1775, he was appointed by it Colonel of the Halifax District revolutionary militia. Having also become a deputy quartermaster eight months later, he proceeded to erect workshops on his plantation to make implements of war, clothing and other supplies for the soldiery. (Robinson, *NC Guide*, 333; Hay ed, *Soldiers from NC*, 499, 502; Heitman, *Historical Register*, 356)

[9] *him*: Butler.

[10] The original of this letter is published in Tarleton, *Campaigns*, 330. It contains the following enciphered subscription: 'My letters to Phillips are in the new cypher. He has not the old one.' A reprint appears in Bass, *The Green Dragoon*, 175.

Haldane to Tarleton, 5th May 1781
86(11): C

5th May 1781

Lt Colonel Tarleton

To enable you to correspond with General Phillips, substitute the following numbers (instead of those in the inner circle of your present cypher): 12 etc ———.

From — to — sets the cypher.

From — to — mark the terminations of words.

From — to — are expletives.

If you do not comprehend my meaning, leave an officer and some dragoons at Cobb's Mill and a cypher shall be sent.

H HALDANE

Cornwallis to Tarleton, 6th May 1781
86(15): C

Nahunta Creek
6th May 1781, 3 am

Lt Colonel Tarleton

Dear Tarleton

Tho I believe I have frequently mentioned it in conversation, I find upon recollection that I did not say explicitly in my letter that *I cannot advance beyond Cobb's Mill until I hear from you, because I have only provisions to carry me back from thence*. Take your measures accordingly and send express after express when you have any thing particular to say.

Yours very sincerely

CORNWALLIS

Tarleton to Cornwallis, 5th May 1781
6(48): ALS

Cobb's
May 5th 1781, 9 pm

Lt General Earl Cornwallis etc etc etc etc

My Lord

Here you will find 4000 *weight of flour*. Cobb's, Lamb's, Viverett's, Muffin's and another mill are all busily employ'd and will furnish any supplies.

I wrote to day by Vicars. Intelligence still the same. *I march in six hours by Lemond's. Rixes Mill is near the ford.*

The cypher to General Phillips I understand.

I shall reach Halifax on the 7th. *Prudence and exertion shall be my guides*. Notes in cypher *shall be often sent. Support I wish as soon as I get the boats*.

I have the honor to be with true attachment and zeal
Your Lordship's most devoted servant

BAN TARLETON

Tarleton to Cornwallis, 6th May 1781   6(56): ALS

May 6th 1781, 11 am

Lt General Earl Cornwallis etc etc etc

My Lord

I am now at Williams' on Tar, a ford half a mile above Lemon's.

I received your Lordship's letter this morning's date. *Viveret's Mill is the best in the country*[11] and wou'd suit the *advanced corps - the light infantry, Guards - here.*

An officer shall be sent from Halifax.

Jackson was at Lemon's. His son went to Halifax and brought account *that Phillips was at Petersburg, La Fayette at Richmond.*[12]

D^y Dawson[13] *came over Roanoke* and says that the *advanced party of the British were at Meherrin, Crawford's Bridge, Monday last*.

I have the honor to be, my Lord,
Your most devoted servant

BAN TARLETON

---

[11] Viverette's Mill was a grist mill on Toisnot Swamp in what is now Wilson County. It lay on Cornwallis's line of march and was operated by Thomas Viverette (1750-1791), a large land owner with more than 9,000 acres in Nash and Edgecombe Counties. (Information from Norma Thacker, 4th May 2005)

[12] Jackson or his son may have been Basil Jackson, to whom Cornwallis refers in his letter of 17th July to Clinton, vol V, ch 51.

[13] *D^y Dawson*: a reference to Dempsey Dawson, a land owner of Nash County. (Nash County, North Carolina, Deeds, Deed Book F-13)

[*Postscripts to the duplicate (6(58))*:]

PS

Colonel Hunter's[14].

PS, 6 pm

Have taken a prisoner. Intelligence the same. Brigadier General Jones has sent an express to Butler at Ramsey's Mill from Halifax.

Cornwallis to Tarleton, 6th May 1781   86(17): ADf

Cobb's Mill
6th May 1781

Lt Colonel Tarleton etc etc etc

Dear Tarleton

Butcher[15] *is returned*. Says that on Friday last some British troops were within a few miles of Halifax. You will hear more particularly. *The light company of the Guards will be at Williams' early on the 8th, and the brigade at Viveret's. If accounts are good, every exertion shall be made*.

[CORNWALLIS]

[*Subscribed in the duplicate:*]

Captain Dundas[16] has the old cypher and will act according to your orders.

---

[14] Thomas Hunter's plantation lay on the north side of Stony Creek in Nash County, which had been formed out of Edgecombe County in 1777. In April 1776 Hunter was commissioned a field officer in the Edgecombe revolutionary militia. (Joseph W Watson, *Abstracts of Early Deeds of Nash County, North Carolina, 1777-1868* (Arrow Printing Co, 1966), 72, 265, 267; Wheeler, *Historical Sketches*, i, 81)

[15] Butcher has not been positively identified. He may, for example, have been Isaac Butcher, a private in the Royal North Carolina Regiment. If so, he would have been sent out in view of his probable familiarity with the way ahead. (Clark, *Loyalists in the Southern Campaign*, i, 398)

[16] Of Sanson, Berwickshire, the Hon Francis Dundas (1759?-1824) was a younger son of Lord Arniston, who held various important judicial offices in Scotland. He was commissioned an ensign in the 1st Regiment of Foot Guards (the Grenadier Guards) on 4th April 1775 and was promoted there to lieutenant on 23rd January 1778, a rank which carried with it a captaincy. He came out to North America in May 1777 and took part in the Battles of Brandywine, Germantown, and Monmouth. Having been frequently employed on detached service during 1778-9, he came south with the Brigade of Guards in late 1780, commanding its light company, which formed the van of the army during the winter campaign and in Virginia. He would be among the troops taken prisoner at Yorktown. In 1794 he served as Adjutant General under Grey in the reduction of Guadeloupe and Martinique and from 1796 to 1803 commanded at the Cape of Good Hope, where he also served for two periods as acting Governor. He went

Tarleton to Cornwallis, 7th May 1781　　　　　　　　　　　　　　　6(60): ALS

Halifax
May 7th 1781
½ past 2 pm

Lt General Earl Cornwallis etc etc etc

My Lord

I have cut up several. This bank commands. One gun wou'd have all the boats. I have got one large one. The rest are gone down adrift. I have sent after them. The enemy have a work opposite with a 4 pounder. *Three letters I have sent to Phillips.* I have sent out for two men and shall dispatch an officer's party to night *as soon as I know circumstantially about Phillips.*

Your most devoted servant

BAN TARLETON

PS, 8 o'clock pm

Mr Elbeck[17], a friend, says that on Fayette's arrival at Richmond Phillips went either on board or crossed James River from *Petersburg*. I leave your Lordship to judge. *I have* taken every step.

I have wrote Phillips 4 times. *The country I have passed* is most plentiful. *I must have support.*

BT

---

　　on to command on the Kentish coast. A full general, he died at Dunbarton while Governor of the Castle. (*ODNB*; *Army Lists*)

[17] Montfort Elbeck was a Justice of the Peace for Halifax County, one of eleven appointed for the county by an ordinance of the revolutionary legislature in December 1776. He had previously served Halifax Court under the Crown. (Walter Clark, *The State Records of North Carolina, Laws 1715-1776* (Goldsboro NC, 1904), xxiii, 994; Bute County, North Carolina, Deeds, Deed Book 2, 33)

Cornwallis to Tarleton, 8th May 1781[18]   86(23): C

Camp at Crowell's Plantation near Tarr River
8th May 1781, am

Dear Tarleton

I cannot venture to pass the Roanoke without some certain information of Phillips or of the state of things in Virginia. You will read and forward the inclosed letter[19]. Not having been able *to mount the light company of the Guards, I think they would only embarrass you. You may stay two or three days at Halifax* if you think it safe. *If in that time you hear any thing certain and favourable of Phillips,* let me know and *I will move forward immediately. If not, return by whatever road you please and join me near Cobb's or Viverett's Mill, fixing every possible channel of intelligence at any price, for I look northward if possible.* I understand that General Butler is at Wake Court House with a few militia. Our accounts of Lord Rawdon's success continue to be confirmed.

[CORNWALLIS]

Tarleton to Cornwallis, 8th May 1781   6(69): ALS

Near Halifax
May 8th 1781

Lt General Earl Cornwallis etc etc etc

My Lord

I have got 300 stand of arms, one pair colours, 20 hogsheads of rum, *boats enough, meal without*. The enemy are gone. I have sent a flag after them to exchange prisoners. *I have sent to Phillips* again and again. I hear nothing new.

Your devoted servant

BAN TARLETON
Lt Colonel Commandant, British Legion

---

[18] The original of this letter containing inconsequential differences is published in Tarleton, *Campaigns*, 331. It is reprinted in this form, but with a material inaccuracy, in Bass, *The Green Dragoon*, 176.

[19] *the inclosed letter*: Cornwallis to Phillips, 8th May, p 151.

Cornwallis to Tarleton, 8th May 1781[20]   *86(22): ADf*

Crowell's Plantation
May 8th 1781, pm

Dear Tarleton

I have just received yours of this date with more satisfaction than that of yesterday. The light company of the Guards shall proceed immediately and I will follow as fast as possible. You will of course secure the opposite bank when Sutherland arrives.

[CORNWALLIS]

Cornwallis to Tarleton, 14th May 1781   *86(31): ADf*

Halifax
May 14th 1781

Lt Colonel Tarleton

Dear Tarleton

I have heard *from Phillips at Petersburgh waiting to co-operate with me.*[21] *I shall march* with all possible expedition. *You will wait for me or join me where you think it* most expedient. *La Fayette is in considerable force on the other side of the Appomattok opposite to Petersburgh*.

Yours sincerely

[CORNWALLIS]

Tarleton to Cornwallis, 15th May 1781   *6(66): ALS*

May 15th 1781, 11 am

Lt General Earl Cornwallis etc etc etc etc

My Lord

You will have seen Colonel Simcoe before this reaches you.

---

[20] Published in Tarleton, *Campaigns*, 332, and reprinted in Bass, *The Green Dragoon*, 176.

[21] See Arnold to Cornwallis, 12th May, p 152.

I wish you joy, my Lord, cordially. *I have fallen back to Hicks' Ford*. I shall there wait your Lordship's orders. I wrote yesterday for the light company Guards to go to General Jones.

I imagine you will call every thing and come this way.

Your most devoted servant

BAN TARLETON

[*Subscribed*:]

I have surprized a major and a few men here.

Cornwallis to Tarleton, 15th May 1781[22]

86(33): C

Jones's Plantation[23]
15th May 1781

Lt Colonel Tarleton

Dear Tarleton

I am making all possible expedition and hope to be at the Nottoway on Friday evening. I would have you proceed tomorrow to the Nottoway and remain near Simcoe's infantry. Arnold is ordered to march immediately to meet me on the Nottoway. Wayne's having joined La Fayette makes me rather uneasy for Arnold untill we join. If you should hear of any movement of the enemy in force to disturb Arnold's march, you will give him every assistance in your power. Continue to let me hear from you. I have not received your letter of yesterday.

I am with great truth
Very sincerely yours

CORNWALLIS

§ - §

---

[22] An extract omitting the penultimate and final sentences is published in Tarleton, *Campaigns*, 333.

[23] *Jones's Plantation*: 'Ochoneche', two miles from Halifax. It was the seat of Willie Jones, a delegate to Congress.

3 - To or from Craig

Craig to Cornwallis, 29th April 1781   5(260): ALS

Willmington
29th April
2 o'clock morning

My Lord

The inclos'd[24] was this moment deliver'd to me. I have only detain'd it till I copied it to secure a duplicate in case of accident. A Captain Hutchinson[25] is likewise arriv'd, who left Charlestown Thursday, where he says they had no particular accounts from the country but that accidents of people being shot on the road etc happen'd daily within 6 miles of Charlestown. He spoke at sea with the *Cormorant* sloop bound for Charlestown with dispatches and informed the captain that your Lordship was here. The pilot who brought Balfour's letter from George Town says Watson march'd in there on Monday morning and left it again on Tuesday towards the southward, but that some troops under Captain Saunders remain'd there. I shall keep the ferry at Swan's for the return of my party. I have sent so many people besides [blank][26] towards [blank][27] that I think we cannot fail hearing soon. The *Delight* sail'd early this morning and Cane yesterday morning.

Your Lordship's most obedient and devoted servant

J H CRAIG

[*Subscribed:*]

Be good enough to send me your route for 3 or 4 days as it may affect the manner in which I may communicate with you.

---

[24] Balfour to Cornwallis, 20th April, p 170.

[25] No record of Hutchinson has come to light. He was probably master of a transport, victualler, or merchant vessel.

[26] *[blank]*: the name of the emissary. Perhaps his name was Ray, to whom Craig refers in his letter of 2nd May, p 167.

[27] *[blank]*: probably Rawdon or Camden.

Cornwallis to Craig, 3rd May 1781   *86(3): C*

Reeves's Plantation
8 miles from Dickson's Ford on the Nuse
3rd May 1781

Major Craig

Dear Sir

The difficulties of effecting the junction are so great that I would decide to embark if sufficient provisions and transports were in Cape Fear. The state of your provisions makes it impossible to return before their arrival as all might starve together, but I shall move slowly forward in readiness to come back when they arrive. Six weeks' or two months' provisions for 3,000 would do. Manage every ration of your own stock; even, if necessary, curtail the allowance. Keep some small vessels constantly going between Balfour and you. Take every means you can to correspond with me. Send the inclosed[28] and a copy of this to Balfour.

Faithfully yours

CORNWALLIS

Cornwallis to Craig, 4th May 1781   *86(5): C*

4th May 1781

Major Craig

Dear Sir

I wrote to you yesterday to say that *when transports and provisions arrive in Cape Fear, I will return to embark. Give me early notice* and communicate this to Balfour immediately.

Faithfully yours

CORNWALLIS

---

[28] *the inclosed*: Cornwallis to Balfour, 3rd May, p 176.

Craig to Cornwallis, 2nd May 1781[29]   *6(24): ALS*

Willmington
2nd May 1781
8 o'clock pm

My Lord

The letters of which you have copies and extracts on the other side[30] arriv'd in the course of last night by a private vessel, but it was not possible for me to dispatch them sooner to you. I have no intelligence of any sort to add to them, *neither Ray*[31] *nor any other of three I sent being yet return'd*. I have accounts of two vessels coming with dispatches for your Lordship from General Phillips being both carried into Beauford. Lieutenants Rutherford and Anderson[32], both of the 82nd, were entrusted with your letters[33] and fortunately had just notice enough of their situation to destroy them. As these gentlemen had just return'd from a captivity of 18 months, may I beg your Lordship's remembrance of them in case of exchange. Gordon[34] and his party arriv'd yesterday evening. My horses almost all laid up for some time. *Letters from exceeding good authority are now in this river* which mention *the reinforcement being at Corke between* the 3rd and 7th of February, *waiting only for a wind, bound either for Charlestown or this place*. Your Lordship's letter for Colonel Balfour[35] went last night.

Your faithfully devoted and obedient servant

J H CRAIG

---

[29] Cornwallis had not received this letter when he wrote to Craig on 12th May. See p 168.

[30] *The letters..*: Balfour to Cornwallis, 26th April, enclosing Rawdon's of the 19th and 21st. See pp 177-9.

[31] Ray or Rae was such a common surname in North Carolina, possessed by a number of loyalists, that identifying the person involved is idle speculation.

[32] Andrew Rutherford and Robert Anderson had been commissioned lieutenants in the 82nd Regiment on 8th and 19th January 1778 respectively. In the spring of 1779 they were on passage to New York when they were shipwrecked off the coast of New Jersey and fortunate to escape being drowned. Taken prisoner and paroled to Reading, they were later exchanged. (*Army Lists*)

[33] *your letters*: those of 8th and 18th April from Phillips and one of 13th April from Clinton. See vol V, ch 50 and 51.

[34] Perhaps John Gordon and his men, who were very soon to be formed at Wilmington into the North Carolina Independent Dragoons. Captained by Gordon, they became a highly disciplined troop of some sixty men, but before long Gordon was to be killed in a skirmish, being replaced by Robert Gillies. When Wilmington was evacuated in November, the troop removed to Charlestown. On 29th August 1782 Gillies was killed in a skirmish with Marion, the troop was soon after broken up, and the effective men were drafted into the South Carolina Royalist Regiment. (Nan Cole and Todd Braisted, 'An Introduction to North Carolina Loyalist Units', *The On-Line Institute for Advanced Loyalist Studies*, 6th June 2006; Clark, *Loyalists in the Southern Campaign*, i, 405-6)

[35] *Your Lordship's letter..*: of 30th April, p 175.

Craig to Cornwallis, 5th May 1781 6(54): ALS

Willmington
5th May 1781

My Lord

The bearer deliver'd me your letter of the 3rd this day at one o'clock and I have only to say in answer to it that you may depend on the strictest attention being paid to every word in it. I hope you have receiv'd the letters I sent you the 2nd instant from Balfour and Lord Rawdon. I have not since heard one syllable from that quarter, by which I think we may hope *all is going on well*. I find great difficulty in *procuring vessels to go to* Charlestown but I think all difficulties are to be overcome. I subjoin the state of our provisions for 1,500 men from this day. Tho' I have wrote it to you twice already, I cannot help repeating that, from what *I think* good authority, which particularly concludes the paragraph with 'and this you may rely on', *the reinforcement waited only a wind at Cork* 7th February, *bound for Charlestown or this. Flour* 150 *days, rum the same, salt meat* 60 *days*.

Your Lordship's most respectfully devot'd servant

J H CRAIG

Cornwallis to Craig, 8th May 1781 86(19): C

Camp near Tarr River
8th May 1781

Major Craig

Dear Sir

I have fresh hopes of a junction with General Phillips. I shall proceed to Halifax, from whence you shall hear from me.

Faithfully yours

CORNWALLIS

Cornwallis to Craig, 12th May 1781 86(27): C

Halifax
12th May 1781

Dear Sir

I have secured the passage of the Roanoke *but have not heard from General Phillips. I will join him if practicable.* I hear of Lord Rawdon's success from all quarters. *This, even if the junction is not effected, will probably make embarkation unnecessary. You will therefore in concert with Balfour make preparations for your removal*, which will depend on the circumstances already settled between us.

Yours etc

CORNWALLIS

[*Subscribed*:]

The letters you sent on the 2nd *have miscarried*.

If you receive this letter by the [*blank date*], you will give *the bearer, Lewis Hind[36], 20 guineas*.

[*Postscript to the duplicate and triplicate*:]

14th May 1781

I have heard from Phillips at Petersburgh. I pass the Roanoke tomorrow.

Ten guineas to be paid the bearer.

[*Postscript to the triplicate*:]

Thirty guineas to the bearer if delivered by the 22nd.

Craig to Cornwallis, 10th May 1781   *6(62A): ALS*

Willmington
10th May, 9 pm

I have this moment receiv'd the following words from Balfour: '*Greene is beat and we shall do well*.' Accept my sincerest congratulations. No arrivals from Charles Town.

JHC

PS

Note left Charles Town 7th in evening.

---

[36] There is reason to suspect that, with the mishearing and misspelling of names, Cornwallis may be referring to Lewis Hines (*c*. 1750-*c*. 1791), a resident of Duplin County, through which Cornwallis's line of march had progressed. If so, Hines, who had been serving in the North Carolina revolutionary militia, was guilty of duplicitous behaviour, whether toward his revolutionary comrades or toward Cornwallis, whose letter he may have failed to deliver (but whose duplicate or triplicate would in that event arrive). Hines may have been related to Benjamin Hinds (*sic*) of Duplin County, now a loyalist militiaman, who was being treated in HM Hospital at Wilmington. In later life Hines would move to New Hanover County, where he died. (Virginia L and Oscar M Bizzell, *Revolutionary War Records of Duplin-Sampson Counties: Contributions to Genealogy* (© 1997); Demond, *Loyalists in NC*, 236)

Craig to Cornwallis, 13th May 1781   *6(70): ALS*

Willmington
13th May 1781

My Lord

As I have sent three expresses with the first accounts I receiv'd, I make no doubt but before this you will have heard of Lord Rawdon's having copied your Lordship's example before Camden. I have just open'd a letter from him for your Lordship[37] confirming the glorious news. As it was wrote immediately after the action, it contains no particulars but that the loss of the rebels trebles that of his Lordship. Greene sav'd his canon by sending it off very early. One officer only, of the Volunteers of Ireland, is kill'd. It happen'd at 10 o'clock of the morning of the 25th. Lord Rawdon has between three and four hundred militia with him and was join'd before the action by the South Carolina Regiment from Ninety Six. Greene was posted on Hobkirk's Hill just beyond Log Town. I have another letter from Lord Rawdon, of which the following is the only part necessary to be copied: '*Lee and Marion were so near I could not follow the success. Greene has rallied at Rugeley's, where Lee, Marion, Sumpter and Pickens will join him tomorrow. McArthur, I hear, is at Thompson's with a reinforcement for me. What it is I know not, but I hope it will enable me to clear the country. Watson is not to be found.*' *This letter is dated the 27th. The man who brought it was in the action and seems* pretty distinct. Lord Rawdon *was in no want of provisions, had about 1,200 in the action, Greene supposed 3,000. No* arrivals from Charlestown. The men here recover fast. General Hospital report this morning only 150. *A General Caswell is collecting some men on the Nuse*.

Your most faithfull servant

J H CRAIG

§ - §

4 - To or from Balfour

Balfour to Cornwallis, 20th April 1781[38]   *5(231): ALS*

Charles Town
20th April 1781

By the inclosed letters your Lordship will see Lord Rawdon's opinions of the movements of the enemy, and from all circumstances which have come to my knowledge they appear to be well founded.

---

[37] *a letter..*: Rawdon to Cornwallis, 25th April, p 179.

[38] Enclosed with Craig's letter of 29th April, p 165.

The letters came to me yesterday and this morning, and I hasten the pilot boat to give you the earliest notice of it, although the convoy will sail the moment they can get over the bar.

I apprehend Greene would not have crossed Rockey River and the Yadkin had he not meant seriously to come into this province.

From what you mentioned in your letter[39] of coming after the rebell army in case of their movement this way, I was at a loss whether to send the supplys for the army or not, but upon considering all circumstances I conceived it best to send them. I have wrote severall letters to Lt Colonel Watson, ordering him to move to Camden instantly, but I fear it is now too late. Although for these six weeks past he has had repeated orders to that purpose, yet he has never made his appearance, nor does Lord Rawdon or I conceive where he is or what he can be about. I now send to him to give him every intelligence I can and to get him if possible on this side the Santee. He has the 64th Regiment and the light infantry[40] with him.

I have attempted to get to Lord Rawdon by every means in my power to inform him of the state of the posts and the asistance I could give him in case of the worst happening, for should Greene's force get to Camden, and with his cavalry in his rear betwixt him and Santee, his situation would be very allarming, nor do I think myself justifiable in crossing to asist him. Lee, I suppose, has joined Marrion and crossed the Pedee below, while their principal force moves by Charlotte. Sumpter and Pickens, by my intelligence from Cruger, are to move towards Ninety Six. I give your Lordship exactly as I have received them the authorrtys for supposing Greene's force to be advancing, and principaly coming from Lord Rawdon, having myself no positive evidence or intelligence of the enemy's movements, but this you know may very probably happen from the distance and all the communications being totaly stopped, which has been the case for some time past.

The enemy in partys of two and three hundred have over run all the country to the southward, and I had detached McArthur with the debris of the British to Pocotaligo in order to cover that country and relieve Fenwick[41], who with the militia were posted in a redoubt there. We came too late for the purpose of saving Fenwick, who was taken partly from his own imprudence and from the treachery of the militia, but McArthur, having forced the enemy to retire, must now be recalled to Dorchester, where a post must be established to

---

[39] *your letter*: Balfour is referring to Cornwallis's of 5th or 6th April, pp 42-4.

[40] *light infantry*: Watson's corps of Provincial light infantry.

[41] Edward Fenwick had been commissioned captain of a troop of horse known as the South Carolina Light Dragoons on 22nd January 1781, but confusingly he is also referred to in contemporary papers as a colonel. Educated in England, he was married to a daughter of John Stuart, the deceased Superintendant of Indian Affairs, and was the son of a deceased wealthy planter who had bred fine race horses on John's Island. As now related by Balfour, he had just been captured by William Harden at Pocotaligo but would be exchanged under the cartel with Greene. As the tide turned in favour of the revolutionaries, he apparently had a change of heart and began secretly to supply them with valuable information about British strength and troop movements. It was not in time to save him from being included in the Banishment and Confiscation Act passed by the revolutionary assembly, but he later obtained the support of Greene and Henry Laurens for his removal from it, which was effected in 1785. (Raymond, 'British American Corps'; Clark, *Loyalists in the Southern Campaign*, i. 87-9; Lambert, *SC Loyalists, passim*; Gibbes, *Documentary History*, iii, 53-5; The SC Banishment and Confiscation Act 1782)

prevent the enemy coming to our gates.

The situation of the posts at present will be, viz, at Monk's Corner 200 infantry and fifty mounted, at Dorchester 150 infantry and sixty mounted, at Nielson's 56 infantry, at Motte's House 54 infantry, at Congarees 76 infantry with militia, and at George Town 86 infantry with twenty mounted.

Lord Rawdon has at Camden the 63rd, Fanning's corps, Volunteers of Ireland and York Volunteers — the 64th and light infantry with Watson, who cannot now get to him. Cruger has Innes's corps joined to him.

From this you will judge of our situation if the enemy realy come in force and lead the country to join them, which they are very ripe for.

The retreat of Lord Rawdon to this side of the Santee in case of Greene's army actualy coming to Camden I cannot help thinking the best and safest measure, as I doubt[42] much the kind of troops he has will be rather too dangerous to trust to when they find themselves surrounded. In this case I can facilitate his retiring, by the post at Monk's Corner.

Should Greene have only sent Lee with his light troops, they cannot so very materialy affect us as to oblige the retreat from *any* of our posts, although they will totaly ruin the country, which indeed is now pretty nearly so, and will cut all our communications, which with raising the country militia may finaly lead to very serious consequences.

Your Lordship's moving into this province with your present force can only be (I humbly conceive) by the low road to George Town, where I shall place some provisions in *case* you may think proper to take that route, but if you do not intend coming I shall contract the posts as much as possible and do my uttmost to cover the country untill your operations are felt in another quarter. This push of Greene's to draw back your force I conceive might have been foiled had Watson's corps been with Lord Rawdon, but situated and posted as the force is now, I think the hazard is very great to Lord Rawdon's corps *if Green* is *actualy* with his army advancing into this province, nor can I doubt of the whole falling, except the town, in that case.

The delay of the cussed frigate's not getting over the barr prevents your receiving Clinton's instructions to Phillips[43], and they being on board these two days prevents my copying them for you by this opportunity, but they are principaly to instruct him to do every thing in his power to relieve Arnold and afterwards to make such movements towards Petersburgh or otherwise as might best assist your operations, to communicate with you, and to look upon himself as under your orders untill he heared further from him. He mentions also the taking finaly some posts in the Chesapeak when the other services may have been performed etc.

---

[42] *doubt*: used in the now archaic sense of 'fear'.

[43] *Clinton's instructions..*: see Clinton to Phillips, 10th March, vol V, ch 50.

These are the principal points of the instructions.

A packet is just arrived from England with a mail for New York, to which place she proceeds immediately, and I have wrote to Sir Henry Clinton to inform him of Greene's movements and the *probability* of their obliging your return to this province, and *this* I have done in a guarded and cautious manner.

There is not one publick letter for you, and I learn that the *Cormorant* sloop of war, who sailed two days before this packet, was sent with your dispatches. No probability of a speedy reinforcement, nor can I learn when they come or where from.

I have taken all the horses in town and country and will be able to give you asistance in mounted infantry or horses if you wish it.

The hurry of this letter will apologise for its innacuracys and the method it is written in, and trust to your goodness for excusing all the libertys used in it.

I ever am
Most sincerly and faithfuly yours

N BALFOUR

PS

The letter of Lord Rawdon's to McInnon was supposing him to be up at Motte's House with a corps, but he had retreated two days before to the Corner by my order.

The supplys sail the moment they can get over the barr, as I did not think it proper to keep them.

Enclosure (1)
Rawdon to Balfour, 12th April 1781   *5(236): ACS*

Camden
April 12th 1781

Lt Colonel Balfour etc etc

Sir

A soldier of Colonel Hamilton's regiment made prisoner by the enemy and just escap'd from them arriv'd here this morning. He asserts that he left Greene's army on Sunday the 8th instant some miles on this side of Deep River marching towards Salisbury. He was inform'd that Lord Cornwallis march'd from Cross Creek to Wilmington on Thursday the 5th, and he heard it report'd, since he cross'd the Pedee, that Greene got to Salisbury on the 10th. The story tallies so much with some flying reports which I have heard that, altho' it is not probable, I cannot disregard it. Lord Cornwallis may have written to me and his letters may have fail'd. All that I can do is muster what force is within my reach till I have prov'd the truth of my information. For this reason I have been forc'd to send after McKinnon, requiring that corps to come hither directly. I know nothing of Watson. You shall hear from me the moment that I learn any thing further.

I have the honor to be, sir,
Your most obedient servant

RAWDON

Enclosure (2)
Rawdon to Balfour, 13th April 1781

5(239): ALS

Camden
April 13th 1781

Lt Colonel Balfour etc etc

Sir

The information which I sent to you yesterday is certainly true. *Lee passed the Pedee two days ago* and *I conjecture will join Marion.* Of Watson I can learn nothing for certain. The report is that he is still in Britain's Neck beyond the Pedee. Coffin has not yet returned, nor has he sent any report to me. *I fear he will get into a scrape. He has disobeyed my orders. I have a fortnight's meal at least. This post is infamous, but if we are tried, we shall do what becomes us. I am sure from all accounts Camden is Greene's object.*

I have the honor to be, sir,
Your most obedient servant

RAWDON

[*Subscribed*:]

I desired Colonel Doyle to apply to you for information about all matters here.

Enclosure (3)
Rawdon to Balfour, 15th April 1781

5(238): LS

Camden
April 15th 1781

Lt Colonel Balfour etc etc etc

Sir

By the intelligence which I have received yesterday and this day, *Greene was to march this morning from Rockey River for Camden. We shall not be alarmed by the visit. I fear Lord Cornwallis is really gone to Wilmington. Watson certainly cannot get to me.*

I have the honor to be, sir,
Your most obedient servant

RAWDON

[*Subscribed in Rawdon's hand:*]

Coffin returned the night before last. He killed fourteen of the enemy and took a few without any loss on his part.

Enclosure (4)
Rawdon to Small, 15th April 1781

5(235): *ALS*

Camden
April 15th 1781

Lt Colonel Small etc etc

Sir

I have already written two letters to you requesting that you would move hither with your corps. It is reported that Mr Greene has passed the Pedee above us and that Colonel Lee has been sent with a detachment into our rear. I wish to have you here as soon as possible until I shall be enabled to prove the truth of this information.

I have the honor to be, sir,
Your most obedient servant

RAWDON

[*Subscribed:*]

Should the reports be true, the enemy could not have been nearer than between fifty and sixty miles from hence this morning.

Cornwallis to Balfour, 30th April 1781

85(55): *ADf*

Duplin Court House
April 30th 1781

Dear Balfour

I received last night yours of the 20th and hope before this time you have got my letters[44] by the *Delight*. The die is cast. The thought of Camden distresses me but I can give no

---

[44] *my letters*: Cornwallis to Balfour, 21st, 22nd and 24th April, pp 121-3.

assistance unless my present move should recall Greene. Should it not, collect all your force and, if you can, get the garrison of Ninety Six. If there can be any means of assisting Lord Rawdon without hazard to Charlestown, you will do it. If not, think only for the present of the security of that place and send[45] without delay the transports and provisions to Cape Fear.

Yours very sincerely

CORNWALLIS[46]

Cornwallis to Balfour, 3rd May 1781

86(1): C

Reeves's Plantation
8 miles from Dickson's Ford on the Nuse
3rd May 1781

Lt Colonel Balfour

Dear Balfour

I shall not repeat what I have said to Craig[47]. The difficulties I allude to are principally the troops becoming sickly and many of the mills being useless by the dryness of the season, which prevents my keeping up my stock of provisions so as to enable me to return if necessary from any point of the march to Wilmington.

Dispatch transports and provisions. Perhaps it will be proper for you to lay an embargo on provisions, to turn out of town all parole men and disaffected people with their families and many Negroes, and to shut your gates against many of the poor country people and all Negroes that your stock of provisions may hold out.

Yours very sincerely

CORNWALLIS

---

[45] The words after 'send' are substituted for: 'as soon as possible for Craig. I shall proceed as fast as possible to James River.'

[46] The following subscription is deleted: 'You will send only transports to bring off Craig with a little more provisions than would be necessary for him, having the other transports with provisions ready to sail in case of my being obliged to return to Wilmington, which nothing but the most absolute necessity shall drive me to do.'

[47] See Cornwallis to Craig, 3rd May, p 166.

Balfour to Cornwallis, 26th April 1781[48]   6(23): LS

Charles Town
26th April 1781

By the inclosed two letters you will see that Greene has got to Camden. I have therefore stopt the supplies sailing till I hear from your Lordship, as you mentioned your positive intentions[49] *to return into this province if you found Greene had penetrated into it in your absence. Lt Colonel Watson cannot get to Camden, being at present just coming from George Town on this side the Santee* in order to proceed up towards *McCord's Ferry* and there wait *events*, as his crossing would be very dangerous untill we know more of Greene's movements.

Lee and Marion have taken a post which Watson established at Wright's Bluff.

McArthur with *three hundred infantry and one hundred mounted and tolerably* well appointed are towards *Nelson's Ferry* to cover the country, and another corps is *at Dorchester*.

By letters from *Cruger he is very much alarmed by a force under Sumpter and Pickens*.

The enemy seem to have made a general push at the different posts in order to affect your Lordship's movements and draw you back, *and I own it appears to me that the force now at Camden is not equal to clear* the country and *drive Greene back without your assistance*.

The movements of Lt Colonel Watson and *the unfortunate idea* of giving him the 64th Regiment *has been of more prejudice* than it is possible to describe, and it has not *only lost us* so very considerable *a force but* the troops *have been let down and the enemy of course* have gained much *ground* by it.

The disaffection of the militia is also almost *universal* and they have *joined the enemy* wherever *they have come*. Those to the southward are the worst. *One Harding*[50] *leads the enemy in that quarter and has overrun* all the country to the southward *of Dorchester* with a very few men.

They have adopted the system of murdering every militia officer of ours as well as every man (although unarmed) who is known to be a loyalist. *The terror this mode of conduct has struck* you will easily *suppose. Some immediate stop must be put to it or the consequences will be very fatal* and we shall not have *one loyalist* in the *country, as they are crowding to*

---

[48] Enclosed with Craig's letter of 2nd May, p 167, but see note 29.

[49] *you mentioned..*: see Cornwallis to Balfour, 5th and 6th April, pp 42-4.

[50] William Harden (1743-1785) was a native of what was later Barnwell County. In February 1776 he had been commissioned by the Provincial Congress as captain of an artillery company at Beaufort. After the capitulation of Benjamin Lincoln in May 1780 he joined Marion as a colonel of militia and since the beginning of 1781 had begun to overrun the area to the west and south-west of Charlestown. Among his recent exploits was the capture of a captain and twenty-five men on the Four Holes, together with the taking of Fort Balfour at Pocotaligo with its garrison of some ninety men. (McCrady, *SC in the Rev 1780-1783*, passim)

town from all quarters. I will not detain the express longer than to assure you that I am

Most sincerely and faithfully yours

N BALFOUR

Enclosure (1)
Rawdon to Balfour, 19th April 1781   *6(24): C*

Camden
19th April, 2 afternoon

Lt Colonel Balfour

Sir

Green has just appeared before us. We are under no apprehension. Neither Fraser[51] nor Watson have joined me, so I must be quite defensive etc etc.

[I have the honor to be] etc

RAWDON

Enclosure (2)
Rawdon to Balfour, 21st April 1781   *6(24): C*

Camden
21st April, 4 afternoon

Lt Colonel Balfour

Sir

Nothing has happened hitherto but skirmishing for some ground which rather commands our works. The enemy must get it, for I cannot afford to risque the men necessary to maintain it. From the report of prisoners whom we have taken I do not think Greene has above five and twenty hundred men, so that, were I distressed, I would at all events attack his camp. If Watson and Fraser join me I shall hope to drive him out of the country. I have been forced to abandon the ferry as I could not support it. The boats I have sent lower down the river.

Green has but four or six pieces of cannon. If he tries any thing, think it will be by assault. Nobody can get from hence to Lord Cornwallis. I wish I could clear the country without bringing his Lordship back.

---

[51] *Fraser*: commanding the South Carolina Royalist Regiment.

I have the honor to be etc

RAWDON

PS

Fraser will be here in two hours. If Watson comes tonight, we shall do business tomorrow.

§ - §

5 - From Rawdon

Rawdon to Cornwallis, 25th April 1781[52]   *6(27): LS*

Camden
April 25th 1781
6 evening

Earl Cornwallis etc etc etc

My dear Lord

General Greene arrived before us on the 19th. As Watson had not joined me, I remained on the defensive, but, hearing that Lee, Sumter and Marion were coming to Greene, and the South Carolina Regiment having got safe to me from Ninety Six, I thought it best to risque an action. We therefore attacked Greene at ten o'clock this morning. He was strongly posted on Hobkirk's Hill just beyond Log Town. After a severe action we routed him totally. His cannon escaped by going off very early, and the enemy's superiority in cavalry prevented our making many prisoners. I cannot yet tell the loss on either part, but I think the enemy's trebles ours. Lieutenant Jewell[53] of my regiment is the only officer killed. Major Campbell and some others are wounded. Excuse this scrawl, my dear Lord, for I am overcome with fatigue. I will send your Lordship a more particular account as soon as possible.

I have the honor to be with great respect
Your Lordship's very faithfull and affectionate servant

RAWDON

---

[52] Published without the antepenultimate and penultimate sentences in Ross ed, *Cornwallis Correspondence*, i, 97. It and Rawdon's following letter were received by Cornwallis before he wrote on 20th May to Clinton, enclosing copies. See vol V, ch 51.

[53] Lt John Jewell, Volunteers of Ireland. (Raymond, 'British American Corps')

Rawdon to Cornwallis, 26th April 1781[54]

5(262): LS

Camden
April 26th 1781

Lt General Earl Cornwallis etc etc etc

My Lord

About a fortnight ago some reports reached me by which I suspected that Major General Greene was bending his course towards this post. Very shortly after, I received intelligence that Lt Colonel Lee had crossed the Pedee and had joined Brigadier General Marion upon Black River. I considered this movement as intended to draw me from Camden whilst General Greene by forced marches thro' a deserted tract of country should attempt to surprize the weakened post.

I therefore contented myself with dispatching orders to recall Lt Colonel Watson, who had been long detached with a considerable corps for the purpose of dispersing the plunderers that infested our eastern frontier.

I now received clearer information of General Greene's approach. I was ignorant of his numbers, but as I had not at that time had any intimation of your Lordship's march to Wilmington, I thought it my duty to maintain the post.

Some of our militia exhibited upon this occasion great zeal and fidelity, coming voluntarily from considerable distances to offer their service, but as my stock of provisions was but scanty, I could only accept the assistance of those who would otherwise have been exposed to suffer from the enemy. On the 19th General Greene appeared before us. I was so weak in troops, considering the extent I had to defend, that I would not risque men to harrass him as he advanced. Three days after, the South Carolina Regiment, which I had summoned from Ninety Six, arrived, and altho' I had been obliged to abandon the ferry, I fortunately secured the passage of that corps into Camden. At the same time I received a letter from Lt Colonel Balfour giving me notice of your Lordship's situation and signifying to me your Lordship's wish that I should retire within the Santee. The necessity of the measure was obvious, but it was no longer in my power. The efforts of the enemy to examine our works, and in particular an attempt to destroy our mill, had in the mean time occasioned some skirmishing. From the prisoners whom we made in these excursions I gathered that General Greene's army was by no means so numerous as I had apprehended, but that reinforcement was daily expected by them.

The position which Marion had taken near the High Hills of Santee precluded the hope of Lt Colonel Watson's joining me. I therefore conceived some immediate effort necessary, and indeed I did not think that the disparity of numbers was such as should justify a bare defence. I had procured information that the enemy with a view of hazarding an assault had sent their

---

[54] A copy of this letter is published in Davies ed, *Docs of the Am Rev*, xx, 122. It omits the enclosure and otherwise contains several inconsequential inaccuracies.

cannon and baggage a day's march in their rear, but that abandoning the resolution, they had detached all their militia to bring up again their artillery. Altho' my intelligence was somewhat tardy, I hoped I should still be in time to avail myself of this conjuncture. By arming our musicians, our drummers and in short every thing that could carry a firelock, I mustered above nine hundred for the field, sixty of whom were dragoons. With this force and two six pounders we marched about 10 o'clock yesterday morning, leaving our redoubts to the care of the militia and a few sick soldiers. The enemy were posted upon Hobkirk's Hill, a very strong ridge, about two miles distant from our front. By filing close to the swamps we got into the wood unperceived and, taking an extensive circuit, came down upon the enemy's left flank. We were so fortunate in our march that we were not discovered till the flank companies of the Voluntiers of Ireland, which led our column, fell in with the enemy's picquets. The picquets, tho' supported, were instantly driven in and followed to their camp. The enemy were in much confusion but, notwithstanding, formed and received us bravely. I believe they imagined us to be much weaker than we were. Their artillery (three six pounders) had unluckily arrived a few minutes before the attack began, of which circumstance they gave us notice by heavy showers of grape shot. I had ordered Lt Colonel Campbell to lead the attack with the 63rd and King's American Regiments, which he performed with great spirit. The extent of the enemy's line soon obliged me to throw forward the Voluntiers of Ireland also. Those three corps quickly gained the summit of the hill, and, giving room for the rest of our force to act, the rout of the enemy was immediately decided. We pursued them about three miles, but, the enemy's cavalry greatly surpassing ours as to number, horses and appointments, our dragoons could not risque much, nor could I suffer the infantry to break their order in hopes of overtaking the fugitives. A part of the enemy's cavalry got into our rear, exacted paroles from several officers who lay wounded on the ground from which we had first driven the enemy, and carried off several wounded men, probably with intent to deceive the country people respecting the event of the action. I have the honor to enclose a return of our loss. The enemy's killed and wounded were scattered over such an extent of ground that I cannot ascertain how much they suffered. I believe the computation would be low, were it rated at five hundred. We brought off above a hundred prisoners, exclusive of a number who, finding their retreat cut off, went into Camden and claimed protection as deserters.

The enemy's cannon escaped by mere accident. It was run down a steep hill among some thick brushwood, where we passed without observing it, and it was carried off whilst we pursued the infantry in a contrary direction. By what I can learn from the officers whom we have taken, General Green had about 1,500 Continentals. The number of his militia I do not know, nor do I believe they were at all engaged. His Majesty's troops behaved most gallantly. I am under great obligations to Lt Colonel Campbell, Major Campbell, Major Fraser, Major Coffin, Captain St Leger, Captain Kane[55] and Captain Robinson[56]

---

[55] Born in Ireland, Bernard Kane (1751-?) had been serving as a captain in the New York Volunteers since 10th November 1776 and was now its most senior captain. At the close of the war he would be placed on the Provincial half-pay list. (Treasury 64/23(1), WO 65/164(31) and WO 65/165(2) (National Archives, Kew))

[56] Morris Robinson (see p 48, note 29), who had been convalescing at Camden after commanding the post at William Thomson's house. (Todd Braisted to the editor, 24th August 2006)

commanding the different corps or detachments, as likewise to Lieutenant Laye[57] of the Royal Artillery, for their animated exertions. Major of Brigade Doyle distinguished himself very much, and Lieutenants Rankin and Stark, who acted as my aides de camp, deserve my warm praises.

I learn that the enemy are endeavouring to collect their scattered corps about fourteen miles from hence behind the farthest branch of Granny's Quarter Creek.

I hope this success may give me an opening to get across the Santee as the spirit of revolt appears strongly in the interior country. At the worst, we will maintain this post, whatsoever force may be assembled against it.

I have the honor to be, my Lord, with great respect
Your most faithful and affectionate servant

RAWDON

Enclosure
Return of killed, wounded and missing   *5(267): DS*

RETURN of the Killed, Wounded and Missing of the Troops under the Command of the RT HON COLONEL LORD RAWDON in the Action on Hobkirk's Hill near CAMDEN, April the 25th 1781

RANKS	RA[58]	63rd	VI	NYV	KAR	SCR	DC	TOTAL
KILLED								
Lieutenants			1					1

---

[57] Francis Laye (1752-1828) entered the Royal Regiment of Artillery as a cadet on 1st March 1768 and was commissioned a 2nd lieutenant three years later. In 1773 he embarked with an artillery detachment for New York and in 1774 was posted to Boston. He went on to take part in various engagements and campaigns in the northern theatre: Bunker Hill; the New York campaign, including White Plains; actions in the Jerseys; the Philadelphia campaign, including Brandywine; Germantown; and Monmouth. On 7th July 1779 he was promoted to 1st lieutenant and in late 1780 came south with Leslie. Remaining in South Carolina in command of the artillery detachment at Camden, he was severely wounded in the Battle of Hobkirk's Hill and had the misfortune to be made prisoner and paroled on the battlefield. Sent home because of his wounds, he proceeded to rise steadily in his regiment, taking part in the Flanders campaign in 1793 and commanding the artillery in the reduction of French islands in the West Indies some seven years later. In 1810 he became a major general, in 1817 Colonel Commandant, and in 1819 a lt general. He died at Newcastle-upon-Tyne. (J Philippart, *The Royal Military Calendar: Containing the service of every general officer...from the date of their first commission* (London, 1815); *Royal Regiment of Artillery*, 13; *Army Lists*; *Appletons'*)

[58] The abbreviations in this row refer respectively to the Royal Artillery, 63rd Regiment, Volunteers of Ireland, New York Volunteers, King's American Regiment, South Carolina Royalist Regiment, and Detachment of Convalescents.

Serjeants		1	1		1	1		4
Rank & File		12	11	1	3	6		33
WOUNDED								
Major			1					1
Captains						1	2	3
Lieutenants	1	1	2		1			5
Ensigns		1	2					3
Serjeants			5	2	4	1		12
Drummers		1			1			2
Rank & File	1	36	65	10	29	10		151
MISSING								
Serjeants				1	1			2
Drummers		1	1					2
Rank & File		3	10	14	3	5	4	39
TOTAL	2	56	99	28	43	24	6	258

Names and rank of the officers:

    Royal Artillery: wounded, Lieutenant Laye (paroled)

    63rd Regiment: wounded, Lieutenant McLeroth (paroled), Ensign Loyd (paroled)

    Volunteers of Ireland: killed, Lieutenant Jewell; wounded, Major Campbell, Lieutenant Moffat, Lieutenant Black (paroled), Ensign Britton and Ensign Harris

    King's American Regiment: wounded, Lieutenant Wightman (paroled)

    South Carolina Royalists: wounded, Captain Dawkins

    Detachment of Convalescents: wounded, Captain Robinson and Captain Harrison

RAWDON
Colonel, Voluntiers of Ireland

§ - §

6 - Troop return

State of the troops marching to Virginia, 1st May 1781   103(29): D

State of the Troops that marched with the Army under the command of Lt General Earl Cornwallis, 1st May 1781									Total
Rank & File present and fit for duty									Total
British					German	Provincial		
Guards	23rd	33rd	71st 2nd Batt	82nd Lt comp^y	Bose	Legion	NCV[59] Lt comp^y	
387	194	209	175	36	228	173	33	1,435

§ - §

7 - Intercepted letters

Jones to Jones, 14th May 1781   105(26): ALS

North Carolina
May 14th 1781

Colonel Joseph Jones

To be left at Captain Robert Watkin

Dear Colonel

I have this moment return'd from Mr Willie Jones's seat (two miles from Halifax). There I learnt the enemies cavalry had pas'd last evening, said to be on there way to Virginia, but I rather suppose there object is to supprise a party of militia which was collected by General Williamson[60] about forty miles below this. It is certain the enemy have a large fatigue party

---

[59] *NCV*: North Carolina Volunteers, that is to say, the Royal North Carolina Regiment.

[60] No general or field officer with the name of Williamson has been identified in the locality indicated by Jones. Some forty miles downriver from Halifax lies Martin County, whose revolutionary militia were commanded by Colonel William Williams, after whom the county seat Williamston was later named. Perhaps Jones, a Virginian

on this side of the river preparing materials to build a fourt. From this we may conjecture they do not mean to join the troops at Petersburgh so early as was expected. I hope, as this is the case, the Marquis will oblige Philips to retire from Petersburgh.

I am, dear Colonel,
Yours most respectfully

CHURCHHILL JONES[61]

Jones to Washington, 14th May 1781 — 105(28): ALS

North Carolina
May 14th 1781

George Washington Esq[62]
Aid de camp to the Marquis de Lafayette

My dear George

I have this moment return'd from Ochoneche, the seat of Mr Willie Jones, where I learnt the enemies cavalry past late last evening, suppos'd by the inhabitants to be five hundred in number. As people unacquainted with cavalry generally magnify them, I presume they do not exceed two or three hundred. They gave out, as they pas'd, they were on there march to Virginia, but I conceive there intention is to surprise a few hundred militia collected by General Williamson about forty miles below this. The accounts that I have collected relative to his Lordship's intentions are rather contradictory. It is certain there is a large party on this side of the river preparing materials for the building a fourt oposite the ferry. Pray, my friend, write me by the return of the bearer what is going forward with you, whether the Pensylvania line is with you, whether Philips will not be compel'd to leave Petersburgh with the loss of at least one half his army.

I am yours affectionately

CHURCHHILL JONES

---

not necessarily familiar with North Carolina, is confusedly referring to him. (Robinson, *NC Guide*, 293; Hay ed, *Soldiers from NC*, 499, 502; Wheeler, *Historical Sketches*, i, 78, 85)

[61] Churchhill Jones was a Virginian who had been commissioned a captain in the 3rd Continental Light Dragoons on 1st June 1777. His troop had taken part in the Battle of Cowpens. After the war he was awarded 4,011 acres. (Heitman, *Historical Register*, 323; Gwathmey, *Historical Register*, 426)

[62] Now serving as an aide-de-camp to Lafayette, George Augustine Washington (1758-1793) was an ensign in the 2nd Virginia Continental Regiment and would be promoted to lieutenant on 26th May. After the war he was awarded 5,666 acres. His remains are interred in the Washington family vault at Mount Vernon. (Heitman, op cit, 573; Gwathmey, op cit, 808)

Jones to Lafayette, 14th May 1781 — 105(30): ALS

North Carolina
May 14th 1781

The Hon Major General Marquis de Lafayette
Wilton

Sir

I have just return'd from the seat of Mr Willie Jones, two miles from Halifax, where I heard the whole of enemies cavalry past last evening, said to be on there way to Petersburgh, and that the infantry were to follow this evening. As yet I cannot learn that any of them have cros'd the Ronoke except a large fatigue party preparing materials for the purpose of building a fort on this side of the river oposite the town.

As the enemy march'd a different road from the one we came, I thought it advisable to send some horse men a few miles to discover if possible there intentions. On there return they reported the enemy left North Hamton Court House (NC) this morning after six o'clock. I have understood since my arrival in this neighbourhood that General Williamson has collected three or four hundred militia about forty miles from this place, which I presume the cavalry are in pursuit of and not on there march to Petersburgh. General Jones, having mov'd higher up the river than I suppos'd him when I wrote you yesterday, determin'd me to visit post[63] first. I shall now proceed to his camp, leaving a party of observation that should the enemy make a movement I may be able to give you the earliest information.

I have the honour to be
Your very humble servant

CHURCHHILL JONES
Captain, Light Dragoons

§ - §

---

[63] *post*: used in the now archaic sense of 'with haste'.

Index[1]

Actions —
    near Alamance Creek, 26;
    off the Capes of Virginia, 39-40, 114, 125;
    at Clapp's Mill, 15-16;
    at Cowan's Ford, 4, 13-14, 44;
    at Georgetown, 45;
    Pyle's massacre, 5-6, 15;
    at Tarrant's Tavern, 14, 44;
    at Wetzell's Mill, 16, 26
Anderson, Robert, 167n
Arbuthnot, Marriot (I, 7), 39-40, 125, 127, 131-2
Ardesoif, John Plummer (I, 306), 126-7
Arnold, Benedict (III, 55), 21, 37, 39, 51, 106, 115, 149, 152-5, 164
Avery, ——, 126

Balfour, Nisbet (I, 35-7), 25, 28-45, 52, 78, 101-3, 105, 108, 113, 121-4, 130, 133, 165-180 —
    describes the critical situation in SC as Greene advances and arrives at Camden, 170-5, 177-9;
    looks to Cornwallis to return to SC, 171, 173, 177;
    cannot drive Greene back without Cornwallis's assistance, 177
Barclay, Thomas, 51n
Barkley, Andrew (III, 49), 31, 33-5, 37-8, 40, 42, 123, 129-133
Barry, Henry ('Harry') (III, 97), 41
Battle of Cowpens, 3, 12, 45, 117
Battle of Guilford (*see also* 'Winter campaign'), 7-9, 17-20, 39, 41, 46, 63-73, 109, 114 —
    Cornwallis's troops taking part in the Battle, 8;
    his casualties in the Battle, 8, 42, 64-70;
    care of his seriously wounded left at New Garden Meeting House, 70-3;
    care of enemy's wounded, 79-80
Biggs, Robert, 129n
Bowdler, John, 71
Bowes, Frederick, 51n
Brice, Francis, 140n
Brigade of Guards, composition of, 137
British strategy and tactics, 3-7, 9, 101-3
Brodrick, The Hon Henry (I, 22), 12, 20, 40, 42, 46, 77-85, 87, 107, 111, 117, 123, 130, 132
Brown, Thomas (II, 351), 134
Browne, ——, 157
Bull, William (III, 44), 11
Butcher, ——, 160n
Butler, John (II, 350), 17, 23, 92-3, 157, 160, 162
Buy, Johann Christian du, (III, 37), 19

Camden, extraordinary disadvantages of post at, 174
Campbell, George (III, 97), 181
Campbell, James, 112n
Campbell, John (III, 115), 179, 181
Campbell, William (II, 134), 49
Cape Fear River, navigation of, 9, 27, 34, 38, 42, 46, 104-5, 110
Captured troops —
    threat to send enemy's to the West Indies, 42, 75, 77, 85-6;
    maltreatment of British, 74-6;
    NC delegates to Congress delaying general exchange of, 91;
    cartel for exchange and relief of in the Southern Department, 11-12, 74-89
Carne, Charles Loder, 37n, 165
Carrington, Edward, 77n-8, 80-5, 88-9
Caswell, The Hon Richard (I, 60), 157, 170
Clinton, Sir Henry, KB, 109-113
Cobham, Thomas, 35n-6
Coffin, John (II, 94), 49, 51, 174-5, 181
Cornwall, The Rt Hon Charles Wolfran, 118-9n, 120
Cornwallis, Charles, Earl (*see also* 'British strategy and tactics', 'Winter campaign' etc) —
    his motives for pressing ahead, despite Cowpens, with the winter campaign, 3;
    his conduct of the winter campaign, 4-9;
    his own accounts of that campaign, 12-21, 25-6, 42, 44-6, 104-6, 109-110, 114;
    negotiates with Greene a cartel for the exchange and relief of prisoners in the Southern Department, 74-89;
    assures Balfour that he will return to SC if Greene attempts any serious move towards it but reveals to Phillips his contradictory preference for undertaking desultory opera-

---

[1] The letter 'n' after the number of a page indicates the presence there of biographical or identifying information. Such information appearing in another volume is indicated in brackets immediately after a person's name.

Cornwallis, Charles, Earl (*continued*)
tions in Virginia, 44, 101, 115, 122;
his ostensible reasons for marching to Virginia, 106-8, 111-3, 116, 122;
his real reasons for marching to Virginia and the absurdity of his decision, 101-3
Cornwallis, Frederick, 87n-9
Craig, James Henry (III, 33) (*see also* 'Wilmington, British post at'), 21, 25-41, 43, 51, 101, 105, 123-4, 126, 165-170, 176 —
the written instructions under which he is acting at Wilmington, 30-1;
does not see eye to eye with Andrew Barkley, 35
Creyk (pronounced 'Creek'), Richard (III, 132), 125-7
Cruden, John (I, 219), 36
Cruger, John Harris (I, 152 and 258), 50, 171, 177
Cunningham, Robert (I, 117), 50
Curry, Nicholas, 54n

Dart, Thomas, 71
Davidson, William Lee (II, 45), 4, 13, 14, 44, 92, 94
Dawson, Dempsey, 159n
Despard, John (II, 235), 63, 65
Doyle, John (I, 185), 182
Doyle, Wellbore Ellis (II, 119), 52
Dundas, The Hon Francis, 160n
Dunglas, Lord: *see* 'Home, William'
Dunlop, James, 39n, 40

Elbeck, Montfort, 161n

Fenwick, Edward, 171n
Fincannon, William, 58n
Fort Granby, 47
Fox, Charles James, 50n
Fraser, Thomas (I, 243), 48-9, 52, 178-9, 181
Fraser, Thomas, 136
French expeditionary forces, 39
Frytag, Martin, 93n

Georgetown, British post at, 45, 94
Germain, Lord George, 11-20, 52, 104-9
Giles, Edward, 92n
Goodricke, ——, 46
Gordon, John, 167n
Grant, ——, 46
Greene, Nathanael (III, 10), 4-10, 12-17, 21, 23-4, 26, 34, 41-2, 44-6, 49, 70-1, 73-89, 94-6, 101-3, 107-110, 112-3, 116, 139 —
his motives for offering battle at Guilford, 7;
marches for Camden and arrives in its vicinity, 10, 103, 107, 116, 121-2, 171-5, 177-180;
is defeated at the Battle of Hobkirk's Hill, 149, 152, 157, 162, 168-170, 179-183

Hagens: *see* 'Heaggins, William'
Haldane, Henry (II, 14), 107, 118, 158
Hall, Francis, 14n
Hamilton, John (I, 55), 17
Hampton, Wade (III, 75), 47
Harden, William, 177n
Harnett Jr, Cornelius, 135n
Harralson, ——, 97
Harrison, John (I, 161), 48
Harvey, John, 90
Heaggins, William (III, 192), 94n
Hill, West (I, 204), 43, 69-71, 73
Hines, Lewis, 169n
Home (pronounced 'Hume'), William, Lord Dunglas, 43n
Hood, Samuel, Viscount Hood, 50
Hopkins, David, 53n
Hospitals or surgeons —
attending the wounded at New Garden Meeting House, 43, 69-71, 73;
attending the sick and wounded on their voyage to Charlestown, 43;
at Wilmington, 170
House of Commons, thanks of, to Clinton, Arbuthnot and Cornwallis, 119
Hovenden, Moore (III, 139), 134
Howard, John (III, 37), 20, 50
Hunter, ——, 125
Hunter, Thomas, 160n
Hutcheson, Robert, 136n
Hutchinson, ——, 165n

Inglis (pronounced 'Inguls'), John, 28, 124-5n, 126-9, 131-2, 134-5, 149
Innes, Alexander (I, 17), 51

Jackson, ——, 159n
Jewell, John, 179n
Johnson, George, 24
Jones, Allen (III, 412), 160, 164, 186
Jones, Churchhill, 184-5n, 186
Jones, Joseph, 184
Jones, Willie, 164n, 184-6
Justin, John, 24

Kane: *see* 'Carne, Charles Loder'
Kane, Bernard, 181n
Kennedy, ——, 125

Lafayette, Marie Joseph Paul Yves Roch Gilbert du Motier, Marquis de, 152-4, 159, 163-4, 185-6
Lancaster, ——— (III, 151), 51
Laye, Francis, 182n
Lee, Henry ('Light Horse Harry') (III, 252), 5, 6, 10, 21, 94, 170-2, 174-5, 177, 179, 180
Lee's Legion (I, 44), 16, 17, 21, 92, 94
Leslie, The Hon Alexander (III, 3-4), 13, 17-19, 34, 36, 44, 110
Lillington, John Alexander, 27n-8
Lincoln, Benjamin, 91
Locke, Francis, 96n
Long, Nicholas, 157n
Lovelace, Robert, 136-7n

MacAlester, Hector, 138-9n
Macleod, John (I, 210), 17-18, 20, 66, 107, 117
Malmedy, François Lellorquis, Marquis de (I, 19), 110
Manson, Daniel (I, 21), 32, 36, 134
Marbury, Joseph, 96n
March to Virginia —
    Cornwallis's force, 149, 184;
    summary of, 149
Marion, Francis (III, 4-5), 27, 35, 47-50, 52, 170-1, 174, 177, 179, 180
Martin, Josiah (I, 66), 20, 59, 105, 130, 140
Mates, medicines, and hospital stores, 4, 39, 40, 43, 70
Mawbey, Sir Joseph, Bt, 50n
Maxwell, Andrew (I, 252), 47, 49
Maynard, ———, 43, 105
McArthur, Archibald (I, 87), 170-1, 177
McKinnon, John (I, 127), 173-4
McLeroth, Robert (III, 77), 47-9, 51
Militia, revolutionary —
    Georgia, 7, 45;
    North Carolina, 7, 13, 14, 17, 19, 31-4, 36, 38, 42, 51, 92, 133-4, 155, 181;
    Overmountain, 16, 17;
    South Carolina, 7, 13, 171-2, 177;
    Virginia, 8, 17, 19, 41, 46
Militia, royal —
    defection, disaffection, or infidelity of in SC, 171, 177;
    zeal and fidelity of as Greene menaces Camden, 180
Montagu, George, 128n
Morgan, Daniel (III, 11-12), 3-4, 12-14, 34, 45, 74-6, 92, 96, 107, 117, 133
Moultrie, William (I, 373), 78
Murphey, Archibald, 96-7n
Murphey, James, 97

Nash, The Hon Abner (II, 337), 36, 38, 133, 157

Nesbitt, Colebrook, 32n-3, 36, 51, 133
North Carolina —
    its terrain and rivers present great difficulties for an invading army, 106, 111;
    the vigilance and severity of its revolutionary government, 115;
    a proposed basis for offensive operations there, 138-9
North Carolina loyalists —
    supineness of, 5-6, 9, 106, 110, 114;
    well inclined inhabitants of Black River, 27;
    reports of large parties in arms to the southward, 35;
    their property appropriated by the revolutionaries, 93
Norton, The Hon Chapple, 50n

O'Hara, ———, 46
O'Hara, Charles (III, 4), 4, 13, 18, 19, 22-3, 110, 115, 137

Pensacola, 52, 92
Peters, Thomas (III, 109), 43
Phillips, John (II, 331), 53-4
Phillips, William, 29, 92, 101-2, 107-9, 113-6, 123, 129, 130, 139, 149, 151-7, 159, 161-3, 167-9, 185
    summary of his instructions from Clinton, 172
Pickens, Andrew (I, 79), 5-7, 44, 49, 122, 170-1, 177
Pierce Jr, William, 71n, 73
Pitcairn, Thomas, 32n, 34, 133
Preston, William, 16n
Proclamations —
    of 20th February, 55;
    of 18th March, 58-9
Pyle, John, 5-6, 15n

Rankin, William (III, 240), 182
Rawdon, Francis, Lord (I, 151-2), 12, 39, 42, 44-52, 102, 105, 107-8, 116, 121-2, 168 —
    seeks to be relieved due to ill health, 49, 52;
    his situation as Greene advances on and arrives at Camden, 170-5, 178-9;
    defeats Greene at the Battle of Hobkirk's Hill, 149, 152, 157, 162, 168-170, 179-183;
    quits Camden and retires within the Santee, 149-150
Ray, ———, 165(?), 167n
Ray, Duncan, 58n
Reeves, John, 134n
Regiment, Maryland state, 92

Regiments or corps, British —
> Brigade of Guards, 13, 15, 17-18, 44, 115, 137, 159, 160, 162-4;
> 23rd (Royal Welch Fusiliers), 13, 14, 17-18, 43;
> 33rd, 17-18;
> 63rd, 172, 181;
> 64th, 171-2, 177;
> 71st, 17-18, 136;
> 82nd, 133;
> 84th, 48;
> Grenadiers, 18;
> Light infantry, 14, 15, 18, 34, 40, 134, 149, 159, 160, 162-4;
> Royal Artillery, 13, 17-18

Regiments or corps, British American —
> British Legion cavalry, 13-18;
> Harrison's corps, 48;
> King's American Regiment (Fanning's corps), 48, 172, 181;
> New York Volunteers, 47-9, 172;
> Provincial light infantry (Watson's corps), 171-2, 174, 177-180;
> Royal North Carolina Regiment (Hamilton's corps), 17, 173;
> South Carolina Royalist Regiment (Innes's corps), 48-9, 179, 180;
> Volunteers of Ireland (Rawdon's corps), 172, 181

Regiments or corps, Continental, 8, 17, 19, 21, 92, 109, 116, 152, 181, 185

Regiments or corps, Hessian —
> von Bose, 13, 17-19, 93;
> Jägers, 18, 110, 123

Reid, John, 71

Returns —
> of Cornwallis's rank and file fit for duty during the winter campaign, 61-2;
> of Cornwallis's casualties in NC prior to the Battle of Guilford, 62-3;
> of Cornwallis's troops at that Battle, 63;
> of Cornwallis's casualties in that Battle, 64-5;
> of weaponry captured at that Battle, 66;
> of wounded left at New Garden Meeting House, 66-9;
> of dead and deserters at New Garden Meeting House, 69-70;
> of provisions supplied by Quakers for the wounded at New Garden Meeting House, 72;
> of John Peasley's regiment of NC revolutionary militia, 89-90;
> of the troops at Wilmington on 15th April, 142-5;
> of the rank and file fit for duty on Cornwallis's march to Virginia, 184;
> of Rawdon's casualties in the Battle of Hobkirk's Hill, 182-3

Richardson Francis, 137
Ring, William, 71
Robinson, ——, 46
Robinson, Morris, 48n, 181
Robinson, William, 71
Rodney, Sir George Brydges (I, 11), 52
Ross, Alexander (I, 73), 11, 29, 70, 106, 118
Royal Navy, 123-132 —
> Ships: *Amphitrite*, 109, 112, 114, 126n, 129; *Assurance*, 125; *Blonde*, 40, 127, 131-2; *Carysfort*, 130; *Cormorant*, 165, 173; *Delight*, 28, 124-9, 131-2, 135, 165, 175; *Iris*, 126n, 128; *Loyalist*, 28, 39, 40, 124-8, 131; *Otter*, 125-8; *Pearl*, 121, 126n, 128; *Royal Oak*, 132; *Sandwich*, 50

Rutherford, Andrew, 167n

St Augustine, 52, 92
St Leger, Hayes (III, 160), 181
Saunders, John (III, 57), 165
Scheer, ——, 93n
Schutz, ——, 19, 43, 46, 105
Scots Highlanders —
> decline to embody, 59-60, 110

Sharpe, William, 91n
Simcoe, John Graves (I, 10), 153, 163-4
Slaves, 93, 96, 176
Small, John (III, 97), 48, 175
South Carolina —
> communication cut between Charlestown and Camden as Greene advances into SC, 171;
> communication between all British posts to be cut soon afterwards, 172;
> the country to the southward overrun by parties of the enemy, 171, 177;
> whole country ripe to defect, 172;
> adverse effect of Greene, Lee and Marion, 172;
> Fort Balfour at Pocotaligo captured, 171;
> Fort Watson at Wright's Bluff captured, 177;
> murder of loyalists by the enemy and its effect, 47, 150, 177-8;
> strength of lesser British posts, 172

Spillard, Maurice, 53n
Stedman, Charles (I, 212), 4, 6
Stevens, Edward (II, 62), 5
Stuart, The Hon James (III, 42), 46
Summons to arms, 57-9
Sumter, Thomas (I, 149), 13, 52-4, 92, 94, 122,

170-1, 177, 179 —
  his foray down the Congaree and Wateree, 47-9;
  murders loyalists in cold blood, 47;
  denounces penalty of death on those who do not join him, 47
Sutherland, Alexander (III, 121), 36, 40, 163

Talbot, ——, 46
Tarleton, Banastre (I, 154-7), 5, 6, 13-18, 20, 23-4, 44, 94, 103, 107, 110, 117, 149, 155-164
Teare, ——, 70
Trott, ——, von, 105

Vallancey, George Preston, 153n
Vaughan, The Hon John (I, 11), 52
Vickers, Benjamin, 156n, 159
Virginia state troops and eighteen months' men, 7, 17, 21, 46, 92, 109

Wallace, James, 79n, 80
Warrants —
  to raise men for the Royal North Carolina Regiment, 55-6;
  to raise a Provincial company, 56-7
Washington, George Augustine, 185n
Washington, William (I, 46), 3, 18, 21
Watkin, Robert, 184
Watson, John Watson Tadwell (II, 199), 48-9, 52, 165, 170-2, 174, 177-180
Wayne, Anthony, 96, 152, 164
Webster, James (I, 9), 4, 13-15, 17-18, 20, 43, 50-1, 105, 111, 115
White, Anthony Walton (II, 133), 21
Whitlock, James and Sylvias, 93
Williams, ——, 97
Williams, Otho Holland (II, 339), 4-6
Williamson, ——, 184n-6
Wilmington, British post at —
  location of and matters appertaining to, 28, 34;
  strength of detachment at, 34;
  fortification of, 38;
  operations of detachment at, 31-4, 133-5;
  illness among detachment at, 36;
  paroling of inhabitants at, 34-5;
  inadequate stock of supplies at for replenishing Cornwallis during the winter campaign, 28;
  supplying with medicines, hospital stores, and necessaries for Cornwallis after the Battle of Guilford, 39;
  petition of certain inhabitants at to become British subjects, 140-1;
  provisions in store at on 5th May, 101, 168;
  conditional instructions to evacuate, 168
Wilmington, refitment at —
  location of Cornwallis's encampment, 29;
  urgent request to Balfour for shoes, necessaries of all kinds, and cavalry clothing and appointments, 42-4;
  wounded to be sent to Charlestown, 43;
  in utmost distress for money, 43;
  the absurdity of Cornwallis's decision to march to Virginia and the real reasons for it, 101-3
Wilmowsky, ——, von, 43n, 105
Winter campaign (*see also* 'Battle of Guilford') —
  summary of, together with Cornwallis's force, 3-10, 12-20;
  factors influencing Cornwallis to proceed with, 3, 12-13;
  destroys all his superfluous baggage, almost all his waggons, and his store of flour and rum after Cowpens, 4, 13;
  his pursuit of Greene, 4-7, 13-17, 44-5;
  fatigue of his troops in initially driving Greene out of NC, 45;
  his immediate plan thereafter, 21, 25;
  his want of cavalry and infantry appointments, together with other supplies, 25, 26, 28, 45;
  his motive for engaging the enemy at Guilford, 7, 16;
  the considerations leading him to march to Wilmington, 9, 42, 46, 104-5, 110

Yorke, John, 111n
Young Henry, 31n, 51

§ - §